D1152810

British Small An...

Practical

y

Publish
Veteri
Kingsl
Shurdi
Glouc

Printec
Typese

Copyr
No pa
stored
means,
recordi
the co

The pu
respon
and m
this pu
by indi

First E
Revise

ISBN

Animalcare are delighted to have been asked to sponsor the new edition of Practical Veterinary Nursing. The two major changes in veterinary nursing practice over the past twenty years have been the shift in emphasis from agricultural to companion animals, and the increased role and importance of the veterinary nurse. These factors have had a major impact on the industry supplying the veterinary profession. In order to improve the quality of care, veterinary practices require better equipped and informed nursing staff. Consequently, the industry has had to adapt to meet these requirements.

This has been achieved in several ways. The process of product development requires a large amount of research to ensure that the product designed meets the needs of the veterinary profession. The investigative process requires input from veterinary nurses to ensure that the product is effective and convenient to use. When promoting products through advertisements and sales campaigns the material is designed to be interesting and informative to both the nursing staff and veterinary surgeons in the practice. Veterinary nurses are increasingly the member of staff who is responsible for liaising with company representatives. They are therefore the source of significant product orders. This makes them very important people to Animalcare, and indeed to most veterinary supply companies.

Animalcare's involvement stretches beyond supplying product information at practice level to addressing nurses groups on fluid therapy, bandaging and compression fixation. The future offers many opportunities to improve the care and welfare of patients. As Animalcare continues to source products of value to veterinary surgeons, we appreciate the role of the veterinary nurse in this process.

N. McFerran
General Manager, Animalcare Ltd

CONTENTS

PREFACE TO THIRD EDITION

The previous editions of PRACTICAL VETERINARY NURSING, first published in 1985, revised in 1991 and edited by Colin Price have proved a very valuable source of information for veterinary nursing students. There have been extensive changes in the veterinary nursing profession since the first edition and this, the third edition, goes some way to update and extend the scope of the publication.

All the authors work closely with veterinary nurses and appreciate their importance as part of the veterinary team. The first-hand experience of the Veterinary Nurse authors improves the overall relevance of the book.

The recent changes in the veterinary nursing examination system and the availability of a further qualification, the Diploma in Advanced Veterinary Nursing (Surgical), would themselves have merited the book's revision. However, the proposed replacement of the present Veterinary Nursing Scheme with National Council for Vocational Qualifications (N.C.V.Q.) modules will further change veterinary nursing education. The N.C.V.Q. qualifications are designed around practice based and assessed practical tasks. This makes this publication of greater relevance to both veterinary nursing students and to the member of staff in the Approved Training Centre responsible for their training.

As with the previous editions this is not a comprehensive textbook but an easy to use reference manual to assist both the veterinary nursing student and the tutor with practical tasks of importance.

ACKNOWLEDGEMENTS

This publication is the result of enthusiastic hard work by both veterinary surgeons and veterinary nurses. I hope it has resulted in a handbook which will prove of lasting use to all veterinary nurses.

I would like to express my thanks to the authors for their forbearance with me in the preparation of this book, to the members of Publication Committee of the BSAVA for their assistance and especially Harvey Locke for his continued advice and support.

I wish to thank the nurses that gave permission for their photographs to be used on the front cover.

Finally my thanks to Matthew Poulson who has been responsible for the typesetting and some of the diagrams. His professional approach, patience and ability to keep a very tight schedule has been an enormous assistance.

Gillian Simpson

FOREWORD

The first two editions of Practical Veterinary Nursing have been well received and have proved to be useful books over the years. As the name suggests, this publication has attempted to concentrate on practical aspects of nursing and has thus complemented the more standard texts such as Jones's Animal Nursing.

In recent years, there has been drastic changes to the Veterinary Nursing syllabus, such that a revision of this useful book was essential. Gillian Simpson and her team of authors have successfully risen to the challenge and addressed all the new issues in a clear and concise manner retaining the practical emphasis of the booklet. This will ensure that this edition will remain an invaluable help to all new veterinary nursing trainees.

I would like to give my personal thanks to Gillian Simpson and all those associated with the production of this excellent book. I would also like to thank Animalcare Ltd who have provided financial support for this venture.

Ray L. Butcher MA VetMB MRCVS
President BSAVA 1993-94

RADIOGRAPHY

RADIOGRAPHY EQUIPMENT

X-ray machines
There are 3 different types of machine available. The major limiting factor in terms of output is the maximum mAs the machine is capable of producing, this tends to increase with the size of the machine. A kilovoltage range of 50-70 is adequate for most small animal radiographs.
1) **Portable machines** -low weight transformers located within the tube head. Output limited in older machines (up to 30 mA). High frequency models with greater output have been recently developed.
2) **Mobile machines** – transformers larger, mounted on wheels to form the base of the unit. Maximum output ranges from 100-500mA.
3) **Fixed machines** – high powered machines built into the room with special electrical connection to the mains. Tube head mounted on a gantry.

Intensifying screens
Contain luminescent phosphors which emit light when irradiated, greatly reducing the exposure necessary to produce a diagnostic image.
1) Calcium tungstate – used for many years, emits blue light.
2) Rare earth phosphors – convert X-ray energy to light energy more efficiency than calcium tungstate. Emit either blue or green light, the film type and safe lights must be matched accordingly.

Screens of differing speed and definition are available, these properties should match the qualities of the film used.

Cassettes
Cassettes are light-tight containers designed to protect film and screens and to hold them together in close contact. Some are designed to hold a stationary grid as well.

LAYERS OF A CASSETTE

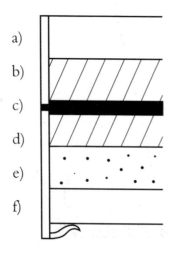

a)

b)

c)

d)

e)

f)

a) Front – made of material such as plastic or carbon fibre which X-rays can penetrate

b) Front screen

c) X-ray film, inserted between screens when cassette opened in darkroom

d) Back screen

e) Felt pressure pad to maintain film – screen contact

f) Back – constructed of a metal to absorb X-rays.

X-ray film

1) Standard X-ray film consists of a layer of photographic emulsion bound to either side of a polyester base, ie. it is double coated. The size of the grains in the emulsion determine the film characteristics, film speed increases with grain size with resultant loss of definition. These qualities should correspond with those of the intensifying screen. Medium speed films are most commonly used in veterinary practice.

2) Nonscreen film comes in light-tight envelopes and is used where high definition is desirable and thick cassettes cannot be inserted , eg. intraoral views of the nasal cavity. Higher exposure factors are required, and some makes require longer processing times.

Grids

1) Grids are used to reduce the amount of scattered radiation reaching the film, therefore improving radiographic contrast.

2) A grid is contructed of many fine strips of lead which alternate with strips of radiolucent material. The lead acts as a filter to absorb X-rays which are not travelling in the line of the primary beam.

3) The grid lines are faintly visible on the developed film. To overcome this specialised systems which move the grid back and forth during the exposure can be incorporated into the X-ray table eg.the Potter-Bucky system.

3) As some useful X-rays will also be absorbed, higher exposure factors are required when a grid is used. The amount the mAs must be multiplied to compensate for this is known as the grid factor, and is usually marked on the grid. The use of grids should be restricted to radiography of regions thicker than 10cm, when scatter becomes significant.

4) The grid ratio describes the height of the lead strips relative to the distance between them, a ratio of 8:1 being suitable for a general purpose grid.

5) The lead strips may be parallel to one another, or in the case of a focussed grid, diverge with the X-ray beam. Focussed grids should only be used at the specified film-focus distance.

GRIDS

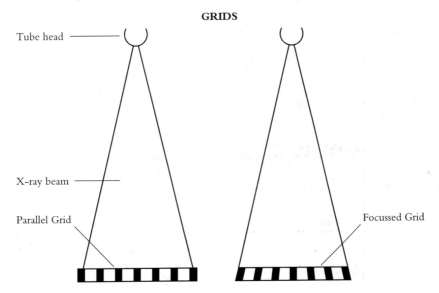

Tube head

X-ray beam

Parallel Grid

Focussed Grid

RESTRAINT FOR RADIOGRAPHY

1) General anaesthesia. Removes need for manual restraint and reduces movement blur. Necessary for selected views, some contrast studies and when animal in such pain (eg. fractures) that other means of restraint rendered inhumane. Seldom practicable in large animal radiography.

2) Sedation. The majority of routine small animal radiographs can be obtained with a combination of sedation and positional aids such as cradles and sandbags. And with tactful handling of the patient prior to making the exposure, manual restraint is seldom necessary.

3) Conscious patients. Occasionally the patient's condition (eg severe respiratory distress, shock) dictates that radiographs be taken fully conscious. This should be strictly supervised to reduce exposure of personnel to a minimum.

EXPOSURE CHARTS

To produce consistently diagnostic quality radiographs, a chart should be formulated for each individual X-ray machine.

The following influence the exposure and should be stated on the chart

1) the region radiographed
2) the species and size of the subject
3) the film-focus distance (it is simplest to use only one FFD)
4) the film/screen type
5) whether or not a grid is used
6) the kV, mA and the exposure time (or the combined mAs). If the kV is raised by 10, the mAs should be halved to get an equivalent exposure.

To penetrate dry plaster of Paris, double the mAs. Double this again if plaster is still wet.

NB. Processing must be standardised.

DARKROOM PROTOCOL

Poor darkroom technique results in poor quality radiographs – it is important to standardise all procedures and ensure that more than one person in the practice is familar with them. Practise good housekeeping in the darkroom to prevent contamination of films by chemical splashes, water and dust.

1) Check that the developer has been heated to the recommended temperature, usually 20°C (68°F), before starting to develop the film. This temperature should be maintained throughout the developing process by means of a thermostatically controlled heater or water jacket. The developer tank should be covered by a lid to reduce oxidation.

2) Turn off all the lights in the darkroom except the safelights. Check that the filter in the safelight is appropriate for the type of film in use (ie. whether blue or green sensitive).

3) Unload the cassette and place it within the stainless steel hanger. Work on the dry bench and handle the film by its edges only and as little as possible.

4) Place the film in the developer and agitate thoroughly to get rid of air bubbles and coat the emulsion evenly. Start the stop clock. Develop for precisely the recommended time (varies according to the formulation of the developer, usually between 3 and 5 minutes) at the correct temperature. Resist the temptation to view the film.

5) Meanwhile, dry hands thoroughly, return to the dry bench and reload the cassette. Remember to replace the lid of the film box securely!

6) When the stop clock rings, remove the film from the developer, replace the tank lid, and drain the film fully. Immerse the film in the wash tank a couple of times to arrest development and remove some of the chemical.

7) Place the film in the fixer tank to fix and harden for a minimum of 10–15 minutes. Fixer solution removes the undeveloped halides and allows the image to be viewed under white light. The film may be viewed after it has cleared (ie. no longer has a milky appearance- approximately 3 minutes) but should be replaced in the bath for the full time. Fixing time is not as critical as development time in that it does not matter if the film remains in the bath for longer than 15 minutes.

8) Remove the film from the fixer and wash in running water for a minimum of 30 minutes to remove as much chemical as possible.

9) Hang film to dry in a dust free atmosphere in its hanger or by a single hook placed in one corner. Channel hangers tend to hinder drying of edges. Take care to ensure wet films do not touch each other.

Automatic processing

1) Once the processor has reached working temperature, pass a used film through the machine to clean the rollers if the processor has not been in use that day.

2) Under safe light conditions remove the film from the cassette and insert into the processor – the film is fed automatically into the rollers. Wait for the warning light to go out or tone to sound before opening the door or turning on the lights.

3) Allow the developed film to emerge fully from the machine, do not pull it from the rollers.

IDENTIFICATION OF RADIOGRAPHS

1) The name of the practice, the date and the patient identity or case number should be marked on every radiograph.

2) Means of identification
   a) Lead letters. The film beneath the letter remains unexposed.
   b) Engraved perspex tablets. Modern equivalent of lead letters.
   c) Lead impregnated tape. Information written onto the tape will be transferred onto the film when the tape is stuck onto a cassette and an exposure made.
   d) Lead blocker and light marker. A lead blocker is fitted to the corner of the cassette, ensuring that a small part of the film is left unexposed. This corner of the film is inserted into a light marker in the darkroom. A piece of paper with the required details written onto it is inserted between the light source and the film, so that when the marker is activated the light flashes and imprints the details directly onto the film.

3) Additional markers
   a) Right and left, medial and lateral etc.
   b) Lead clockface, or marking film time numerically when doing a sequential study.
   c) Pre- and post- op.
   d) Metallic probes to outline or indicate fistulae etc.

FILING
The film should not be filed until it is completely dry.
Label the envelope with the same details marked on the radiograph.

FILM FAULTS

Fault	Cause	Remedy
Film too dark	1) Overexposure 2) Overdevelopment 3) Excessive fogging	1) Reduce kV, mAs 2) Check temperature of developer and time of development 3) Check safelight, cassettes and film storage conditions
Film and background density too light (common fault)	Underdevelopment	Check developer temperature, time of development, replenishment procedures.
Film too pale but background black	Underexposure	Increase mAs, kV
Image blurred	1) Movement of animal 2) Tube head or film movement 3) Poor screen/film contact	1) Review restraint procedure and consider anaesthesia 2) Stabilise equipment 3) Check cassette pressure pad
White specks	1) Dust, hairs, dirt inside cassette 2) Fixer splashes before development	1) Clean the screens 2) Improve darkroom technique
Black spots	Developer splashes	Avoid splashes
Crimp marks	Excess pressure from fingernails	Handle film by edges only
Clear white spots surrounded by ring	Airbubble marks	Agitate during development
Streaking	1) Lack of agitation 2) Dirty hangers 3) Inadequate rinsing 4) Drying marks	Correct darkroom technique
"Lightning flash" black streaks	Static marks	Remove film slowly from box when reloading cassette
Edge of film underexposed	Grid cut-off	Correct use of grid, ensure aligned properly and right way up

POSITIONING TIPS FOR SMALL ANIMAL RADIOGRAPHY

The following is a guide only. For more complete description see references.

Thorax
1) Use a high kV, low mAs exposure, keeping exposure time to minimum, and obtain film on maximum inspiration. However, if respiratory movement blur still a problem take film on expiration.
2) Ensure forelimbs pulled well forward on lateral view.
3) If animal dyspnoeic obtain dorsoventral view to rule out large pleural effusion or pneumothorax before positioning for lateral or ventrodorsal views.

Abdomen
1) Use high mAs, low kV setting to maximise contrast.
2) May need two exposures for lateral views in deep chested breeds, increase setting for cranial abdomen, decrease for caudal abdomen.

Spine
1) Often requires general anaesthesia for accurate positioning and to reduce discomfort.
2) Pad animal carefully to bring spine parallel to table top on lateral view.
3) Collimate closely over suspicious areas as only the disc spaces closest to the centre of the primary beam can be assessed fully.

Pelvis
1) For best results obtain under general anaesthesia.
2) Ventrodorsal view with hips in extension for hip dysplasia scheme. "Frog leg" view with hips naturally abducted useful to avoid damaging during positioning when radiographing trauma cases.

Skull
1) Dorsoventral view can be obtained under sedation, ventrodorsal and other views usually require general anaesthesia.
2) Tympanic bullae best assessed with open mouth rostrocaudal view – animal lies on back , hard palate vertical and lower jaw pulled back with ties. Beam directed vertically level with hard palate.
3) Use oblique views to separate upper and lower arcades when assessing tooth roots.
4) The nasal cavity is best assessed with the intraoral view using nonscreen film. Place the corner of the film into the mouth as far caudally as possible.

CONTRAST MEDIA

Definition

Contrast media are used to visualise soft tissue structures which are difficult to identify clearly on plain films due to lack of surrounding contrast. Their use can provide information regarding the position, shape, size, internal surface and, in some cases, function of the tissue under examination.

1) Positive contrast media contain elements of high atomic number (eg. iodine or barium), so are more opaque than surrounding tissues.
2) Negative contrast agents are gases (room air or carbon dioxide) with low specific gravity, so are less opaque.

Good quality plain films should always be obtained prior to a contrast study-
1) to check exposure factors and positioning.
2) to ensure the animal is adequately prepared for the study (eg. has an empty stomach before a barium meal).
3) to ensure the diagnosis is not apparent from the plain film.
4) to select the correct contrast technique and judge the amount of material necessary.

Types of positive contrast agent

1) **Barium**
   eg. Micropaque Standard suspension (Nicholas).
   a) Used for examination of the gastrointestinal tract.
   b) Inert and insoluble, is not absorbed by gastro-intestinal tract or acted upon by its secretions. Provides excellent mucosal detail.
   c) Can remain in situ indefinitely if leaks through a perforation of the bowel or is aspirated into the lower airways and may provoke a foreign body reaction.
   d) Available as powder, ready made suspension, or thick paste. Store at room temperature in a dry place.

2) **Water soluble iodine preparations**

   a) **Conventional**
      eg. Conray and Gastro-Conray (May & Baker), Urografin and Gastrografin (Schering), Hypaque (Sterling Research).
      i) Contain either the **sodium or meglumine salts of either iothalamic, metrizoic or diatrizoic acid (tri-iodinated benzoic acids).**
      ii) Hypertonic, soluble and carry an ionic charge.
      iii) Excreted by the kidneys after I/V administration.
      iv) Most often given by the intravenous route, may also be given via a urinary catheter into the lower urinary tract for selected studies, or per os for examination of the gastro-intestinal system when a perforation is suspected. Because these solutions are hypertonic, they exert an osmotic effect as they pass through the intestines, and are progressively diluted by gastro-intestinal secretions. They therefore give poorer contrast and mucosal detail than barium.

v) Side effects which may result from I/V use include a drop in blood pressure or very rarely, an anaphylactic reaction. Disturbances in fluid and electrolyte balance should be corrected before their use. If given to conscious animals, the animal may whine or retch on administration.

b) **Lower osmolar, ionic media**
   eg.Hexabrix (May & Baker).
   i) **Sodium and meglumine ioxaglate** produce fewer side effects than conventional media as they are less hypertonic. They are therefore more suitable for use in gastro-intestinal studies as they are less diluted by gastro-intestinal secretions so provide better contrast and improved mucosal detail than the conventional media above.

c) **Lower osmolar, non-ionic media**
   eg. Niopam (E.Merck) and Omnipaque (Nyegaard).
   i) Unlike the above, these agents do not carry an ionic charge, so are therefore safe for use in myelography. They may also be used in intravenous studies.
   ii) Iopamidol (Niopam) and iohexol (Omnipaque) are the most widely used examples. Because metrizamide is only available as a freeze dried powder which must be made up shortly before use, and is more expensive, it is less commonly used.

Preparation and storage

a) All the water soluble contrast media (with the exception of metrizamide) are available in bottled sterile solutions of varying iodine concentrations.
b) They should be stored at room temperature below 30°C, protected from light and secondary irradiation. Care should be taken to maintain their sterility when aliquots are withdrawn.

Other iodine containing positive contrast agents, now rarely used –

3) **Cholecystopaques**
   eg. Biligram and Biliscopin (Schering).
   These are water soluble organic iodine compounds which, if given I/V or orally, are then excreted by the liver, outlining the gall bladder and bile ducts.

4) **Viscous and oily agents**
   a) Viscous agents (eg. Dionosil Aqueous (Glaxo)) are used for bronchography and contain a suspension of propyliodone in either water or arachis oil.
   b) Oily iodine agents (eg. Pantopaque (Wintrop))are immiscible with water, so cannot be given I/V, and are only slowly eliminated from the body. They have limited use eg. lymphangiography.

USE OF CONTRAST MEDIA

Examination of the gastro-intestinal tract

i) **Method.** The technique used is selected according to the region of the gastro-intestinal tract to be investigated. A fine colloidal suspension of barium sulphate is routinely used, unless a perforation is suspected, when organic iodine preparions are preferable.

ii) **Preparation.** The alimentary tract should be emptied by withholding food for 24 hours, and judicious use of enemata, although this is not usually necessary in the case with vomiting or inappetence.

iii) **Sedation.** General anaesthesia, heavy sedation and use of opiates should be avoided as this reduces the rate of passage of the contrast agent and increases the risk of aspiration. Light sedation with low doses of a phenothiazine derivative (eg. acepromazine maleate) may be necessary.

Techniques

a) **Oesophagus**

i) Smear thick barium paste onto the tongue and hard palate or allow the animal to eat a small barium meal (eg. 20-30ml of 100% w/v barium sulphate suspension added to a small amount of palatable tinned food).
Do NOT use liquid barium alone in an animal with swallowing difficulties – there is a high risk of aspiration.

ii) As soon as contrast has been given, position animal in lateral recumbancy and take exposure.

b) **Stomach**

i) Administer 100% w/v barium suspension either by syringe or plastic bottle with nozzle introduced into corner of the mouth (allowing the animal time to swallow), or via a stomach tube.

ii) Amount needed varies (15-100ml) according to size of animal, speed of administration and rate of gastric emptying.

iii) Take left lateral and VD views before right lateral and DV views to delay passage of contrast into duodenum. All 4 views should be obtained.

iv) Alternately, perform a double contrast gastrogram, using both barium and air for better visualisation of the mucosal pattern.
Premedicate animal with acepromazine and give glucagon I/V (0.1 mg total dose of glucagon for up to 8kg body weight, 0.2mg for 8-20kg, and 0.3mg for over 20kg) to reduce speed of gastric emptying.
Give 2ml/kg of high density, low viscosity barium sulphate suspension (170-200% w/v) via a stomach tube, using a syringe and 3 way tap. Inflate stomach with approximately 20ml/kg room air, remove stomach tube, and slowly rotate patient to coat mucosa with contrast.
Obtain 4 views as above.
Effervescent formulae of barium sulphate are available to produce a similar effect.

c) **Small intestine**
   i)   For optimum visualisation administer 25% w/v barium made up by diluting 100% w/v suspension with water, at 8-12ml/kg for cats and small dogs, 5-7ml/kg for larger dogs.
   ii) In practice however, the small intestine is most often examined in the same positive contrast study as the stomach.
   iii) Take a series of films, lateral and ventrodorsal views, at intervals determined by rate of transit and suspected pathology, usually between 5-20 minutes apart.

d) **Large intestine**
   i)   Can be visualised at the end of the study when barium given orally ("follow through"), but as barium is mixed with faeces by then lesions are easily missed.
   ii) Preferable to give as barium enema, about 10ml/kg of 20% w/v barium suspension. Colon should be prepared by cleansing enema of warm water at least 2-3hrs prior to study. Barium slowly introduced by enema syringe, gravity feed tube and funnel or ready prepared bags, or via a Foley catheter and large syringe. The animal should be sedated or anaesthetised, and a purse-string suture may be placed round the anus to prevent leakage of contrast.
   iii) Take lateral and ventrodorsal views and then remove contrast and inflate colon with air to produce double contrast study, which provides better mucosal detail.

Examination of the urinary tract

Contrast media containing water soluble iodine (eg. Conray, Urografin) is used for positive contrast examinations of the urinary tract. The large bowel should be empty as faeces can obscure the structures under examination. General anaesthesia is usually preferable to sedation for these studies.

a) **Kidney and ureters**
   Water soluble iodine containing media are excreted via the kidneys following intravenous injection, allowing the upper urinary tract to be readily visualised. The examination is known as intravenous urography (IVU), and made be performed in two ways:
   i) **Low volume, rapid injection IVU.** This is the most commonly used technique. A total dose of 600-800 mg/kg iodine is injected intravenously as a rapid bolus. Using 60-70% contrast media (300-400mg iodine/ml) this is a dose of 2ml/kg. The initial film should be taken 10 seconds from the start of injection to demonstrate the renal arteries and parenchyma. Subsequent films are taken at one minute, and every five minutes thereafter.
   ii) **High volume, drip infusion IVU.** A more dilute solution of contrast media (150 mg iodine /ml) is given slowly over a 15 minute period to a total dose of 1200mg iodine/kg. Contrast media is available at this concentration or may be diluted from more concentrated preparations with sterile saline. Films are taken every five minutes for twenty minutes.This technique will not demonstrate the renal parenchyma with the same clarity, but shows the ureters better than the previous technique.

With both techniques, it is preferable to start with the animal anaesthetised and lying in dorsal recumbancy, with a cannula in the cephalic vein for administration of the contrast agent. The initial films are taken in the ventrodorsal projection, with lateral views taken subsequently. Compression of the caudal abdomen with a broad band is occasionally used to delay flow of contrast into the bladder with the low volume technique, but this can produce distortion of the renal pelvices and ureters. Both techniques may be usefully combined with a pneumocystogram to improve visualisation of the ureteric openings.

b) **Bladder**
   i) Pneumocytography.The bladder is catheterised and emptied. The bladder is then inflated with air using a three way tap and syringe or bulb insufflator until moderately distended. The amount of air required varies considerably with the animal's size, the distensibility of the bladder, and the extent of leakage of air back around the catheter, so is best judged by gentle palpation of the bladder through the abdominal wall.
   ii) Positive contrast cystography.The technique is similar to pneumocystography but positive contrast (50-300ml of 5-10% w/v water soluble iodine containing media) introduced in place of air.
   iii) Double contrast cystography is the best means of visualising the bladder. First catheterise and empty the bladder. A small volume (3-5ml) of 20% contrast media is then introduced via the catheter and a three way tap. The animal is then rotated to coat the mucosa, and the bladder inflated with air as described above.

For all three techniques, the lateral view of the caudal abdomen is most useful, and a ventrodorsal view may often not be necessary.

c) **Retrograde urethrography in the male dog**

5-10ml of a 50/50 mixture of KY jelly and water soluble contrast media (150-200mg iodine/ml) is introduced via a catheter placed just inside the penile urethra. The mixture is best made up the day before to get rid of bubbles. Two lateral views, hindlegs drawn forward then back, allow the whole urethra to be seen. Ventrodorsal views are less commonly taken but are occasionally helpful.

d) **Retrograde vagino-urethrography in the bitch**

A plastic urinary dog catheter is placed just inside the vulval lips of the anaesthetised bitch which are then gently clamped shut with atraumatic bowel forceps. Water soluble contrast media, 200mg iodine/ml, can then be introduced carefully avoiding excess pressure, to a volume of 1ml/kg. Only the lateral view is taken.

Before removing the catheter after completion of studies of the lower urinary tract, some attempt should be made to withdraw the contrast media.

Myelography

In myelography the spinal cord is outlined by the injection of contrast media into the subarachnoid space so that it mixes freely with the cerebrospinal fluid that bathes the cord.

i)   General anaesthesia is essential. The injection is most often made into the cisterna magna with the animal in lateral recumbancy and the head held flexed by an assistant at 90° to the spine. The skin caudal to the occipital crest should be clipped and surgically prepared. Care should be taken to ensure that the endotracheal tube is not kinked.

ii) A 21-23 gauge spinal or hypodermic needle is introduced carefully into the subarachnoid space, and CSF will flow from the needle. The syringe can then be attached and the contrast media injected slowly.

iii) ONLY low osmolar, non-ionic water soluble contrast agents should be used. Other agents have toxic effects on the CNS. A dose of 0.3ml/kg of 330mg/ml iopamidol or iohexol (maximum 9ml total dose), can be used.

iv) The head and neck should then be raised or the table tilted for a few minutes, to encourage the flow of contrast down the spinal canal. Lateral radiographs are taken sequentially to follow the passage of contrast caudally, with ventrodorsal and collimated views taken when a lesion is identified.

v)   After the procedure the animal's head should continue be be raised while it recovers from general anaesthesia. Sometimes seizure activity occurs on recovery, this is usually readily controlled with intravenous diazapam.

vi) Lumbar myelography is technically more difficult, the needle being inserted between the 4th and 5th, or 5th and 6th lumbar vetrebrae, and is best performed under image intensification.

Arthrography

The shoulder joint of dogs may be injected with 1-1.5ml water soluble contrast media, air or both, to help identify lesions which are not clearly visible on plain films. General anaesthesia and surgical preparation of the skin overlying the joint are required. There are few indications for the technique- it is most often performed to demonstrate the extent of osteochrondtis dessicans.

The cardiovascular system

The heart and selected vessels may be visualised by intravascular injection of water soluble contrast media. In most cases it is necessary to make an exposure immediately after injection, and rapid film changing equipment is required to follow the flow of contrast through the area under investigation. These studies are most often performed in referral centres.

RADIOGRAPHY FOR THE BVA/KENNEL CLUB HIP DYSPLASIA SCHEME

In order to reduce the incidence and severity of hip dysplasia in the dog, owners of dogs which are known to have a breed predistribution to hip dysplasia may have the dog's hips radiographed and scored by a panel of veterinary radiologists in order to select only those animals with good hip conformation for breeding.

Practice procedure

1) Only dogs over 12 months of age may be submitted to the scheme. There is no upper age limit.

2) Whenever possible obtain consent for general anaesthesia, as this is the best means of obtaining a standard technique for positioning and reduces the need for repeat radiographs and manual restraint.

3) The following information must be marked on the radiograph prior to development.
    a) the dog's Kennel Club number (obtained from the top right hand corner of the original Kennel Club Registration Certificate). This is usually written on lead impregnated tape.
    b) the date
    c) a right or left marker.
    This labelling should be located in a standarised way to avoid obscuring anatomical features.

4) The dog should lie in dorsal recumbancy, the trunk supported by a cradle, with the hips in full extension and the femora parallel to one another. Inward rotation of the stifles, which can then be secured with tape or a bandage, is necessary to achieve this.

5) The testes or ovaries may be covered with a lead gonad shield (ensuring the hips are not obscured). This is good practice generally when radiographing animals intended for breeding.

6) The radiograph, accompanied by the combined declaration form and scoring sheet (signed by the owner and the veterinary surgeon), and the fee, should then by sent to the BVA panel. If the hips are obviously bad, some owners are reluctant to submit the film, but they should be encouraged to do so as this is the only means of accurately assessing the average score for the breed.

7) The BVA panel of scrutineers will reject any poor quality radiographs and a further charge may be payable for examination of a repeat film. If the film quality is satisfactory, each hip is assessed and scored according to the appearance of nine radiographic features. The higher the score, the worse the hips are judged to be affected, with a maximum score of 53 for each hip, 106 per dog.

8) The radiograph and two copies of the completed scoring sheet are returned to the veterinary practice. One copy is retained and filed, the second passed on to the owner.

9) Radiographs may be re-submitted once if the client wishes to appeal against the original score. A further fee is payable, and the radiograph scored by the chief scrutineer, whose decision is final.

10) The names of dogs with scores of 8 or less, with not more than 6 on one hip, may be published in the Kennel Gazette, subject to the owner's consent.

LABELLING FOR THE HIP DYSPLASIA SCHEME

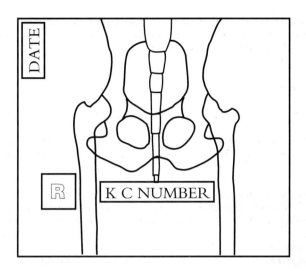

FLUOROSCOPY

Modern fluoroscopic apparatus links a fluorescent screen with an image intensifier to produce a radiographic image which can be viewed on a television monitor. This allows continous updating of the image during exposure to X-rays ("screening") so that movements of body tissues such as the heart beat and gut peristalsis can be observed. Fluoroscopy is useful in interventional techniques such as placement of cardiac pacemakers and lumbar puncture, and in contrast studies such as angiography.

Production of the image

1) The source of the X-rays is a conventional tube head, with the beam closely collimated to the area under investigation.

2) The cassette is replaced by a fluorescent screen , the crystals of which emit light when exposed to X-rays, producing a radiographic image.

3) An image intensifier increases the brightness of this image and increases the visible detail, allowing a great reduction in the amount of radiation required to produce a diagnostic image. A photocathode reacts to the light produced by the fluorescent screen, and emits electrons. These are accelerated towards a photo-anode by applying a voltage across a vacuum which greatly increases their energy. The photo-anode converts the electrical signal back into a visible light image, which can be recorded by a cine or television camera. (The black and white areas of a conventional radiograph are reversed, giving a positive image).

4) During screening, the guidelines for radiation protection during conventional radiography should be adopted.

ULTRASOUND

Ultrasonography is the use of high frequency sound waves which are reflected by the tissues of the body to produce an image. It has many applications including obstetrics, evaluation of abdominal soft tissues, and echocardiography.

Production of the image

1) Sound waves are produced by applying a voltage to piezo-electric crystals housed within the head of the transducer (or probe).
2) The sound waves travel harmlessly through the tissues, and are reflected by them according to different tissue characteristics.
3) The reflected waves return to the transducer which relays information about the depth of tissue from which they have been reflected and the strength of the echo. This is displayed on a screen as a two-dimensional cross-sectional image when the machine is operating in B ("brightness") mode. This image can be rapidly updated so that movement of body tissues (eg. heart beat, gut peristalsis) can be observed – this is referred to as real-time imaging.
4) Machines may also be equipped with a Doppler facillity which evaluates signals reflected by rapidly moving particles – this is most often used to assess blood flow through cardiac chambers and blood vessels.
5) Various designs of transducer are available – the sector scanner which produces a pie-shaped image on the screen is most widely used in small animal work. Linear array scanners are more suitable for rectal use in large animal obstetrics and for scanning equine tendons.
6) The detail visible within the tissues increases with the frequency of the ultrasound waves produced by the probe, but at the expense of penetrating ability of the beam. Frequencies of 5MHz are appropriate for cardiac and abdominal imaging in medium and large dogs, 7.5MHz for small dogs and cats, 7.5-10MHz for ophthalmic imaging.

Patient preparation

1) The animal's hair usually has to be clipped over the area under examination as ultrasound does not penetrate air and close contact with the skin is essential. The skin may then be cleansed with spirit. Liberal amounts of coupling gel should be applied to the head of the probe.
2) Most animals tolerate the procedure well, and only a minority will require sedation.
3) There is no evidence to suggest that ultrasound is harmful at the intensities used for diagnostic purposes.

CARE, MAINTENENCE AND USE OF RADIOGRAPHIC EQUIPMENT.

Care of the X-ray set

1) A report by the installer confirming that the equipment is satisfactory should be provided before it is put to use. It is the responsibility of the manufacturer and supplier of the equipment to ensure that the equipment does not emit unnecessary radiation and that it functions properly.
2) The machine should be serviced periodically according to the degree it is used and at least yearly.

Care of Cassettes and Intensifying Screens

1) Cassettes and screens are readily damaged and should be handled with care. If dropped this may reduce film/screen contact, producing areas of unsharpness on the developed film. Test for this by placing wire mesh on top of cassette and taking exposure at a large film/focal distance. Poor contact will show as blurring of the image.
2) Test for light leakage by loading with film and leaving in normally lit room for an hour. Develop the film, any blackening around the edges indicates damage and cassette should be replaced.
3) The screen surface should not be touched with the fingers and can be permanently damaged by developer or fixer splashes.
4) Dust and animal hair must be removed from the cassette with a soft brush, and the screens cleaned regularily, at least on a monthly basis. Damp cotton wool and a mild soap (which should then be lightly rinsed off with water), or proprietary cleaner with anti-static properties, can be used to clean the screens using figure-of-eight motions. Stand vertically to dry in a dust free room before reloading with film, and label the outside of the cassette with the date of cleaning. At all other times cassettes should be kept closed.
5) If there is a risk of blood or urine leaking into a cassette during an examination, it should be placed within a plastic bag.
6) If more than one type of screen is used, the cassette should be clearly labelled to indicate which is in place.

Care of Stationary Grids, Protective Clothing and Positioning Aids

1) **Grids.** Grids are expensive and fragile. The corners especially are easily damaged. Store in a case or box and clean regularly with a damp cloth. Special grid cassettes are available which have a recess in the front to house a grid.
2) **Protective clothing.** Lead aprons should never be folded but should instead be hung up, over wide rollers rather than narrow hangers, when not in use. The base of the fingers of gloves are particularly prone to cracking and must be checked carefully. Defects may not be obvious externally, and so radiographing the clothing (by laying it over a cassette and taking a moderately high exposure) should be performed periodically to detect any flaw. Routinely clean clothing with soap and water.
3) **Positioning aids.** Plastic or clingfilm covered foam cushions, sandbags and cradles should be kept clean, and wiped free of contrast media.

Care of X-ray Film

1) Mark delivery date on boxes of film and use in date order. Note expiry date.
2) Always stand boxes vertically as film emulsion is pressure sensitive.
3) Unopened boxes should be stored in a cool, dry place away from strong chemical fumes and the source of radiation if storage fogging is to be avoided. (In hot, humid climates they may be best in cold storage.)
4) Opened boxes should be kept in the darkroom, protected from white light and radiation. They should not be put into cold storage after opening. The inner wrapper should be carefully folded over and the box securely closed immediately after a film is removed.
5) Film should be handled gently and by the edges only.

Care of Darkroom Equipment and Chemicals.

1) The wet tanks should be emptied and cleaned thoroughly at intervals dependent on the number of films processed, but approximately every six weeks. Made up solutions should never be kept for longer than 3 months as they oxidise and become unfit for use.
2) Fresh developer and fixer can then be made up according to the manufacturer's instructions. The developer should be kept covered to prevent oxidation, and the wash tank and water jacket filled.
3) The number of films taken should be recorded and the tanks topped up with the correct replenisher solution at weekly intervals.(NB. Topping up should only be done with replenisher, not with water or the original developer solution). As a rough guide to the amount of developer replenisher required, one large film will absorb about 60ml of developer. Usual practice is to replenish a volume equal to that of the original developer before the solutions are thrown away and fresh developer made up.
4) Keep separate wet and dry benches, and mop up any splashes.
5) Avoid at all costs contamination of developer by fixer (eg. never use the same stirrer for both solutions)- if this occurs the developer must be immediately replaced.

Care of the Automatic Processor

1) Switch on machine first thing in the morning. Allow time to warm up and then pass an old used film through the machine to clean rollers.
2) Leave on stand-by ready for immediate use for the rest of the day.
3) Switch off at the end of each day and wipe clean exposed parts with a damp cloth.
4) Rollers should be removed and cleaned with water once a week.
5) Check and top up chemicals with appropriate replenisher as required.
6) Machine should be serviced by an engineer regularly.

CARE, MAINTENANCE AND USE OF ULTRASOUND EQUIPMENT

1) Ultrasound machines generally require very little in the way of routine maintainence provided they are handled carefully. New machines usually carry a 12 month warranty, and when this expires a maintainence contract may be offered. This may not be available to purchasers of secondhand machines.

2) The most likely part of the machine to be damaged is the transducer (or probe). As these are delicate and extremely expensive items, great care should be taken to avoid dropping them.

3) During an investigation, mechanical transducers should be put into freeze mode whenever they are not in contact with the patient to reduce wear, and at the end of the study before the machine is turned off.

4) After each use the transducer, keyboard and screen controls should be wiped clean of acoustic gel, and the transducer either disconnected from the machine and replaced in its case, or secured within its attachment to the machine.

5) Some makes of ultrasound machine have simple dust filters which require frequent emptying-ask the supplier to demonstrate the procedure.

RADIATION PROTECTION

Nature of injury

X rays are a form of ionising radiation, causing ionisation and excitation of the atomic lattice of the body tissues through which they pass, leaving the cells in a state of high chemical reactivity. A number of serious biological effects may then occur, either as the result of a single massive exposure or by more insidious accumulative doses.

Legislation

1) The **Ionising Radiation Regulations 1985** (and the supporting Approved Code of Practice, *The protection of persons against ionising radiation arising from any work activity*) were established to minimise the risk to personnel.

2) In 1988, the National Radiological Protection Board and the Health and Safety Executive published a booklet entitled Guidance notes for the Protection of Persons against Ionising Radiations arising from Veterinary use, which indicates the practical arrangements which should be employed in order to comply with the legal requirements of the Regulations. It is a good practice policy to keep a copy in the room used for radiography.

Responsibility within the practice

1) A **radiation protection adviser** (RPA) approved by the Health and Safety Executive should be appointed by the practice. Their role is to provide specialist advice, and to inspect the premises and equipment where there is any doubt over safety aspects. They are either holders of the Diploma in Veterinary Radiology or health physicists with an interest in veterinary radiology.

2) The practice should also appoint a **radiation protection supervisor** (RPS) to implement and supervise day to day safe running of the machine. This is usually a senior member of staff actively involved in radiography.

3) In veterinary work, it is unlikely that any member of staff would be exposed to radiation greater than 3/10ths the dose limits defined by the Regulations. Therefore they do not need to be classified, provided they only operate under a **Written System of Work**, which indicates the estimated personal doses which might be expected to arise from operation of the system, gives details of the monitoring arrangements (eg. personal dosemeters) used to verify these estimates and requires that the X-ray set be isolated from the electrical supply after each radiographic session.

4) The Written System of Work should form part of the more general **local rules**, which should be drawn up with the advice of the RPA, and displayed in the X-ray room and copies given to anyone carrying out radiography. Additional information provided by the local rules will vary from practice to practice but may include the names of the RPA and RPS, a description of the controlled area, the procedure to be followed when taking radiographs, the use of protective clothing and details of a contingency plan to be followed in the event of a fault or incident.

Controlled areas

1) An RPA's advice will normally be sought to determine the extent of a controlled area. With permanently installed equipment this area needs to be physically demarcated and access to it restricted, therefore it is most usual to designate the whole room in which X-rays are taken as the controlled area.

2) Entry to the room should be restricted by use of illuminated warning notices and the international radiation trefoil. When mobile equipment is used outside, for example in large animal work, portable warning signs should be erected, and when possible any horizontal beam directed towards a thick wall.

SAFE PROCEDURES FOR RADIOGRAPHY

1) Radiography should only be undertaken where there is definite clinical justification for the procedure.

2) Whenever possible, x-ray examinations should take place in a designated room with the beam directed vertically downwards onto an examination table.

3) Ensure that only persons whose presence is required and who understand the procedure remain in the room. Unless they can stand behind a lead screen, they must wear a protective lead apron. They should try to remain at least 2 metres from the X-ray tube and the animal being radiographed. Close the door to the room.

4) Avoid using manual restraint. A combination of restraining aids and sedation or general anaesthesia should be used instead in the great majority of small animal patients, unless this is contra-indicated by the animal's condition. If , in exceptional circumstances, manual restraint is necessary;
   a) pregnant women or anyone under 16 years of age should not be asked to hold the animal
   b) those holding the animal must wear lead sleeves or gloves as well as an apron, and should be positioned as far as possible from the primary beam.
   c) manual restraint should not be permitted unless the X-ray set is fitted with a light beam diaphragm to ensure that no part of the person holding the animal is within the path of the primary beam.
   d) if accidental exposure of personnel to the primary beam occurs, inform the RPS.

5) The beam should be collimated maximally to reduce the amount of scattered radiation. The field size must always be smaller than the cassette used.

6) Use of a grid increases the exposure values needed and therefore should only be practised when the part of the animal being radiographed exceeds 10cm thickness.

7) Use the fastest suitable film/screen combination to reduce exposure values to a minimum.

8) To avoid unnecessary repetition of radiographs use standardised exposure charts, keep permanent records of exposures used for each animal and the quality of the films obtained, and practise good darkroom techniques.

9) If the exposure button jams, immediately turn the machine off at the mains. Inform the RPS and the service engineer.

REFERENCES

LEE R. (Ed) (1989) *A Guide to Diagnostic Radiography and Radiology in Small Animal Practice*, BSAVA publications.

DOUGLAS S.W., HERRTAGE M.E. and WILLIAMSON H.D. (1987) *Principles of Veterinary Radiography*, 4th Edition, Balliere Tindall.

National Radiological Protection Board, HMSO. *Guidance Notes for the Protection of Persons Against Ionising Radiations Arising from Veterinary Use*. (1988).

BVA Publications, *Health and Safety at Work Act. A Guide for Veterinary Practices*. (1989).

SURGERY

GENERAL THEATRE ORGANISATION

The theatre suite consists of a patient preparation area, operating room, surgeons scrub-up area and an instrument preparation and storage area. Other areas in or near theatre may include a recovery room and a changing room for theatre personnel.

The operating room should contain the minimum furniture necessary which must be easily removeable to allow regular cleaning. Fixtures and fittings (e.g. x-ray viewers) should be flush within the wall, this prevents dust collection and makes cleaning easier.

A strict theatre protocol must be enforced. Personnel entering theatre must change into clean theatre clothing and footwear. Hats and masks should be worn by everyone. The number of people in theatre can contribute to the risk of infection. The more people, the higher the risk, therefore personnel in theatre should be kept to the minimum.

The operating room should always be left clean, tidy and ready for use.

Cleaning Routine

1) Daily: damp dust all surfaces in the theatre using a cloth and antiseptic solution at the beginning and end of each day.
   Clean the table, scrub sinks and all dirty areas between operative procedures.
   At the end of the day wash all floors and tables properly.
2) Weekly: Remove all furniture and clean walls, floors and equipment thoroughly.
   All rooms connected with theatre should have a thorough weekly clean.

Planning the surgery list

All operative procedures can be divided into one of the following categories:-

1) Clean: sterile surgery with no breaks in aseptic technique.
2) Clean/Contaminated: sterile surgery where there is potential for contamination e.g. gastro-intestinal surgery.
3) Contaminated: sterile surgery where contamination will occur e.g. gut anastomosis
4) Dirty: surgery of a non sterile area e.g. oral surgery.

To minimise risk of infection the operating list for each day should be planned taking the above categories into account. Priority should be given to any surgery involving implants followed by all the 'clean' surgery. Contaminated or dirty surgery should be left until last.

PREPARATION OF THE PATIENT

Pre-operative preparation

Bathing: If the patient is very dirty a pre-operative bath may be advisable. Ideally all patients undergoing surgery involving prosthesis (e.g. hip replacement) should be bathed.

Clipping: Clipping should be carried out in the prep area. Clip a large neat area around the surgical site. Consider clipping before anaesthesia if the patient is amenable, the site accessible and not too painful. Patients that do not permit clipping before anaesthesia must be clipped in the prep area of theatre. Clipping more than 12 hours before surgery may increase skin bacteria. To minimise this and therefore reduce the risk of infection, patients which are clipped before going to theatre should have the area cleaned with a skin scrub solution immediately after clipping.

Starvation: Food should normally be withdrawn twelve hours prior to surgery. Access to water should be allowed until the time of premedication or 30 minutes before anaesthesia. Special consideration may be needed in some cases such as Diabetics or paediatrics when fasting for 12 hours is not recommended.

Enema: An enema may be necessary to evacuate the bowel before surgery (e.g. rectal surgery). Bathing may be required afterwards.

Medication or eye drops: Antibiotics or other medication may need to be given prior to surgery to reach peak levels during the time of surgery.

Procedures following anaesthesia

These should be carried out in the prep area.

Catheterisation of the bladder: to monitor urine output, to empty the bladder prior to abdominal surgery or to prevent iatrogenic damage to the bladder.

Purse string suture: usually around the anus, preventing contamination during surgery in this region.

Throat pack: to prevent blood and debris passing down the trachea during oral or nasal surgery.

Tourniquet: using an Esmarch bandage to provide a blood free surgical site.

Foot bandage: to reduce the risk of contamination during surgery the foot or un-clipped part of the distal limb should be covered with a dressing.

Wounds: any wounds should be dressed to avoid further contamination.

PREPARATION OF THE OPERATIVE SITE

Clipping

Clipping should be carried out in the prep area. Clip a large straight-edged area around the surgical site. Remove surplus hairs using a vacuum cleaner or equivalent. Special attention should be paid to hair removal as small loose hairs are difficult to remove and may be carried into theatre. Use good sharp clipper blades as skin irritation increases the likelihood of wound interference by the patient. Using an open razor will also increase skin damage and irritation. When clipping around open wounds use a sterile water soluable lubricant in the wound to prevent contamination from clipped hairs, this can be washed out afterwards. The clippers should be cleaned and lubricated after each patient. The blades should be removed at regular intervals for sterilisation by spraying with a proprietory clipper disinfectant/lubricant particularly after cases which may be infected.

Skin preparation

Aim: to destroy micro-organisms in the operative site.

Solutions used: Chlorhexidine: Hibiscrub: Pitman-Moore
                                         Nolvasan: Willows Francis
                      Povidone Iodine: Pevidine: BK Veterinary Products
                                         Betidine: Napp Laboratories

Initial prep. should be done in the prep area before moving into theatre. Mechanical cleaning and skin contact times are important. Take care not to wet the coat too much during preparation.

Method

1) Using lint free swabs, water and scrub solution start at the intended area of surgical incision, using small circular movements, work towards the edges of the clipped area. Discard swabs and repeat.
2) Rinse with methylated spirit and repeat.
3) Keep repeating the procedure until the swabs indicate that the area is clean (i.e. no more surface dirt can be removed).
4) This procedure should be repeated once the patient is positioned in theatre. The final prep should be applied in a sterile manner, preferably by the surgical team using sterile swabs on sponge holding forceps.

Areas which involve mucous membranes (e.g. mouth and eyes) or open wounds require a different method of pre surgical preparation. In these areas, as chlorhexidine may be irritant, a dilute solution of povidine (0.1%) should be used with sterile water or saline.

PREPARATION OF THE SURGICAL TEAM

Scrubbing

Aim: to significantly reduce the number of micro-organisms on the hands and arms of the surgical team.

Before starting the surgical scrub the team should remove all jewellery and watches, nails should be short and clean.

The 5 minute scrub routine can be divided into stages of approximately one minute each.

1) Wash hands and arms to elbows with a non-perfumed, non coloured soap and rinse, ensuring the water flows away from the hands.
2) Wash hands and arms in the same manner with a scrub solution (e.g. Hibiscrub). Rinse as before.
3) Using a sterile brush and scrub solution the palm of each hand and all 4 surfaces of each finger should be scrubbed. Allow 1 minute for each hand, rinse the brush before changing to the second hand. Backs of hands and arms need not be scrubbed as this may lead to sore and damaged skin.
4) Finally wash hands to mid fore-arm with the scrub solution and rinse.

Scrub solutions should be kept in an elbow operated dispenser. Hands should be kept above elbows to allow water to drain down, arms should be kept away from the torso. Hands should not be shaken dry.

To dry hands and arms, pick up the towel and keeping the same surface uppermost dry the first hand on one quarter of the towel and the second hand on the next quarter. Dry from the wrist to the elbow in one movement in the third quarter and repeat on the other arm in the remaining quarter.

Gowning

The surgical gown is folded with the inside outermost (see Figure 1) This prevents handling the outside of the gown with ungloved hands.

Holding the gown away from the body it is gently shaken down. The hands are put in the sleeve holes and arms extended forward. An un-scrubbed assistant then adjusts and secures the gown. Most gowns secure at the back (see Figure 2) so the assistant must only touch the ties at the back of the gown, this area is then considered non-sterile. Some gowns wrap completely around and are secured at the side by the wearer (see Figure 3). These give all round sterility as there is no need for an un-scrubbed assistant to touch the gown.

Practical Veterinary Nursing

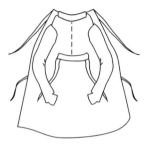

1) Lie flat out

2) Fold side to middle

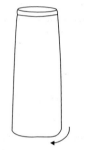

3) Fold over other side to edge

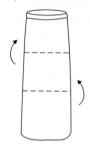

4) Fold lengthways

**FIGURE 1
FOLDING A GOWN**

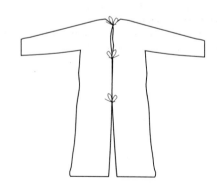

**FIGURE 2
BACK TIE GOWN**

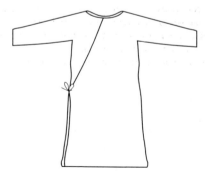

**FIGURE 3
SIDE TIE GOWN**

Gloving

Even after a through scrub up routine the hands and arms can not be considered sterile and may still harbour micro-organisms. To protect the patient from the risk of infection sterile gloves should be worn for all surgical procedures. The starch free gloves now available are better than the powdered variety as it has been shown that powder may interfere with wound healing.
Surgical gloves should be laid out onto a sterile surface ready to be put on.

There are two main gloving methods available:-

A) **Closed Gloving**; this is the best method for gloving prior to surgical procedures as there is less risk of contamination. (see Figure 4).

   1) Keep hands inside cuffs.
   2) Turn glove packet upside down.
   3) Pick up right glove with right hand by the rolled rim folded over (glove fingers should be pointing down towards the elbow).
   4) Take hold of the other side of the rolled rim with the left hand and pull over the top of the right hand.
   5) Push the hand forward into the glove and adjust, still keeping the other hand inside the cuff.
   6) Repeat the procedure with the left hand.

B) **Open Gloving**; this may still be used for sterile but non invasive procedures (see Figure 5).

   1) With hands outside the cuffs the right glove is picked up with the left hand. Only the inner surface of the glove should be handled. Pull onto the right hand but do not unfold the cuff. Hook the thumb underneath the cuff as the hand is pushed into the glove.
   2) Pick up the left glove underneath the fold with the gloved fingers of the right hand. Pull onto the left hand pulling the cuff back over the thumb.
   3) Pull the cuff of the left glove back over the gown cuff with the fingers of the right hand.
   4) Repeat this with the right glove and adjust.

Once gowned and gloved the wearer should not risk contamination by unnecessary movement. The hands should be kept up, preferably clasped together in front of the chest until surgery begins. Scrubbed personnel should not turn their backs to any sterile area, particularly when wearing gowns secured at the back as this will obviously increase the risk of contamination.

Double gloving should be considered when there is an increased risk of contamination e.g. for draping the patient, or for procedures that involve entry into the intestinal tract. The outer gloves may be removed when the high risk of contamination has passed (e.g. when suturing of the intestines is complete).

Damaged or contaminated gloves should be removed and replaced as soon as possible. Removal can be performed by an unscrubbed assistant who takes hold of the glove on the palm and back of the hand. Grasping the cuff of the gown through the glove the assistant pulls the glove off while pulling the cuff over the surgeons hand. This enables the surgeon to re-glove using the closed method.

Practical Veterinary Nursing

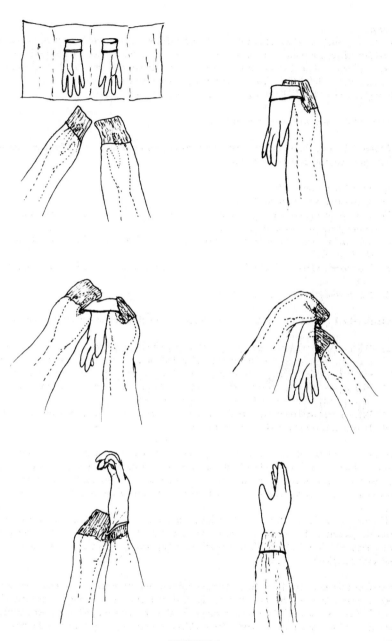

FIGURE 4
CLOSED GLOVING

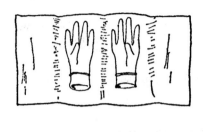

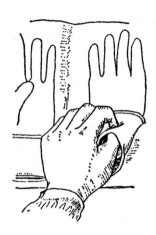

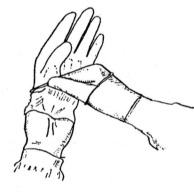

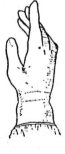

FIGURE 5
OPEN GLOVING

Practical Veterinary Nursing

DRAPING

Aim: To prevent contamination of the surgical site. Drapes should cover the entire patient and table leaving only the surgical site exposed.

Materials available: Reusable : linen.
Disposable: paper, plastic, paper based materials.

1) Reusable drapes:

Advantages:	cheaper
	usually more conforming (than paper)
Disadvantages:	porous, therefore allow 'strike through contamination' when wet.
	time consuming to wash and fold
	can become encrusted after heavy use

2) Disposable drapes:

Advantages:	water resistant therefore prevent contamination
	labour saving
Disadvantages:	expensive
	can be less conforming
	need to keep a large stock.

All types of drapes come in different shapes and sizes. Deciding which to use depends on the type of surgery being performed and personal preference of the surgeon. Fenestrated drapes can be made with different sized 'windows' depending on the intended use. Alternatively four plain drapes can be used to make a suitable fenestration. Drapes should be secured with towel clips to prevent them moving and exposing the un-prepared area during surgery.

PREPARATION OF THE INSTRUMENT TROLLEY

The trolley containing sterile instruments for surgery should be laid out by the nurse just prior to surgery. The best method is by using a pair of sterile cheatle forceps. The trolley should be of a suitable size for the number of instruments required, it should be prepared with a water resistant base to prevent 'strike through contamination' when wet. A double thickness of sterile linen drape is then placed on top. If necessary the instruments can be covered with a sterile drape until ready for use .

An alternative method for preparation of the instrument trolley is for the assistant to lay out the trolley by hand once gowned and gloved. This method may save time, but increases the risk of the assistant contaminating themselves.

The theatre nurse should be able to use her knowledge of the surgical technique to anticipate which instruments may be required. These should be put onto the trolley ready for use, anything extra that may be needed should be close at hand.

INSTRUMENTS

Most surgical instruments are made of stainless steel, those with tungsten carbide edges (usually indicated by gold coloured handles) are generally more durable. Instrument packs should be kept as simple as possible but contain sufficient instruments to cover all eventualities during surgery. Example of a general set:-

Sponge holding forceps x 2
Towel clips: Bachhaus towel clips x 6
Scalpel handles x 2 (sizes 3&4)
Tissue forceps: Allis tissue forceps x 4
Dissecting forceps: non-toothed x 2, toothed x 2
Artery forceps: curved x 2, straight x 6, mosquito x 4
Needle holders x 1: Gillies, Mayo's or McPhails
Scissors: straight x 1, curved x 1
Swabs x 10

Common additions to a general pack:-

Retractors: self retaining, handheld
Diathermy leads
Suction tips
Gallipot and receiver

Smaller packs for minor procedures may be useful. It is a good idea to keep index cards with the contents of each pack listed.

Example of a suture set:-

Scalpel handle x 1
Dissecting forceps x 1
Mayo scissors x 1
Artery forceps x 5
Needle holders x 1 (e.g. Gillies)
Gauze swabs x 5

Example of an orthopaedic set:

Osteotome, Chisel
Curette, Mallet
Hohmann retractor

Example of a laparotomy set:

Gossett retractor
Doyen bowel clamps

Example of an ophthalmic set:

Eyelid retractors, Vectis
Iris repositor, Lens expressor

Cleaning
Immediately after use surgical instruments should be cleaned.
> Open all ratchets.
> Rinse in cold water to remove large clots and debris.
> Use an ultra-sonic cleaner or soak in a cleaning solution.
> Scrub with a soft brush, particularly around the teeth or jaws and then check.
> Rinse and dry.
> Lubricate joints if necessary.

Packing
Several different packaging methods are available, methods of sterilisation available may determine how instruments are packed.

1) **Metal drums:** contain aeration holes that must be closed immediately after sterilisation. Good method, but must have an autoclave suitable for sterilising them.
2) **Linen wrap:** usually double wrapped, useful for larger sets and instruments. Must have an autoclave with a drying cycle.
3) **Paper wrap:** useful as it provides a water resistant dust proof outer layer, usually used with linen wrap.
4) **Self seal bags:** expensive, but the method of choice for smaller instruments. Heavy objects may need to be doubled bagged, or sharp ends protected.
5) **Autoclave film:** cheaper than self seal bags, must be secured with autoclave tape. They are easily perforated by sharp objects and it can be difficult to remove instruments without contaminating them.

Ideally instruments should be stored sterile ready for use.
Packs should be kept dry and dust free, labelled with the date of sterilisation and checked regularly. Anything that has perforated its packaging, or has not been used for 3 months after the sterilisation date should be re-packed and sterilised.

METHODS OF STERILISATION

Sterilisation is the complete destruction of all microbes, this can be achieved in different ways. Boiling should not be considered as a method of sterilisation as sufficient temperatures can never be reached by boiling to kill all spores.

1) **Dry heat: hot air ovens**
   Temperature is raised slowly and maintained at 160°C for 1 hour.
   Advantages: does not blunt or dull sharp or fine instruments.
   Disadvantages: instruments are very hot
                    long cycle
                    materials may scorch (linen drapes and gowns)
                    can not use for heat sensitive items

2) **Moist heat: autoclaves**
   Increase in pressure allows for an increase in temperature and a decrease in time.
   > 10 lb sq in at 112°C for 20-30 minutes
   > 15 lb sq in at 121°C for 12-20 minutes
   > 20 lb sq in at 126°C for 10 minutes
   > 30 lb sq in at 134°C for 3 minutes

   To function correctly an autoclave must be operated properly, carefully loaded and the instruments packed correctly. Regular services are essential for maintenance
   Advantages: rapid cycle
                    destroys bacterial spores
                    will not damage linen drapes
                    no toxic residue
   Disadvantages: expensive to install and run
                    unsuitable for delicate instruments e.g. Endoscopes

3) **Chemicals**
   a) **Liquids:** different sterilising solutions are available, you should be familiar with your own solution and the sterilisation times.
   Gluteraldehyde is popular, this disinfects in ten minutes but needs 10 hours to kill spores.
   Advantages: useful for delicate instruments
   Disadvantages: must be rinsed before use
                    may not kill spores if soaking time is not adequate.

   b) **Gases:** Ethylene Oxide: Health and Safety are very strict about the use of ethylene oxide as it is very toxic. However used correctly it is a useful method of sterilisation. This needs 10 hours to kill spores.
   Advantages: effective against all microbes
                    can sterilise heat sensitive items
   Disadvantages: toxic and flammable
                    does not penetrate large items
                    long cycle and airing time
                    expensive

4) **Gamma Irradiation**
   This is not a practical method of sterilisation for veterinary practice. However many of the disposable items used (e.g. catheters and suture materials) have been sterilised by this method.

Practical Veterinary Nursing

CHECKING STERILISATION METHODS

NAME	COMMENTS	USE WITH
Chemical Indicators	These show a colour change when exposed to a given temperature for adequate time.	
	i) Brownes Tube: Small glass tube filled with a liquid that changes colour when a certain temperature is reached and maintained for an adequate period of time. Brownes tubes are available to indicate changes at different temperatures eg. 120°, 130°, 160° & 180°C.	Autoclave Hot Air Oven
	ii) Indicator strips; strips of paper that change colour on exposure to saturated stream for an adequate length of time or exposure to Ethylene oxide gas.	Autoclave Ethylene Oxide
Indicator Tape	This tape has a series of line stripes that change colour.	
	i) Autoclave tape: on exposure to a temperature of 121°C the line stripes change to black.	Autoclave
	ii) Ethylene Oxide tape: on exposure to E.O. gas the line stripes on this green tape turn to red.	Ethylene Oxide
	Both these tapes only indicate an exposure, other requirements such as length of time or steam pressure may not have been reached.	
Spore Tests	These culture test indicators usually contain a controlled count spore population of a certain bacteria. After sterilising the strips are cultured to see if all spores have been killed. The disadvantage of this method is that the results are not immediately available.	Autoclave Hot Air Oven Ethylene Oxide
T.S.T.	T.S.T. strips indicate that temperature, time and pressure have all been adequate for spore destruction. Indicator changes from yellow to purple if all 3 incication criteria are reached.	Autoclave

SUTURES

All suture materials can be divided into two main categories:-
    absorbable or non-absorbable
within these categories they can be further divided
    natural or synthetic
    monofilament or multifilament
    coated or uncoated
Tables 1 & 2 show the most commonly used suture materials.

Alternatives to sutures

1) **Staples:** these are made of metal (usually stainless steel) and are primarily used for skin closure. They are quick to insert and require special instruments to remove them, and are relatively expensive.
They are also available for ligation and anastomis of the intestinal tract.

2) **Tissue adhesive:** may be useful for small superficial wounds.

An ideal suture material should have all of the following characteristics:-
    easy handling
    good knot security
    minimal tissue drag and reactivity
    easily sterilised
    no capillary action
    good retention of tensile strength
    absorption when tissue strength is adequate
    readily available and inexpensive

Unfortunately no suture material contains all these properties. Selection of the appropriate material will be guided by the personal preference of the surgeon. The strength of the tissues in which the suture is to be placed, the speed of healing, and the risk of contamination are also important factors.

Practical Veterinary Nursing

TABLE 1
ABSORBABLE SUTURES

TRADE NAME	SUTURE MATERIAL	MONOFIL. MULTIFIL.	SYNTHETIC OR NATURAL	COATED	DURATION OF TENSILE STRENGTH & ABSORPTION	METHOD OF ABSORPTION	COMMENTS
Coated Vicryl (Ethicon)	Polyglactin 910	Multifilament (Braided)	Synthetic	Yes. (Calcium Stearate)	Retains 55% at 14 days, 20% at 21 days. Absorption 60-90 days	Absorbed by hydrolysis	Most commonly used. Low tissue reactivity
PDS II (Ethicon)	Polydioxanone	Monofilament	Synthetic	No	Retains 14% at 56 days. Absorbed by 180 days	Absorbed by hydrolysis	Monofil. so better in infected sites Very strong.
Dexon (Davis&Geck)	Polyglycolic Acid	Mutlifilament (Braided)	Synthetic	Can be coated with Polasamer	25% stronger than catgut. Retains 20% at 14 days	Absorbed by hydrolysis	Very similar to Vicryl in use and other properties
Maxon (Davis&Geck)	Polyglycolic	Monofilament	Synthetic	No	70% remains @ 14 days 55% @ 21 days Absorption 2 mth	Absorbed by hydrolysis	Similar properties to PDS
Chromic Catgut (Ethicon)	Made from purified animal intestines	Essentially Monofilament	Natural	Yes Chromium Salts	Provides tensile strength for up to 28 days	Absorbed by enzymatic degradation & phagocytosis	Causes a moderate inflammatory reaction
Plain Catgut (Ethicon)	Made from purified animal intestines	Essentially Monofilament	Natural	No	Retains tensile strength for 14 days	Absorbed by enzymatic degradation & phagocytosis	Less strength than chronic catgut & is absorbed faster

TABLE 2
NON-ABSORBABLE SUTURES

TRADE NAME	SUTURE NAME	MONOFIL./ MULTIFIL.	SYNTHETIC/ NATURAL	COATED	KNOT SECURITY	DURATION	COMMENTS
Ethilon (Ethicon)	Monofilament Polyamide 6 & 66	Monofilament	Synthetic	—	Fair	Permanent	Commonly used for general purpose
Novafil (Davis &Geck)	Polybutester	Monfilament	Synthetic	—	Fair	Permanent	Very similar properties to Ethilon & similar usage
Prolene (Ethicon)	Polypropylene	Monfilament	Synthetic	—	Fair	Permanent	Very inert only minimum tissue reaction.
Surgical Stainless Steel Wire		Available in both	Synthetic	—	Excellent	Permanent	Difficult to handle. Sutures may break due to flexibility.
Mersilk (Ethicon)	Braided Silk	Multifilament (Braided)	Natural	—	OK	Eventually may fragment and breakdown.	Has high tissue reactivity
Supramid	Polyamide polymer	Multifilament	Synthetic	Encased in outer tubular sheath.	Good	Outer sheath may easily be broken	OK for skin should not be used buried.

SELECTION OF SUTURE PATTERNS

Suture patterns can be devided into continuous or interrupted and further divided into simple, mattress or tension sutures. Selection of the suture pattern depends on wound tension and personal preference. The most commonly used suture patterns are as follows.

1) **Simple Interrupted Suture:** used as a buried suture, when the suture ends should be cut short, or for skin closure when the suture ends should be left longer. They are easy to insert, maintain good tissue apposition and allow for a certain amount of tissue movement between sutures. Occasional inversion of the skin edges may be seen, or gaping between sutures if the wound is under tension or the sutures placed too far apart.

SIMPLE
INTERRUPTED
SUTURE

2) **Simple Continuous Suture:** often used in the closure of sub-cutaneous tissues, but can also be used in the skin. It is quick to apply and gives good tissue apposition. The main disadvantage is that poor knot strength or a break in the suture line may lead to complete wound breakdown.

SIMPLE
CONTINUOUS
SUTURE

3) **Horizontal Mattress Suture:** often used for closure of skin wounds under moderate tension. They can produce eversion of the skin edges.

HORIZONTAL
MATRESS
SUTURE

4) **Vertical Mattress Suture:** used for closure of skin wounds under moderate tension, can also produce slight eversion of the skin edges but provides good apposition of the wound edges.

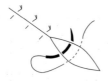

VERTICAL
MATRESS
SUTURE

SURGICAL NEEDLES

Needles can be of two different kinds, atraumatic needles which have the suture material swaged on , or needles with an eye through which the suture material must be threaded. Choice of needle depends on the tissue to be sutured, the accessibility of the site and the preference of the surgeon.

All needles can be classified by shape and type

Most commonly used needle shapes:-

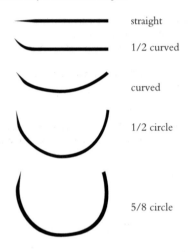

straight

1/2 curved

curved

1/2 circle

5/8 circle

Automatic needle
(Suture material swaged on)

Most commonly used needle types:-

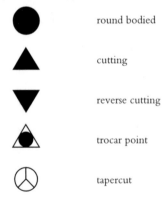

round bodied

cutting

reverse cutting

trocar point

tapercut

ASSISTANCE DURING SURGERY

1) **The Scrub Nurse**

   To be properly prepared for surgery the surgical assistant should be familiar with the procedure being performed. This may mean asking or reading about the technique beforehand.

   The assistant must know which instruments are on the trolley. All swabs needles and sutures should be counted before surgery commences.

   During surgery the assistant must concentrate on what the surgeon is doing in order to anticipate his needs.

   The surgical trolley should be kept tidy, with the instruments laid out in the likely order of use, this enables them to be located and passed promptly on request.

   Instruments should be kept clean and must be passed to the surgeons hand so that they are ready for use (i.e. the right way up).

   Before final closure of the wound all sutures, swabs, needles and instruments should be checked and counted so that nothing is left unaccounted for.

2) **The Circulating Nurse**

   It is useful to have an unscrubbed assistant during surgery. This person can supply extra instruments, connect apparatus (e.g. electrocautery or air drill lines) and generally be available for emergencies.

POST OPERATIVE CARE

As soon as the surgery is over;
1) All drapes should be removed.
2) The wound should be cleaned with a dilute antiseptic solution (e.g. 0.1% Chlorhexidene), treated or dressed if necessary.
3) Observe the patient for normal respiration, check pulse and temperature.
4) Deflate cuff and remove endotracheal tube when the swallowing reflex has returned.
5) Move the patient to a warm quiet comfortable place and continue observation.
6) Observe patient for signs of pain and seek advice on administration of analgesics if necessary.

Post operative Emergencies

1) Respiratory failure or obstruction: watch rate and character of respiration and be prepared to re-intubate.
2) Cardiac failure: check rate, rhythm and character of pulse and colour of mucous membranes. Be prepared to get assistance and have a "cardiac arrest" box available.
3) Shock or circulatory failure: watch colour of mucous membranes and capillary refill time. Weak peripheral pulses may indicate inadequate circulatory volume.
4) Hypothermia or hyperthermia: take temperature immeditiately after surgery and if abnormal take action. If hypothermic the temperature should be raised slowly, heat pads and hot water bottles should always be covered as the recumbent or anaesthetised patients may not be able to move away if the heat is too intense and so can easily be burned.
5) Acute wound breakdown: cover the area with saline soaked swabs or towels, prevent further damage and call for assistance.

BANDAGES AND DRESSINGS

Aims of a bandage:
1) Prevent further damage e.g. fractures.
2) Minimize swelling and haematoma formation.
3) Provide comfort, support and pain relief.
4) Control haemorrhage.
5) Prevent contamination of wounds.
6) Hold dressings and medication in place.

Bandages can be divided into three different layers:
1) Primary or contact layer: should be in close contact with the wound. It is usually a sterile dressing preferably non adherent, although adherent dressings have a place for wound debridement.
2) Secondary or intermediate layer: padding layer which absorbs exudate from the wound. This should be applied firmly but not too tightly.
3) Tertiary or outer layer: usually consists of two layers, the first is a conforming layer, which holds the intermediate layer in place, it should not be applied too tightly. The second layer is usually an extra protective layer, which is normally cohesive or adhesive conforming bandage. These make the bandage more durable.

Rules for bandaging:
1) Collect all materials together before you start.
2) Cleanliness is important for wound dressings.
3) Must be tight enough to stay in place, but not too tight.
4) Avoid sticking adhesive to the skin.
5) Change dressings regulualy, especially when soiled.
6) In fracture cases the joints above and below the fracture must be included.

The following table describes some of the basic materials used in the three different layers of the bandage

BANDAGE LAYER	DESCRIPTION	USES
Primary Contact Layer	Non-adherent open weave paraffin gauze. (Can be impregnated with Chlorhexidine)	Lacerations, skin loss wounds and minor burns
	Dry non-adherent dressings; a cotton acrylic fibre pad with a perforated polyester film.	Clean sutured wounds
	Knitted fabric non-adherent dressings: made from Rayon silk and wool.	Clean wounds, infected or discharging wounds
	Impregnated wound dressings: impregnated with saline to draw wound fluids.	Infected wounds
	Hydroactive and interactive hydrogel dressings: gel or granules used in the wound to promote tissue healing.	Chronic granulating wounds
	Poultice dressings: containing an antiseptic and a substance to draw wound secretions.	Infected wounds, contusions & inflammations
	Woundcare powders: an antiseptic dry dressing.	Abrasions and superficial cuts.
	Haemostatic dressing: calcium alginate	Control haemorrhage
Intermediate Padding Layer	Cotton wool: 100% hospital quality cotton wool.	Used as an absorbant layer and the padding layer in a Robert Jones Dressing
	Gamgee: cotton wool layer with gauze covering.	Same uses as cotton wool
	Orthopaedic padding bandages: many different makes are available in varying sizes. Gamgee in bandage form.	General purpose padding in support dressings
Tertiary Layer	Cotton conforming bandage.	Provides support and holds padding layer in place
	Crepe Bandage: cotton bandage, stockingette.	Useful for areas where support with some 'give' is needed eg thorax
	Cohesive support bandage: adheres to itself not the skin, lightweight and porous.	Useful for an outer layer giving support and protection
	Elastic adhesive bandage.	Same uses as above

CASTS

Casting material can be used in the same way as a bandage to provide support by encircling the whole limb. Alternatively it can be used in conjunction with a support bandage as a gutter splint. The ideal casting material would be:-

high strength to weight ratio
rapid development of strength
radiolucent
easy to remove
easy to handle and apply with no mess
waterproof
durable
re-usable (e.g. gutter splints)
porous
non-irritant to the skin

Indications For Cast Application
Fracture stabilization in young animals.
Post operative management after fracture, tendon or ligament repair.
In fracture cases where there is little or no displacement of the fragments.
Management of limb deformities.
Post skin grafting on the lower limb where movement will disrupt healing.

Prinicples of Application
1) Minimal padding is required under the cast, usually either one layer of orthopaedic padding, bandage or stockingette.
2) Bony prominences should be protected.
3) The limb should be as clean and dry as possible before application.
4) The cast should be neat fitting. A cast which is too tight may lead to ischaemic areas, which may in turn lead to necrosis and sloughing of the skin. A cast which is too loose can also cause sores in areas of contact, it may lead to instability of the fracture site, or if very loose it may fall off.
5) When applying a cast to the lower limb it has been suggested that two toes may be left out. This enables the foot to be checked for signs of poor circulation.

Mangement of casts
1) Once a cast has been applied it should be checked regularly to enable early anticipation of any problems. Daily checks can be made at home by the owner, but the cast should be checked by a veterinary surgeon at least every 10 to 14 days and more regulaly if the patient is a young animal still growing.
2) Owners should be advised to keep the patient quiet, allowing confined or lead exercise only.
3) When the patient is allowed out the cast should be covered with a waterproof dressing to prevent the foot from getting wet, this should be removed once inside otherwise it may cause the foot to sweat.

4) Regular checks should be made for :-
swelling above or below the cast
removal or slippage of the cast
pressure sores around the top or toes
patient interference
cracking or wearing of the cast
dirt or wetness around the foot area
any increase in patients lameness
change in attitude of the patient, no increase in temperament or depression
foul smells or discharges
If in any doubt re-casting should be considered.

Removal of casts

Casts are most easily removed using an electric plaster saw. These are noisy and may cause upset to some patients, sedation may need to be considered. Cast spreaders and manual cutters can also be used.

CARE AND MAINTENANCE OF SURGICAL EQUIPMENT

All instruments and equipment used in surgery are expensive to buy and therefore need to be given proper care and attention to continue to function properly.

Continued heavy use, exposure to heat or corrosive chemicals may significantly reduce the working life of any instrument or equipment.

With this in mind, everything should be cleaned and where necessary lubricated as soon as possible after use. Even items infrequently used should be regularly checked to ensure that they are in working order if needed urgently.

Most large pieces of equipment will come with manufacturers recommendations for cleaning and sterilising, these should be adhered to as far as possible.

Instrument Construction

In order to buy and maintain surgical instruments it is important to have some knowledge of the materials they are made of and how they are manufactured.

Quality and price are naturally connected. Generally instruments made from chrome plated carbon steel are less expensive but do tend to show signs of wear earlier than the better quality but more expensive stainless steel instruments.

Instruments with gold coloured handles have tungsten carbide inserts. These are more durable and give a better grip.

General Instrument Care

1) Instruments should always be handled with care, they should never be dropped or thrown as this may cause stress and damage.

2) Surgical instruments should not be engraved for identification purposes as this damages the surface and can cause corrosion.

3) Certain substances are not recommended for contact with surgical instruments (e.g. iodine) as this may cause unnecessary corrosion. Saline solution may also cause corrosion particularly if allowed to dry on the instrument.

4) Heavy instruments should be separated from lighter more delicate instruments during cleaning to prevent damage.

5) Always clean instruments in cold water first, hot water causes coagulation of protein. Make sure all ratchets are unlocked and joints open during cleaning.

6) Never use steel wool or abrasive powders as they will damage the corrosive resistant film.

Ultrasonic Cleaners

These electrical units are undoubtedly more effective than manual cleaning as they clean in the areas that the brush cannot reach. After the initial rinse in cold water the instruments are put into the wire mesh basket of the ultrasound cleaner, which is then lowered into the cleaning detergent. Using a method of gentle vibration for up to 15 minutes the debris is dislodged from the instruments. The instruments are then rinsed and inspected.

Manufacturers normally recommend a detergent and desired strength. Detergents should have a pH as near to neutral as possible, they should be low foaming and easy to rinse off. If possible distilled or de-ionised water should be used to minimise scale formation, however it is expensive and may not be practical. Water softeners may be used but can leave the surface of the instruments dull.

The cleaning fluid should be changed regularly, usually daily to avoid build up of dirt and scale. The ultrasonic cleaner should never be overloaded.

Inspection After Cleaning

Before packaging and storage all instruments should be dried and checked. Failure to dry instruments properly leads to corrosion in the joints or crevices.

Areas For Attention

Checks should have been made to ensure:

1)   Ease of movement of pivots and hinges.

2)   Alignment of teeth and jaws.

3)   There are no dents and distortion.

4)   There is no evidence of rust or corrosion.

If an instrument is damaged or does not work properly it must be replaced. Using damaged instruments may lead to a poor surgical technique.

Lubrication

Lubrication of all moving parts of the instrument is very important. Most instrument companies recommend a lubricant. Machine oils and grease should be avoided as these mask bacteria during autoclaving and leave an unpleasant film on the surface of the instrument. Antimicrobial water soluble lubricants are the best, but because they are water soluble, instruments should be lubricated after each use.

SPECIALISED EQUIPMENT

1) Orthopaedic Equipment

All orthopaedic instruments used in routine surgery should be checked after use. Osteotomes and chisels may blunt, become chipped or bent, curettes may lose their sharpness.

Internal Fixation Equipment: Instruments intended for internal fixation are especially expensive and therefore need careful attention. Bone drills and taps should be carefully cleaned after use using an ultrasonic cleaner or a soft brush. Small fragments of bone can easily be left within the thread of the drill or tap. The depth gauge should be taken apart to ensure adequate cleaning.

Air drills and hoses: Compressed air machines should never be immersed in liquids. They should be carefully wiped or brushed over, paying particular attention to the quick coupling area but taking care not to allow water into the air inlet. The hose should receive similar treatment, paying particular attention to the attachment ends. Both the drill and the hose should be dried.

All air machines need to be oiled after each use with a lubricant recommended by the manufacturers. This should be put around the quick coupling, the triggers and the air inlet. After oiling the machine should be reconnected to the compressed air and run for approximately 20 to 30 seconds.

Sterilising: Most compressed air machines are recommended for autoclaving, although gas sterilisation can be used. (N.B. battery drills are usually plastic coated and therefore should be gas sterilised.)

Motorised equipment: These are similar to compressed air machines in methods of cleaning but often are electrical and therefore require special attention to the electrical connections. Repeated autoclaving may cause seizure of the motor. Manufacturer's instructions will offer the best advice.

2) Ophthalmic instruments

Most of these instruments are required to be delicate and therefore need care during cleaning so as not to damage the fine workings. Careful manual cleaning with a soft brush is recommended, opening joints and lubricating. Careful inspection is necessary as dirt not seen on a quick check with the naked eye may be seen with the operating microscope or loupes during surgery.

3) Dental Equipment

Hand held instruments: e.g. elevators, scalers, luxators, curettes and extraction forceps. Many of these instruments have fine tips and so need careful handling and storage to avoid damage. With use and repeated autoclaving some of the dental instruments will become blunt, and so need regular sharpening to be of any use. Carefully drawing a curette or scaler along the plastic case of a ball point pen indicates the need for sharpening. A sharp instrument will shave off a fine curl of plastic from the surface. The most popular method for sharpening these instruments is using a Arkansas sharpening stone and oil which is rubbed into the stone before use.

Powered equipment: e.g. ultrasonic cleaners and polishers. These pieces of equipment are expensive to buy and therefore require regular maintenance to give continued use. The manufacturers usually give good instructions which should be followed.

4) Other Theatre Equipment

Although the theatre nurse is not generally expected to carry out routine servicing on all equipment she should be aware of the requirements of that equipment for regular maintenance.

Autoclaves: Sterilisation depends on the correct operation of the autoclave, correct packing of the instruments and correct loading of the chamber. For the autoclave to function properly it must be properly maintained. Before using any autoclave for the first time the manufactures instructions should be read and understood, then daily use can be carried out according to the instructions. Health and Safety requirements suggest that autoclaves should be serviced at least annually preferably every six months.

Suction units: The suction containers, usually plastic or glass jars, should be emptied, cleaned, disinfected and dried immediately after use. (Some newer machines may have disposable containers) An anti-foaming agent is available which can be used in the jars to prevent a build up of foam getting into the motor during use. The filter must be changed regularly, usually weekly, depending on usage. Regular servicing by the manufacturing company is recommended.

Diathermy units: All leads and connections should be checked. The sterilised rubber lead may perish with continual autoclaving. For safety reasons servicing is advisable.

Clippers: Clipper units which are not properly maintained may cause damage to the skin of the patient and therefore increase the likelihood of infection. Sharp blades should be used, blunt or damaged blades must be returned for repair or sharpening. During prolonged use clippers should be stopped and the clipper head sprayed with lubricant. This prevents overheating of the blades and possible thermal injury to the skin. After each use the clippers should be cleaned with a brush and lubricated, the blades should be dismantled cleaned and sterilised daily or following use on an infected animal. Handle carefully, avoid dropping and damaging the outer case and the motor.

Other general equipment

Cryosurgery units: This equipment is now fairly common in veterinary practice. The liquid nitrogen used should be stored in a vacuum flask at low pressure. Protective clothing should be worn when filling any smaller containers for use, this should only be done when necessary. Tips and nozzles should be allowed to thaw before cleaning, the handheld unit should be wiped over.

Endoscopes: Careful handling is essential to prevent damage to the delicate fibres within the scope. Immediately after use the outside of the scope should be wiped, paying particular attention to the most distal end where a soft toothbrush may be used. A long flexible endoscope brush should be pushed through the biopsy channel until it emerges from the distal tip, the brush should then be cleaned before it is withdrawn from the scope. This channel can then be flushed with a dilute antiseptic solution. When dried the endoscope is ready to be sterilised. Two methods of sterilisation are available, either gas, using ethylene oxide or liquid using Gluteraldehyde . For gas sterilisation the endoscope should not be coiled too tightly and the proper airing time allowed before use. For liquid sterilisation the manufactures instructions should be noted as some scopes are not fully immersible. After soaking the scope should be re-flushed with a sterile solution to remove any traces of the sterilisation fluid. Autoclaving is not suitable as the delicate light fibres will be destroyed by heat.

REFERENCES:

McCURNIN (2nd Edition) *Clinical Textbook for Veterinary Technicians*, W.B. Saunders & Co., Philadelphia.

LANE D.R. (Ed) (1989). *Jones's Animal Nursing*, 5th Edition, Pergamon Press, Oxford.

STASHAK. *Equine Wound Management*, Lea & Febiger.

Rocket of London: Instrument Catalogue.

Ethicon: Sutures Catalogue.

WARREN R.G. (1983) Mosby's Fundamentals of Animal Health Technology. In: *Small Animal Surgical Nursing*. Mosby, St Louis.

ANAESTHESIA

THE ANAESTHETIC MACHINE AND ANCILLARY EQUIPMENT

Trolley unit	Four wheels and a variety of shelves.	Good storage facilties but takes up space.
Trolley stand	Three/four wheels. No nitrous oxide storage.	Take up less space, easier to clean and cheaper but limited storage.
Gas cylinders	Carbon Dioxide: Grey. Nitrous Oxide: Blue.	Oxygen: Black with white neck.
Reducing valve	Between the cylinder & flowmeter.	Allows delicate control of gas flow.
Pressure gauge	Incorporated into the regulator.	Indicates gas remaining in cylinder.
Flowmeter	Glass tubes with revolving bobbins: variable or fixed orifice.	Controls gas flow to animal. Calibrated for a particular gas.
Vaporiser	Fluotec most common.	Allows volatile liquid to vaporise.
Reservoir / rebreathing bag	Acts as a gas reservoir.	Allows manual I.P.P.V.
Corrugated tubing	Between the patient and gas source.	
Expiratory valve	Usually situated close to patient in circuit.	Allows gas escape in semi-closed system.
Soda lime canister	Removes CO_2 from expired gas.	Allows re-breathing of expired air.
Soda Lime	90% calcium hydroxide 5% sodium hydroxide 1% potassium hydroxide Silicates to prevent powdering.	The hydroxides combine with the carbon dioxide in the presence of moisture to form carbonates.
Face masks	Flexible rubber, in various sizes to fit both cats and dogs.	Use correct size to ensure good fit around animal's face.
Endotracheal tubes	Rubber (orange) or polythene (clear). Range of sizes: internal diameter in mm stamped on the outside. Tubes usually have an inflatable cuff.	Too big: will cause trauma on insertion. Too small: will not seal in the trachea.
Scavenging systems	Collect waste gases from the circuit and duct them to the exterior.	N.B. Avoid inhaling volatile agents and nitrous oxide, especially during pregnancy.
Ventilators	To provide artificial ventilation. Cycle is controlled by: a) pressure or b) volume or c) time	IPPV (intermittent positive pressure ventilation) can be provided by ventilators or manually, by squeezing the re-breathing bag.

FIGURE 1

ANAESTHETIC EQUIPMENT

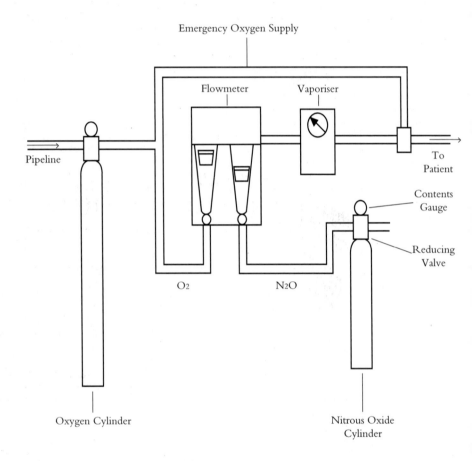

TECHNIQUES FOR ADMINISTERING ANAESTHETIC AGENTS BY INHALATION

There are four different ways of delivering the volatile anaesthetic agent to the animal.

1) **The Open Method**
   Anaesthetic agent is put onto absorbent material and held near the animal's nose and mouth.
   Depth of anaesthesia cannot be controlled.
   Resuscitation is difficult.
   Hypoxia easily develops.
   Pollution of the air with volatile agent is a risk to operators.
   Rarely used except occasionally for anaesthesia of exotic pets.

2) **The Semi-Open Method**
   Anaesthetic agent on absorbent material is placed within a mask.
   Same disadvantages as the open method.

3) **The Semi-Closed Method**
   This requires an anaesthetic machine and a circuit.
   Anaesthetic gas is delivered via a mask or an endotracheal tube.
   Principle: Fresh gas flow must eliminate the expired carbon dioxide from the circuit.
   A flow rate equal to, or preferably greater than, the animal's minute volume is required to ensure carbon dioxide removal.
   Nitrous oxide may be used in these circuits. Not less than 30% oxygen should be adminstered with it.

   a) **Magill Circuit**
      Reservoir bag ~ wide corrugated tube ~ expiratory valve ~ connector ~ endotracheal tube (or mask).

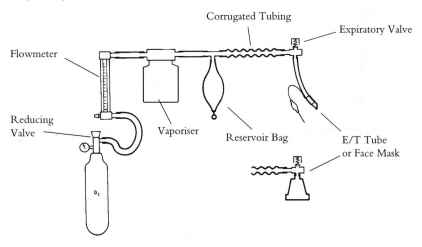

Corrugated Tubing
Expiratory Valve
Flowmeter
Reducing Valve
Vaporiser
Reservoir Bag
E/T Tube or Face Mask
O_2

      A flow rate equal to the minute volume is required.
      Used in animals over 5 kgs.
      In large dogs, the high flow rates required to equal the minute volume become uneconomical.

b) **Ayres T-piece**
No valves therefore little resistance to breathing.
A flow rate of 2.5 – 3 times the minute volume is required.

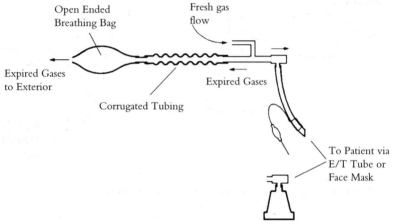

For cats and small dogs up to 10 kg.

c) **The Bain Co-axial Circuit**
This has no valves and hence the circuit offers very little resistance to breathing. Fresh gases pass up the central tube and expired gas flows out of the outer sleeve. A flow rate of 2.5 – 3 times the minute volume is required. The circuit is described by Carlucci and Hird (1978).

d) **The Lack System**
This is a modification of the Magill system which has a double tube through which the animal breathes. The outer tube is inspiratory and the inner expiratory with the valve situated near the anaesthetic machine. Flow rates equal to the minute volume are required. This system is superior in performance to both the Magill and Bain circuits. Its use is further described by Waterman (1986).

4. **The Closed Method**
This also uses an anaesthetic machine and a circuit.
Principle: Soda lime is used within the system to absorb the exhaled carbon dioxide.
Once the carbon dioxide is removed, then the gas mixture may be re-breathed.
Flow rate should be a minimum of 1 litre of oxygen per minute.
Use only in animals over 10kg due to the resistance to breathing caused by the soda lime.
Economic in use of gases and volatile agent.
Heat and moisture are conserved.
Less risk of explosion or pollution of the atmosphere.

a) **The "To-and-Fro" System**

Endotracheal tube ~ connector ~ soda lime canister ~ rebreathing bag.

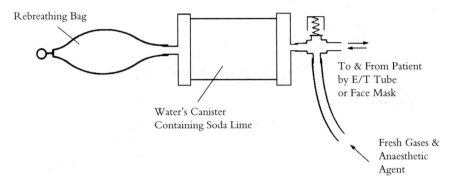

Rebreathing Bag

Water's Canister
Containing Soda Lime

To & From Patient
by E/T Tube
or Face Mask

Fresh Gases &
Anaesthetic
Agent

Most common system in use.
Gases pass through the soda lime on inspiration and expiration.

b) **The Circle System.**

More complex. A unidirectional flow of gas through the system.

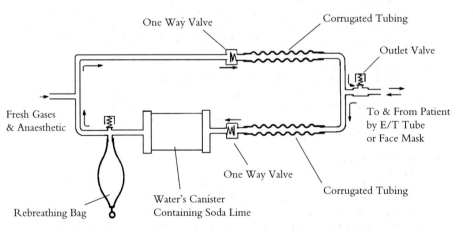

One Way Valve

Corrugated Tubing

Outlet Valve

Fresh Gases
& Anaesthetic

To & From Patient
by E/T Tube
or Face Mask

One Way Valve

Corrugated Tubing

Rebreathing Bag

Water's Canister
Containing Soda Lime

Very efficient in removal of carbon dioxide.
Valves and long tubing create more resistance to breathing than the to-and-fro system.

Flow Rates

Tidal volume: volume of air inspired / expired in a single breath. In the normal dog or cat, this is usually between 10 - 15 ml/kg with lighter animals having the higher value.

Minute volume: volume of air inspired / expired in one minute i.e. the tidal volume x respiratory rate. The respiratory rate varies with size from 30 breaths per minute in smaller animals to 15 in larger dogs.

Flow rates for anaesthetic circuits are estimated from the minute volume.

Intermittent Positive Pressure Ventilation (IPPV)

Artificial ventilation may be used in the following circumstances:

a)   resuscitation of apnoeic patients.
b)   where muscle relaxants have been given.

As the term implies, respiration by this method is under positive pressure and the intrapulmonary and intrapleural pressures are also positive. This reduces both the venous return to the heart and the cardiac output. This is compensated for by venoconstriction, causing a rise in peripheral venous pressure. IPPV should not be used in situations such as hypovolaemic shock, where venoconstriction is already maximal. It is essential to ensure that circulating blood volume is within normal limits. Mean intrathoracic pressure can be reduced by shortening the duration of inspiration and allowing a longer expiratory pause.

MONITORING DEVICES

These fall into two categories:

1) Warning devices attached to the anaesthetic equipment.
   Usually these are attached to the anaesthetic machine and give warning when the gas supply is failing. These devices should work on the oxygen supply.

2) Monitoring devices used to give further information about the patient.

   a) Blood pressure: It would be ideal if information about blood pressure could be obtained during every operation. However, the only completely accurate way of measuring BP is to pass an I/V catheter which, as an invasive technique, is rarely justified. There are several non-invasive techniques which may be used such as **arterial tonometry**, which is the external application of a transducer over an artery. Another technique which is being looked at is **pulse transit time** which involves the measurement of the time taken between a pulse at one site and another.

   b) **Capnography**: This is the measurement of carbon dioxide in the expired air. The information is available as a graph.

   c) **Pulse oximetry**: This is the continuous estimate of arterial haemoglobin saturation with oxygen. It detects hypoxaemia and monitors the function of the lungs in delivering oxygen to the blood. Arterial haemoglobin saturation is estimated by measuring the transmission of light at two wavelengths through a pulsatile vascular bed. The ear is a commonly used site.

SCAVENGING SYSTEMS

The Health and Safety Executive (HSE) consider anaesthetic agents to be hazardous to health. A COSHH assessment must consider the precautions required to limit exposure, and also the means of determining whether or not this is achieved.

Types of scavenging systems

1) Passive – a length of 22mm clear plastic tubing is connected to the scavenge valve of the machine and led outside the building. Tube should be <8ft in length with no upward gradient.
2) Active –Passive – as above but the discharge is into a forced ventilation duct (which is rarely available in veterinary practice). Constant monitoring required.
3) Activated Charcoal Absorbers – do not remove nitrous oxide, cause increased resistance and are often used when they are 'spent'. Regular weighing essential.
4) Active systems – can be installed in any operating theatre. There is a high capacity fan connected to the expiratory valve by a receiver. This is an air break device, carefully designed to prevent too great a suction being applied to the patient.

Personal exposure monitoring

Nitrous oxide is the agent the HSE are most concerned about. The personal exposure of the staff can be measured by dosemeter tubes which are the size of a fountain pen. The BSAVA, in conjunction with Barnsley District General Hospital, has arranged to make available monitoring devices for both halothane and nitrous oxide. (Contact: Dr John O' Sullivan Tel: 0226-730000 ext 2809)

These monitoring tubes should be worn as close to the face as possible. After one wear period i.e. two hours of operating, they should be sealed and returned to the monitoring service. The tubes have a useful life of three weeks but should be returned to the laboratory as quickly as possible. The absorbed gas is driven off by heat and measured by gas chromatography.

Minimising theatre anaesthetic pollution

The purchasing of an approved active scavenging system does not itself guarantee low levels of waste anaesthetic gases. In conjunction with the use of any scavenging system you should observe the following rules.

1) Avoid face-masks wherever possible.

2) Intubate with a correctly fitting tube and inflate the cuff.

3) Turn on the scavenging system before commencing induction of anaesthesia. Check that it is working.

4) DO NOT turn on the nitrous oxide and volatile agent until the circuit is connected to the patient.

5) DO flush the patient circuit with oxygen alone for at least 30 seconds before disconnection.

6) Remember to flush the circuit with oxygen beforehand if you have to disconnect the patient during anaesthesia.

7) Fill vapourisers at the end of an operating session in a well ventilated area.

8) Check pipelines, machines and circuits regularly for leaks and have all equipment serviced annually.

9) Monitor pollution levels on a six-monthly basis.

Reproduced by permission of:
Mr J F R Hird, MA, BVSc, DVA, MRC.Anaes, MRCVS.

DRUGS USED IN ASSOCIATION WITH ANAESTHESIA

Drug groups used in conjunction with anaesthesia:
Local anaesthetics.
Premedicants and sedatives.
Induction agents.
Inhalation agents.
Analgesics.
Muscle relaxants.
Emergency drugs.
Others e.g. atropine, heparin.

LOCAL ANAESTHESIA

SURFACE	Spray Drops Gel / cream	Mucous membranes Cornea Intrasynovial analgesia
INFILTRATION	Injection	Operating site Field blocks
REGIONAL	Injection	Nerve blocks Spinal and epidural analgesia
INTRAVENOUS REGIONAL	Injection	Limbs

Practical Veterinary Nursing

LOCAL ANAESTHETIC DRUGS

DRUG	PREPARATIONS	PROPERTIES	USES	TOXIC SIGNS
LIGNOCAINE	Solutions 0.5% to 3% Cartridges for dental syringes Aerosol spray Gel, creams and ointments Ophthalmic preparations	Excellent surface analgesia Good spread through tissue Minimal tissue irritation Rapid onset of action Action 60-90 minutes	Almost all applications	Drowsiness / sedation Twitching / convulsions Coma / death
PROCAINE	Solutions 1% to 5% - with or without adrenaline	Good analgesia Action 60 minutes Poor tissue penetration Poor suface analgesia	Not good for regional nerve blocks	Twitching / convulsions Coma
PRILOCAINE		Less effective tissue spread Minimal tissue irritation		
AMETHOCAINE	Procaine group	Excellent surface analgesia	Skin and aural preparations	Same as procaine
BUPIVACAINE		Long analgesic action	Prolonged analgesia	
PROPARACAINE			Ophthalmic preparations	

ADRENALINE: Local anaesthetics cause vasodilation, which increases the blood supply to the area. This speeds up absorption, which increases the risk of systemic toxicity and limits the action of the analgesic. Adrenaline, as a vasoconstrictor, counteracts this effect. However, this vasoconstriction can cause undesirable side-effects e.g change in hair colour or necrosis of the anaesthetised part.

PREMEDICATION AND SEDATION

Aims: To calm and control the patient.
        To relieve pre-operative pain.
        To reduce the total dose of anaesthetic.
        To reduce unwanted side-effects of the anaesthetic.

Drug groups used for premedication

Sedatives / tranquillisers / hypnotics.
Analgesics.
Parasympathetic antagonists.

DRUGS COMMONLY USED TO SEDATE ANIMALS

DRUG	DOSE AND ROUTE	PROPERTIES	COMMENTS
ACEPROMAZINE 'ACP' - C-Vet 'BK-Ace' - BK	**Dogs:** S/C, I/M, I/V 0.03 – 0.2 mg/kg Oral: 1 –3 mg/kg **Cats:** I/M, I/V 0.1 – 0.2 mg/kg	Tranquillises and sedates. Anti-emetic. Spasmolytic. Hypotensive. Anti-adrenergic.	Causes hypotension and bradycardia. N.B. Boxers may faint. Reduces dose of barbiturates by half. Convulsions possible in epileptics because threshold is lowered. Sedation much less reliable in cats.
XYLAZINE 'Rompun' - Bayer 'Anased' - BK	**Dogs and cats:** I/M, S/C 1 - 3 mg/kg	Sedation and analgesia. Dose dependent. Reduces cardiac output. Bradycardia and slight hypotension. Vomiting. Muscular tremors.	Animal should be calm before administration. Do not overdose with anaesthetic agent. Do not use in the last third of pregnancy. Use with caution in animals with dehydration or those who have cardiopulmonary disease. Use gloves to handle.
MEDETOMIDINE 'Domitor' - SmithKline Beecham	**Dogs:** S/C, I/M, I/V 10 – 80 µg/kg **Cats:** S/C, I/M 50 – 150 µg/kg	Sedation and analgesia. Dose dependent. Reduces cardiac output. Bradycardia and slight hypotension Vomiting. Muscular tremors.	Animal should be calm before administration. Do not overdose with anaesthetic agent. Use with caution in animals with dehydration or those who have cardiopulmonary disease. Use gloves to handle. Reversal possible by antagonist, atipamezole ('Antisedan').
DIAZEPAM 'Diazemuls' - Dumex 'Valium' - Roche	**Dogs:** I/M 5 – 20 mg.	Sedation is minimal. Anti-convulsant. Muscle relaxant.	Not licensed in U.K. but widely used. Useful prior to ketamine anaesthesia or myelography. Used in cats for control of severe convulsions (2 – 10 mg I/V)

Sedative and analgesic combinations

When sedative and opioid drugs are combined their actions are synergistic.
There are many combinations which are now used, sometimes as premedication prior to general anaesthesia or often as the sole anaesthetic agent for minor procedures.
Opioid combinations should not be used I/V in cats.
Sedation can be profound and respiratory depression is possible. Therefore, the degree of care and monitoring of patients under these drugs should be the same as for general anaesthesia.

SEDATIVE / ANALGESIC COMBINATIONS IN COMMON USE

DRUGS	ROUTE GIVEN	PROPERTIES
ACEPROMAZINE/ PETHIDENE (C.D.)★★	I/M I/V	Good sedation e.g. for radiography. I/V route can cause severe hypotension.
ACEPROMAZINE/ MORPHINE (C.D.)★★	I/M	Good sedation for radiography. 20% of patients may vomit.
ACEPROMAZINE/ BUPRENORPHINE 'Temgesic' – Reckit & Colman (C.D.)★	I/M	Good sedation e.g. for radiography.
MEDETOMIDINE 'Domitor' – SmithKline Beecham / BUTORPHANOL 'Torbugesic' – Willows Francis	I/M	Sedation deeper than medetomidine alone.

★ Controlled drug Schedule 3
★★ Controlled drug Schedule 2

Parasympathetic antagonists

These are included in premedication to reduce salivation and prevent bradycardia.
They are used when muscle relaxants are employed.
Routine use in the dog may not be necessary but it is advisable in the cat, to control salivation.

PARASYMPATHETIC ANTAGONISTS

ATROPINE 'Atricare' Animalcare Atropine sulphate 0.5 mg/ml	S/C, I/M or I/V 0.02-0.1 mg/kg	Pupil widely dilated. *Initial* bradycardia, then tachycardia. Overdose results in convulsions.
GLYCOPYRROLATE 'Robinul' - A.H. Robins Company	I/M 0.01 mg/kg	Causes less tachycardia than atropine.

INTRAVENOUS ANAESTHESIA

Indications: As induction agents prior to inhalational anaesthesia.
                      As the sole anaesthetic agent for minor or short procedures.

Techniques: As a single dose.
                      By incremental doses.
                      As a continuous infusion.

Drug groups used for intravenous anaesthesia

Barbiturates.
Propofol.
Steroids.
Dissociative agents.
Neuroleptanalgesics.

INTRAVENOUS DRUGS: BARBITURATES

DRUG	DOSE AND ROUTE	ACTIONS	COMMENTS
THIOPENTONE SODIUM 'Intraval' - Rhône Mérieux Ltd.	**Dogs and cats:** I/V 2.5% or 1% solution. Stable for 3-7 days. **Given to effect:** calculate around 20-25 mg/kg in unpremedicated, fit dogs. **Half** this dose if premedicated.	Rapid onset of unconsciousness. Short acting. May cause respiratory depression and apnoea. Hypotension, tachycardia, depressed myocardial contractility and coronary perfusion (significant in hypovolaemia or heart disease).	**Very alkaline** (pH 14) so **irritant** if used at concentrations >2.5%. Incremental doses prolong recovery because metabolism by the liver is slow. Thin or uraemic dogs are more sensitive, as are those with liver disease. Greyhounds have a markedly long recovery. Large doses produce restlessness.

METHOHEXITONE
SODIUM
'Brietal' - Elanco
	Dogs and cats: I/V
	1% solution.
	Stable for 6 weeks
	Given to effect: calculate on
	5 mg/kg - give half this dose and
	top up as required. Premedication
	reduces apnoea and muscle spasm.
		Similar to thiopentone but:
		   it is twice as potent as thiopentone,
		   more of a given dose is effective,
		   it is metabolised faster.
		Apnoea is more common.
		Muscle spasm at induction
		and recovery.
			Recovery is not prolonged by infusion or by
			incremental doses..
			Useful in greyhounds and related breeds
			because recovery is not prolonged.

PENTOBARBITONE SODIUM 'SAGATAL' Rhône Mérieux	**Dogs and cats:** I/V 6% solution. **Given to effect:** calculate around 25-30 mg/kg. Make allowances for premedication. In small dogs - use 3% solution.	Induction and recovery prolonged. Long duration of action. Marked respiratory depression. Cardiovascular depression. Hypothermia common.	Metabolism is slow. Marked hyperalgesia and excitement occurs during long induction and recovery. Not recommended as the sole anaesthetic agent Must have oxygen available. Protect against hypothermia. Can be used in **guinea pigs** and **rabbits**, but better anaesthetics available.

INTRAVENOUS DRUGS: PROPOFOL

DRUG	DOSE (DOGS)	DOSE (CATS)	ACTIONS	COMMENTS
PROPOFOL 'Rapinovet' - Pitman–Moore Ltd	**DOG: Induction** Premedicated: 3-4 mg/kg I/V Non-premedicated: 5-6 mg/kg I/V **Maintenance** 0.4 mg/kg as infusion **Recovery** 18 minutes after single dose	**CAT: Induction** 6-7 mg/kg I/V regardless of premedication **Maintenance** 0.51 mg/kg **Recovery** 20-30 minutes after single dose	Rapid unconsciousness. Rapid recovery. Hypotension. Occasional bradycardia. Respiratory depression.	Expensive. Opened vials should be discarded. Rapid hepatic metabolism so non-cumulative. Reduce dose in old, debilitated animals. Care needed in animals with liver disease. Good for brief procedures. Useful induction agent for Caesarian section.

INTRAVENOUS DRUGS: STEROIDS

DRUG	DOSE AND ROUTE	ACTIONS	COMMENTS
ALPHAXOLONE/ ALPHADOLONE SULPHATE 'Saffan' - Pitman-Moore Ltd	**I/M:** 4 mg/kg (as premed. before giving I/V dose). 18 mg/kg - full anaesthesia after 15-20 minutes. **I/V:** 6 mg/kg - to allow intubation. 6 mg/kg followed by 3 mg/kg, given to effect - 10 minutes of anaesthesia. **Increments** 0.5 ml as necessary or 0.24 mg/kg/min as infusion.	I/V induction rapid. Duration of single dose short. Recovery is rapid. Better safety margin than barbiturates. Hypotension and tachycardia. Anaphylactoid reactions occur occasionally as a result of histamine release.	**NOT FOR USE IN DOGS.** Do not store in refrigerator. Discard unused solutions. Repeated doses do not prolong recovery due to rapid hepatic metabolism. Do not use with barbiturates. S/C injection is totally ineffective. Use only for induction in Caesarian section.

DRUG	DOSE AND ROUTE	ACTION	COMMENTS
KETAMINE HCL 'Vetalar' - Parke, Davis and Company.	**Dogs:** not recommended alone **Cats:** I/M 11-22 mg/kg - restraint 20-25 mg/kg - minor surgery IV 10-15 mg/kg	Slow onset of anaesthesia. Eyes remain open. Swallowing reflex persists. Muscle tone enhanced or increased. Dose-related cardiovascular effects. Increased lacrimation and salivation.	Hepatic or renal dysfunction prolong its action. Can be given by all routes, including buccal mucosae Nearly always used in combination with a sedative. Recovery period must be quiet and warm (hypothermia). Protect eyes with ophthalmic ointment. Depth of anaesthesia difficult to judge.
KETAMINE/ XYLAZINE 'Rompun' - Bayer UK Ltd.	**Dogs:** I/M Xylazine 1-2 mg/kg (+ atropine) Ketamine 10 mg/kg, 10 minutes later. **Cats:** I/M Xylazine 1 mg/kg (+ atropine) Ketamine 20-25 mg/kg Given simultaneously if starved, xylazine 20 mins. before, if not starved	Anaesthesia after 5-10 minutes. Anaesthetised for ~30 minutes.	
KETAMINE/ DIAZEPAM	**Dogs:** I/V Diazepam 0.1-0.2 mg/kg Ketamine ~5 mg/kg	Salivation not usually a problem.	Smooth, slow induction in debilitated animals.
KETAMINE/ MEDETOMIDINE	**Cats:** I/M Medetomidine 80 µg/kg Ketamine 5-7 mg/kg	Anaesthesia within 5 minutes. Effect lasts 30-40 minutes. Hypothermia can be a problem.	Atipamezole (Antisedan) useful if recovery prolonged. Full recovery can be 5-8 hours.

INTRAVENOUS DRUGS: DISSOCIATIVE AGENTS (Continued)

DRUG	DOSE AND ROUTE	ACTION	COMMENTS
KETAMINE/ ACEPROMAZINE	**Cats:** I/M Acepromazine maleate 0.1 mg/kg Ketamine 20–25 mg/kg	Anaesthesia within 5 minutes. Effect lasts for 30–40 minutes.	
TILETAMINE	**Dogs:** (+ atropine) I/M 7-15 mg/kg I/V 5-10 mg/kg **Cats:** (+ atropine) I/M 10-15 mg/kg (effect 3-5 minutes) I/V 5-7 mg/kg (effect 1 minute)	Similar to ketamine but: - more potent. - longer lasting. - more pronounced side effects Duration of anaesthesia 20-60 minutes depending on dose.	**Not yet available in U.K.** Zolazepam included to counter muscle rigidity and seizures. Full recovery can be up to 6 hours.

INTRAVENOUS DRUGS: NEUROLEPTANALGESIA

DRUG	DOSE AND ROUTE	PROPERTIES	COMMENTS
Etorphine Methotrimeprazine 'S.A. Immobilon' - C–Vet Ltd.	**Dogs:** I/V 0.05 ml/kg (onset immediate) I/M 0.1 ml/kg (onset 5 minutes) Further half dose can be given I/V.	Deep sedation, hypnosis and analgesia. Anaesthetised for 60–90 minutes. Marked respiratory depression. Bradycardia and hypotension.	For use in minor surgical procedures. Avoid using in old, sick or debilitated animals. Use atropine to counteract bradycardia. May be reversed with diprenorphine (REVIVON) **Very dangerous to man – handle carefully.** KNOW THE EMERGENCY PROCEDURE!
Fentanyl Fluanisone 'Hypnorm' – Janssen Animal Health	**Dogs:** I/M 0.25-0.5 ml/kg S/C Increase dose by 10%	Deep sedation and excellent analgesia. Anaesthetised for ~30 minutes. Bradycardia and respiratory depression. Hypersensitive to sound. Causes defecation.	For minor surgical procedures or premedication Do not use in dogs with respiratory depression. Avoid using in dogs with hepatic/renal disease. May be reversed with naloxone (0.04–1 mg/kg). Useful in **guinea pigs** and **rabbits.**

INHALATION ANAESTHESIA

Inhalational anaesthetics are either gases or volatile liquids.
Some form of anaesthetic circuit is required for administration.

GASES USED IN CONJUNCTION WITH ANAESTHESIA

GAS	CYLINDER	PROPERTIES AND USES
OXYGEN	**Black** with white neck. Pressure 135 atmospheres.	Not inflammable. N.B. In contact with oil or grease, oxygen under pressure will cause a fire.
CARBON DIOXIDE	**Grey.** Pressure 50 atmospheres.	Not inflammable. Increases depth of anaesthesia when volatile agents are used and hence the speed of induction is increased. Use to stimulate respiration after IPPV.
NITROUS OXIDE	**Blue.** Pressure 51 atmospheres.	See next table.

INHALATION AGENTS: Gaseous and volatile anaesthetics.

AGENT	PROPERTIES	PROPERTIES	USES
NITROUS OXIDE	Gas at 51 atmospheres. **Blue** cylinders. Sweet smell, non-irritant. Not inflammable or explosive but supports combustion of other agents.	Potent analgesic but poor anaesthetic. Rapidly eliminated through lungs. Administer with >30% oxygen. Pure oxygen given for 10 minutes after procedure.	Reduces overall requirement for anaesthetic agents. Do not use in closed circuits. Used as a supplement with I/V or volatile agent.
DIETHYL ETHER	Colourless, volatile liquid. B.P. 35°C Inflammable and explosive in oxygen. Decomposed by heat, light and air.	Cardiovascular effects affect anaesthetic depth. Excellent muscle relaxation. Progressive hypotension as anaesthesia deepens. Nausea and vomiting common during recovery. Increases secretion of saliva and mucus.	Useful in cats – relatively safe. Not commonly used. Health & Safety Legislation restricts use. Use in a semi-closed circuit with oxygen and nitrous oxide. Premedicate with atropine.

INHALATION AGENTS: Gaseous and volatile anaesthetics. (Continued)

AGENT	PROPERTIES	PROPERTIES	USES
HALOTHANE Rhone Merieux Ltd	Colourless, volatile liquid. B.P 50°C. Vapour pleasant smelling. Not inflammable or explosive in clinical concentrations. Decomposed by light.	Potent anaesthetic. Hypotension and dysrhythmias may occur. Moderate muscle relaxation. 80% eliminated through the lungs; 20% metabolised and slowly excreted.	Induction: 4%. Maintenance: 0.5% to 2%. Administer with oxygen or oxygen / nitrous oxide in semi-closed systems or oxygen in closed circuits.
METHOXYFLUORANE 'Metofane' - C-Vet Ltd	Volatile liquid. B.P. 104°C. Non-inflammable and non-explosive. Vapour has a fruity odour.	Good analgesic. Pedal and palpebral reflexes are abolished early. Good muscle relaxation. Respiration and blood pressure depressed at deep levels of anaesthesia. Most excreted by the lungs; metabolites excreted in urine for up to 10 days.	Not suitable for induction. Depth of anaesthesia should be judged on muscle relaxation, the swallowing reflex and respiration. Use with most types of anaesthetic circuit. Used with oxygen or oxygen and nitrous oxide.
ENFLURANE	Volatile liquid. B.P. 56.5°C. Concentrations >4.25% are inflammable in 20% oxygen in nitrous oxide.	Potent anaesthetic but less so than halothane. Reasonable muscle relaxation. Hypotension/myocardial depression. Rise in respiratory rate: decrease in tidal volume. Excreted mainly by lungs: up to 2% metabolised.	Expensive so used mainly in closed systems. Induction: up to 5%. Maintenance: 1.5 – 3%. Recovery smooth and relatively rapid.
ISOFLUORANE	Volatile liquid. B.P. 48.4°C.	Myocardial depressant but less so than halothane. Hypotension. Respiratory and heart rate increased. Cardiac rhythm stabilised.	Expensive so used in closed systems. Useful for cardiac conditions. Induction: 4% Maintenance: 1.5 – 2%

ANALGESIA

Drug groups available for analgesia

1) Opioids.
Use for treatment of severe pain following trauma or surgery.
Most opioids are controlled drugs (CD) and are subject to regulations regarding their purchase, storage and use under Schedule 2 and 3 of the Misuse of Drugs Act 1971.
Written records of their use in every animal is essential.

The general effects of the opioid analgesics are listed below:
> Analgesia
> Respiratory depression
> Sedation or excitement
> Nausea, vomiting, defecation
> Depression of the cough reflex

See table **ANALGESIC DRUGS: OPIOIDS**

2) Non-steroidal anti-inflamatory drugs (NSAIDs).
These drugs should not be used for severe pain.
They may be useful for chronic pain or as continuation analgesia after an operation.
NSAIDs can be toxic to cats and dogs and great care must be taken with their dosage.

NSAIDs

DRUG	DOSE AND ROUTE
PHENYLBUTAZONE	**Dogs:** Oral 10 - 20 mg/kg daily **Cats:** Oral 10 mg/kg daily
ASPRIN	**Dogs:** Oral 25 mg/kg t.i.d. **Cats:** Oral 25mg/kg every 48 hours
MEFENAMIC ACID 'Ponstan' - Parke, Davis and Co.	**Dogs:** Oral 10mg/kg b.i.d.
FLUNIXIN 'Finadyne' - Schering Plough	**Dogs:** Oral, I/V 1mg/kg daily
PIROXICAM 'Feldene' - Pfizer Ltd	**Dogs:** 0.3 mg/kg every 48 hours
KETOPROFEN 'Ketofen' - Rhone Meriuex	**Dogs:** Oral 1 mg/kg daily S/C, I/M I/V 2 mg/kg daily **Cats:** Oral 1 mg/kg daily. S/C 2 mg/kg daily

3) Miscellaneous analgesic drugs

Methoxyfluorane 'Metofane' (C-Vet Ltd)
This volatile anaesthetic agent has good analgesic properties. Clearance from the body is slow and therefore the analgesic effect is useful.

Nitrous Oxide
This gas is used in semi-closed circuits with oxygen (66% nitrous oxide: 34% oxygen). It is a good analgesic agent but the analgesia is only effective during nitrous oxide administration.

Xylazine 'Rompun' - (Bayer UK Ltd)
Good analgesic properties. Low doses (0.2 - 0.4 mg/kg I/M) may be useful in controlling visceral pain.

Medetomidine 'Domitor' (SmithKline Beecham)
Good analgesic properties. Use at low doses to avoid side-effects.

ANALGESIC DRUGS: OPOIDS

DRUG	DOSE AND ROUTE	NOTES
MORPHINE (C.D.)	**Dogs:** I/M 0.1 – 0.25 mg/kg Duration 4 – 5 hours **Cats:** I/M, S/C 0.1 – 0.2 mg/kg Duration 6 – 8 hours	Potent, reliable analgesia Do not use in animals with: acute pancreatitis or biliary obstruction Use with care if head injuries are present as it may increase intro-cranial pressure May cause vomiting In **cats** excitement may occur at higher doses.
PAPAVERETUM (C.D.) (Omnopen – Roche)	**Dogs and cats:** I/M 0.2 – 0.4 mg/kg	Contains 50% morphine in a mixture of opium alkaloids Effects are very similar to morphine
PETHIDINE (C.D.)	**Dogs:** I/M I/V 3 – 4 mg/kg Duration – 3 hours **Cats:** I/M 5 mg/kg Duration 2 hours	Less potent than morphine but more rapid onset. Does not cause vomiting or defecation Spasmolytic effect useful for abdominal pain. Use 1 – 2 mg/kg in old dogs or those with hepatic disease Large doses given I/V cause severe hypotension
FENTANYL (C.D.) 'Sublimaze' – Janssen	**Dog:** I/V 2 – 5 µg/kg Duration 20 – 30 minutes.	Potent analgesic with rapid onset Use during surgery or in immediate post-operative period May cause respiratory depression in anaesthetised dog.
PENTAZOCINE (C.D.) 'Fortral' – Winthrop	**Dogs and cats:** I/M 2 mg/kg Duration 2 – 3 hours.	Good post-operative analgesia and sedation Also available in tablets

DRUG	DOSE AND ROUTE	NOTES
BUPRENORPHINE (C.D.) 'Temgesic' - Reckitt & Colman	**Dogs and cats:** I/M 4 – 10 μg/kg Duration ~ 4 hours.	Potent analgesic and sedative with slow onset (give well in advance of the need for analgesia) Variable quality and duration of analgesia
BUTOPHANOL 'Torbugesic' - Willows Francis Veterinary	**Dogs:** I/V, I/M, S/C 0.2 - 0.3 mg/kg Duration 2 hours **Cats:** 0.2 - 0.8 mg/kg	Good sedative properties but analgesia is variable

MUSCLE RELAXANTS

Indications:
To relax skeletal muscles for easier surgical access.
To control respiration during thoracotomy.
To assist reduction of dislocated joints.
For endoscopy.

Drugs used for neuromuscular block

Suxamethonium 'Anectine' (Wellcome)
Pancuronium 'Pavulon' (Organon Technika)
Gallamine 'Flaxedil' (Rhone-Poulenc Rorer)
Alcuronium 'Alloferin' (Roche)
Vercuronium 'Norcuron' (Organon Technica)
Atracurium 'Tracrium' (Wellcome)

Neuromuscular blocking agents have no analgesic or anaesthetic effect.
It is more difficult to assess the level of anaesthesia when muscle relaxants are used.
Paralysis of the respiratory muscles means that IPPV must be available.

SUGGESTED CONTENTS OF A RESUSCITATION TRAY

Airway:
Face masks and E.T tubes.
Laryngoscope or pen torch.
Tracheotomy tube.

Venous access:
Syringes and needles / cannulae / I/V catheters.
Three way tap.
Fluid administration set.

Surgical access:
Skin swabs
Sterile pack: Scalpel handle and blades.
Rat-tooth forceps.
Tissue forceps.
2 prs artery forceps.
Scissors.
Gauze swabs
Suture material
Non-sterile: Scissors, cotton wool, gauze bandage, tape.

Drugs:
Adrenaline 1:1000
Atropine 0.6 mg/ml
Calcium gluconate 10%
Doxapram 20 mg/ml
Isoprenaline 0.2 mg/ml
Lignocaine 20 mg/ml
Naloxone 0.4 mg/ml
Sodium bicarbonate 8.4%
Sodium chloride 0.9%

EMERGENCY PROCEDURES

MANAGEMENT OF EMERGENCIES

RESPIRATORY PROBLEMS **Signs:** Dyspnoea Apnoea Coughing Cyanosis Snoring Altered respiratory rate Respiratory arrest	Stop anaesthetic administration. Check that a pulse is present. Establish a patent airway – intubate if tube is not already in place. Ventilate using either: the anaesthetic circuit. an Ambu bag. anaesthetist's own expirate. Administer 3–4 breaths rapidly followed by 6–12 breaths per minute thereafter, until animal restarts its own respiration.
CARDIOVASCULAR PROBLEMS **Signs:** Weak/ non-existent pulse Long capillary refill time Pale mucous membranes Increased heart rate Absence of wound bleeding Respiratory arrest Dilated pupil / fixed eye Cyanosis No heart beat.	**Hypotension**: Lighten anaesthesia and control haemorrhage. Use a slight head–down tilt and administer I/V fluids rapidly. Give 100% oxygen. Treat any dysrhythmias. **Cardiac arrest:** Stop anaesthetic administration. Ensure an open airway and begin ventilation. External cardiac massage: right lateral recumbency. Massage once every two seconds. Internal cardiac massage. Head down tilt. Rapid I/V fluids. Pressure bandage round abdomen. Drugs: Adrenaline – 1 ml of 1:1000 adrenaline, diluted in 9 ml water. Give 1 ml/10 kg I/V or intra-cardiac. Repeat every 10 minutes. Sodium bicarbonate – 1 mEq/kg (1 ml of 8.4% NaHCO3) I/V if resuscitation is longer than 10 minutes. Defibrillation. Further drug therapy depending on rhythm present:
HYPOTHERMIA **Signs:** Thermometer registers low. Cold extremities. Delayed recovery (normal doses) Respiratory depression. Bradycardia.	Insulate the patient and provide additional heat. Reduce the anaesthetic administration. Finish the procedure as soon as possible. Warm I/V fluids to 37°C before administration.
VOMITING AND REGURGITATION **Signs:** Presence of vomitus Cyanosis and dyspnoea Tachycardia	Removal of vomitus: Lower the head to allow vomitus to drain away. If available, apply suction to remove. Administer oxygen.

Practical Veterinary Nursing

PRE-OPERATIVE PROCEDURE

Reception of patient

1) Confirm that the animal is booked in.
   In emergency, enter the case in the operation records book.

2) Ascertain from the owner what procedure the patient is booked in for.
   Make sure the owner understands what is involved.

3) **The owner must sign the anaesthetic consent form.**

4) Advise the owner when to telephone for information.
   Give the owner some idea of the collection time.

5) Be pleasant and reassuring – remember the owner will be concerned.

Assessment of the patient

1) **Facts**
   Name and address of owner
   Telephone number (for contact in emergency today)
   Name of animal
   Age
   Sex
   Breed
   Weight

2) **History**
   Time of last meal and fluids
   Inappetance / cough / polydipsia / polyuria / vomiting / diarrhoea
   Poor exercise tolerance / history of syncope / abnormal behaviour
   Current drug therapy
   Previous anaesthetic history

3) **Clinical Examination**
   Must be done by the veterinary surgeon in charge of the case but the veterinary nurse may be asked to check the patient's temperature, pulse and respiration.
   Inspection, palpation, percussion, auscultation.

4) **Special Tests**
   The clinical examination might indicate the need for:
   Haematology and/or biochemistry
   Radiography
   ECG
   Ultrasound

PREPARATION FOR GENERAL ANAESTHESIA

Anaesthetic tray

Scissors and/or clippers.
Injection site swabs.
Syringes: 1ml, 2.5ml, 5ml, 10ml and 20 ml as required.
Needles/cannulae: Assorted sizes (19G - 23G) and lengths ($^5/_8$" - 1").
Tape or plaster for strapping intravenous needle.
Local anaesthetic spray, cream or gel for endotracheal tube.
Endotracheal tubes and connectors of relevant sizes.
Mouth gag, spatula or laryngoscope.
Induction agent.

Set up anaesthetic machine

Check the gas levels in the cylinders.
Check that the vaporiser is full.
Check the soda lime canister is full and still active.
Turn on the reducing valves - make sure there are no leaks.
Set up the appropriate circuit, ready for connection to patient.

Pre-medication of patient

Appropriate drugs given on instructions of the veterinary surgeon.

INDUCTION AND MAINTENANCE OF ANAESTHESIA

Induction by I/V injection into the right cephalic vein.

The veterinary nurse stands on the left of the animal.

Her left arm is positioned under the animal's neck with her hand holding the head firmly against her.

Her right arm reaches over the animal's body, supporting it against her own body.

Her right hand grips the animal's right elbow with the palm of her hand behind the olecranon and her thumb across the top of the limb.

The limb should be held in extension.

The injection site is clipped and swabbed to clean the site.

The nurse's thumb should apply pressure to the anterior surface of the limb to raise the vein.

Once the needle/cannula lies in the vein, and on the instructions from the anaesthetist, this pressure is released.

A firm grip must be maintained on the limb until the drug takes effect.

Once the tongue curl reflex is absent, the needle/cannula may then be withdrawn or taped to the leg.

Use a minimum of two tapes, taking care not to occlude the vein.

Heparinised saline may be used to prevent blood clotting in the lumen of the cannula.

Intubation

An assistant holds the head in extension.

A gag may be used between the canine teeth on the lower side.

The endotracheal tube is lightly lubricated with xylocaine gel.

A laryngoscope or spatula may be used to visualise the entrance to the trachea.

In cats, the larynx is sprayed with lignocaine.

The tip of the tube is used to elevate the soft palate and depress the epiglottis so that the arytenoid cartilages may be seen.

The tube is gently passed between the cartilages (easier at inspiration) and positioned in the trachea, midway between larynx and carina.

The cuff is inflated, the tube secured and then the animal is ready to be connected to the correct anaesthetic circuit.

Maintenance

After induction and intubation, relatively high concentrations of volatile anaesthetic are given. e.g. halothane 4% with either oxygen or oxygen and nitrous oxide.

If spontaneous respiration does not start after a short time, turn off the vaporiser, empty the reservoir bag and refill it with oxygen. It may be necessary to inflate the lungs by compressing the reservoir bag. Once respiration is settled at a steady rate and the palpebral reflex just disappears, then the halothane concentration is reduced to 1.5 - 2%, depending on the response of the animal to surgery.

MONITORING ANAESTHESIA

A = Airway   **B = Breathing**   **C = Circulation**

The above must be maintained at all times.

An endotracheal tube does not guarantee a patent airway.

Adequate respiration is essential: IPPV must be available.

Circulation must be maintained.

It may be necessary to give I/V fluids before, during or after the operation.

What to monitor

1) **Respiration:** Pattern and rate. Keep veterinary surgeon informed.
2) **Pulse:** Rate and quality. Use digital or lingual arteries or pass an oesophageal stethoscope.
3) **Mucous membranes:** Colour and capillary refill time. Normal <3 seconds.
4) **Reflexes:** Helps to assess depth of anaesthesia.
5) **Temperature:** Thermometer and palpation of the extremities.
6) **Depth of anaesthesia:** Response to stimuli, cardio-respiratory patterns, muscular relaxation, eye position and pupil size.
7) **Fluids:** Dehydration should be assessed.
8) **ECG:** Obtain a recognisable PQRST complex for monitoring.
9) **Equipment:** Check soda lime state, gas and anaesthetic levels.

Action

Inform the veterinary surgeon **immediately** if:

1) Respiration ceases.
2) The rhythm of the pulse alters/becomes irregular.
3) The heart stops beating.
4) Mucous membranes are cyanotic/pale.
5) The patient is becoming hypothermic.
6) The animal responds to external stimuli..
7) There is an equipment failure.

Tell the veterinary surgeon of your actions and concerns.

REFERENCES

HIRD, J.F.R. and CARLUCCI, F. (1978) A new anaesthetic circuit for use in the dog. *Journal of Small Animal Practice,* **19,** 277.

WATERMAN, A.E. (1986) Clinical evaluation of the Lack coaxial breathing circuit in small animal anaesthesia. *Journal of Small Animal Practice,* **27,** 591.

HILBERRY, A.D.R. (1992) *Manual of Anaesthesia, for Small Animal Practice,* BSAVA.

FLUID
THERAPY

WATER IN THE BODY

Water is under delicate balance in the body and must be controlled to combat variations in input and output. Drinking and eating provide the main inputs plus a small amount of 'manufactured' water from cell metabolism. Water losses occur in many ways, some of which are controllable to some degree by physiologic functions **(sensible losses)** eg:- urine and lactation. Others which are continuosly lost despite a decrease in water intake are described as **insensible losses**, and include the water lost by respiration, perspiration, and defaecation. There is also an obligate urine loss.

Distribution of water in the body

Of the 100% body water 66% is confined to the intracellular compartment (ICF) (fluid within cells) and 33% is outside the cells, extracellular fluid (ECF). Of the 33% of the body water which is extracellular 25% is found in the tissue spaces (interstitial fluid), 8% in the plasma and a small proportion is transcellular fluid formed by active secretion eg CSF, GIT secretions.

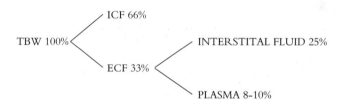

The major cations and anions in extracellular fluid compared to intracellular fluid are listed Table 1.

The amount of water in the body is balanced between input and output and the amount of water in each compartment depends on the free flow of water between these.

INPUT	OUTPUT	
DRINKING	RESPIRATION	
FOOD	SKIN- active/passive	} INSENSIBLE
METABOLISM	FAECAL	
	URINE	} SENSIBLE
	LACTATION	

INSENSIBLE losses are those which cannot be increased or decreased by the body but depend on ambient temperatures and the neccessity of particular body systems to use water e.g: respiratory tract for humidification and lubrication. Because of insensible losses and the requirement of an animal to produce urine to eliminate wastes (obligate urine loss), all animals have a basic requirement for water.

TABLE 1

COMPONENT	ECF	ICF
	mOsmol/l	mOsmol/l
Na+	143	10
K+	5	150
Ca++	2.5	–
Mg++	1	20
Cl-	110	–
HCO3-	24	10
HPO4-	1	5
Organic Acids		
Protein	17.5	90
Glucose		
Urea		
TOTAL	305	305

Daily water requirements

DOG: 40-60 ml/kg/day plus other sensible losses. Obligate loss in urine 20-30ml/kg, insensible loss 20 ml/kg. (Large dogs > small dogs). In general this is 2ml/kg/hr.

CAT: 60 ml/kg/day. Obligate loss in urine 40 ml/ kg, insensible loss 20ml/kg. Kittens 3-4 months of age may require up to 150ml/kg/day.

PYREXIA: Increases requirements by 3ml/kg/°C increase in body temperature.

Imbalances may arise from an inability to keep up input e.g: deprivation of water or an inability to drink. Output can vary with environmental temperatures, pyrexia, humidity, metabolic activity and disease.

DEHYDRATION

Dehydration literally refers to water depletion but is used to describe clinical signs produced by both salt and water depletion. No single clinical sign can indicate dehydration, which is not detectable until 5% or more of body water is lost.

Assessing dehydration

History
May suggest a predisposing cause e.g: anorexia, vomiting, diarrhoea, ptyalism, polyuria, hot weather, trauma.

Physical examination
a) Skin Turgor – Pinch the loose skin over shoulders/dorsolumbar region, the rate of flattening should be assessed, and in normal animals the skin should retract quickly. This is a subjective test and is influenced by posture, age, and how fat the animal is.
b) Eyes – Sunken, prolapse of third eyelid. Less reliable in small animals. Severe deficits produce this.
c) Mucous Membranes – Sticky and viscid, cyanosis or a muddy colour with an increased capilliary refill time.
d) Respiratory rate and depth – Acidosis stimulates an increased rate and depth to excrete CO_2.
e) Muscle weakness.
f) Depression.
g) Thirst.
h) Urine Output – Urine becomes more concentrated as animal becomes more dehydrated leading eventually to anuria and development of toxaemia.

TABLE 2

FLUID DEFECT (%BWt)	CLINICAL SIGNS
0-5%	No clear signs, may be thirst, and depression, urine concentrated
5-7%	Skin elasticity lowered (tenting), sunken eyes, dry mucous membs., pulse rapid and weak, CRT slow, oliguria.
7-10%	Anuria, cold extremities, weak pulse, skin permenantly tented.
10-12%	Collapse, progressive shock.

Laboratory analysis

Laboratory analysis is limited by the practice facilities but simple tests can be done with very little equipment.

a) Packed cell volume – A general rule is, a 1% increase in PCV above normal is equivalent to a loss of 10ml/kg. Unreliable unless previous PCV is known, cheap and quick assessment and can be used as a guide to assessment of clinical improvement.

b) Haemoglobin and Total serum proteins – Both rise in dehydration.

c) Urea and Creatinine – elevations in these products may indicate a 'pre-renal azotaemia', due to decreased kidney perfusion from severe dehydration.

Clinical signs

a) Body weight – limited in the first instance as many owners will not be aware if the exact weight of their animal, can be used to assess fluid replacement.

b) Central venous pressure – CVP will fall when severe dehydration ensues. CVP measurement is very useful for assessing the adequacy of fluid replacement before overhydration results.

c) Urine output – Low during dehydration (oliguria). Normal urine output indicates that replacement is adequate. Output can be measured via active (catheterisation) or passive (collection) methods. 1-2 ml/kg/hr is normal, and less than 0.5ml/kg/hr is defined as oliguria.

FLUID AND ELECTROLYTE DISORDERS

Definitions

1) pH: The negative logarithmic expression of the concentration of hydrogen ions e.g: $[H+] = 1 \times 10^{-6}$ = pH 6.

2) METABOLIC ACIDOSIS: Fixed retention of acid (H+) or loss of alkali.
   CAUSES: Ingestion of acid, ketoacidosis, loss of alkali. (eg: HCO3- in diarrhoea)

3) RESPIRATORY ACIDOSIS: Pulmonary retention of carbon dioxide.
   CAUSES: Impaired ventilation, respiratory arrest.

4) METABOLIC ALKALOSIS: Loss of fixed acid (H+) or gain of alkali.
   CAUSES: Vomiting, hyperaldosteronism, alkali ingestion, some diuretics.

5) RESPIRATORY ALKALOSIS: Excessive loss of carbon dioxide.
   CAUSES: Hyperventilation.

6) HYPOKALAEMIA:
   (Low blood potassium)
   CAUSES: Dilutional: infusion of excessive amounts of K+ deficient fluids.
   Alkalosis: exchange of H+ for K+
   GIT loss: Vomiting/diarrhoea.
   Urinary: High Na+ intake, excess HCO3-, Chronic renal failure. Malnutrition.
   Diuretics. Hyperaldosteronism
   Congenital: Burmese kittens.

7) HYPERKALAEMIA:
   (High blood potassium)
   CAUSES: Oliguric renal failure, urinary obstruction, Hypoadrenocorticism, iatrogenic, massive soft tissue trauma, severe acidosis.

8. HYPONATRAEMIA:
   (Low Blood sodium)
   CAUSES: Na+ loss/ water excess, congestive heart failure, hepatic fibrosis, nephrotic syndrome, ADH deficiency, renal failure.

9. HYPERNATRAEMIA:
   (High blood sodium)
   CAUSES: Dehydration, Diabetes insipidus, diarrhoea, primary hyperaldosteronism (rare), decreased water intake, osmotic diuresis, ingestion of sea water, iatrogenic.

FLUID THERAPY

Definition of terms

ATOM: Smallest particle matter can be broken in to. Consists of an
                             inner core consisting of protons and neutrons surrounded by
                             an electron cloud.

ION: Small water soluble particle that carries one or more positive
                             or negative charges.

CATION: Ions carrying one or more positive charges eg Na ++, H+.

ANION: Ions carrying one or more negative charges eg Cl-, HCO3-.

ELECTROLYTE: Any compound which can conduct an electric current when in
                             solution. eg sodium chloride. Sodium ions & chloride ions.

OSMOSIS: Movement of pure solvent (H_2O) from an area of low
                             concentration through a membrane, to an area of high
                             concentration, so as to equalise the difference.

OSMOTIC PRESSURE: The pressure by which water is drawn through a semi-
                             permeable membrane.
                             Proportionate to the number of particles in the solution.

ISOTONIC SOLUTION: Contain the same osmolality as extracellular fluid (273
                             mOsm/l). Good for rehydration and maintenance. e.g.:
                             Lactated Ringer's, 0.9% Saline, Ringer's, 4% Dextrose in
                             0.18% saline.

HYPOTONIC SOLUTION: Osmolality less than blood and extracellular fluid. Used for
                             hypernatraemia, carbohydrate source, fluid supplement for
                             sodium intolerant conditions. Never for maintenance.

HYPERTONIC SOLUTION: Osmolality greater than blood and extracellular fluid. E.g.
                             Dextrose 5% in 0.9% NaCl (560mOsm/l). Used for partial
                             maintenance once hydrated. Intravenous use only.
                             Contraindicated in dehydration.

Definition

Fluid therapy is the administration of fluid to treat and maintain the hydration, blood volume,
electrolyte and acid-base status of the animal.

Table 3

FLUID	COMPOSITION	USES
HARTMANN'S SOLUTION (LACTATED RINGER'S) eg: Aquapharm No. 11 (Animalcare)	ISOTONIC. Na, K, Cl, HCO3, Ca.	Polyionic – fluid replacement. Alkaliser. Use in acidosis, e.g. persistent diarrhoea. Good first choice if unsure.
NORMAL SALINE 0.9% NaCl eg: Aquapharm No. 1	ISOTONIC. Na, Cl.	Correction of hyponatraemia. Loss of chloride eg : in severe vomiting.
RINGER'S eg: Aquapharm No. 9	ISOTONIC. Na, K, Cl, Ca.	Polyionic – fluid replacement. Acidifier. Use in alkalosis, e.g. persistent vomiting.
5% DEXTROSE eg: Aquapharm No. 6	ISOTONIC Dextrose	Correction of hypernatraemia. eg: Cardiac conditions where Na++ is contraindicated.
0.18%NaCL + 4% DEXTROSE eg: Aquapharm No. 18	ISOTONIC Dextrose, Na, Cl.	Maintenance.
PLASMA EXPANDERS eg: Haemacel, (Hoechst)	ISOTONIC Gelatin Dextrans	Increase the osmotic pressure and increase blood volume.
BLOOD	ISOTONIC	Replacement of blood, plasma, platelets and clotting factors. May be administered with colloids.
PLASMA	ISOTONIC	Replacement of plasma and increase of blood volume.

ROUTES FOR ADMINISTRATION

When selecting the route for administration one should consider the reason for fluid therapy and the fluid to be administered.

Oral
The alimentary tract has the largest area for absorption of fluid and the fluid administered does not have to be sterile or physiological and is therefore cheaper. However, where there is vomiting or if the absorption from the tract is impaired by disease or reduced perfusion as in shock an alternative route is required. If the animal is dysphagic, fluid can be administered through a nasogastric/naso-oesophageal tube or gastrostomy tube. Puppies and kittens can be fed through stomach tubes.

Parenteral
All fluids must be given at body temperature, especially when delivered at fast rates of infusion.

Rectal
The colon has a large area for absorption of fluid and the fluid administered does not have to be sterile. However this route is not suitable in cases where diarrhoea is present and often precipitates diarrhoea. It is seldom used.

Intraperitoneal
The peritoneum has a large surface area for absorption, although this is impaired if the animal is in shock. Aseptic technique is required and only polyionic isotonic solutions must be used. The animal is placed in dorsal recumbancy and the fluid is administered through a needle placed in the abdomen caudal to the umbilicus. Often used in small mammals and young animals.

Subcutaneous
Although intravenous fluids are preferable, this is a good route of administration of fluid for maintenance requirements in small animals (eg: rats, guinea pigs). It is of little value in shocked or dehydrated animals. The fluid must be non-irritant and isotonic. The total volume should be administered in different sites; 100ml/site in the cat, 40ml/site in the dog and should be delivered through a wide bore needle (20 gauge) over the shoulders, back and hind quarters. Massage the injection sites gently.

Intravenous
This is the only effective route for fluid administration in severe dehydration or shock. It is also the only route through which hypertonic solutions can be delivered to treat acid-base imbalances or to administer parenteral nutrition. Surgical preparation of the administration site is necessary, constant monitoring for catheter patency, fluid rate and the onset of phlebitis is required. The catheter should be changed every 48-72 hours.
Most large peripheral veins are acceptable to use, although the cephalic is the most convenient and therefore, most commonly used. The recurrent tarsal veins and jugulars can also be utilised.

Intraosseous
This route is usually restricted to patients which do not have an accessible vein, eg. animals in severe shock with collapsed veins or where veins have been damaged by repeated venipuncture and in very small animals and birds. It is only suitable for the administration of hypotonic fluids.

INTRAVENOUS FLUID ADMINISTRATION

Veins used

Cephalic or radial vein
Saphenous or recurrent tarsal vein
Femoral vein
Jugular vein

Never take blood samples from any vein other than the jugular vein. The jugular vein gives the best sample and you run the risk of damaging a peripheral vein that you may need for fluid administration.

Equipment required

Intravenous catheter
Most catheters used in veterinary medicine are described as "over the needle". They come in various sizes and designs, for use in particular veins and are teflon coated plastic. In general it is not acceptable to use a needle for the administration of fluid because it is rigid and causes too much damage to the vein.

Administration set
The administration set delivers the fluid from the bag into the vein. Extension leads can be used to increase the length of the set. There are three different sets;
The normal administration set delivers 15-20 drops per ml.
The paediatric or burette set is more accurate and delivers 60 drops per ml.
The blood transfusion administration set has a nylon filter to remove aggregates of blood cells.

Fluid
Fluid should be kept in an incubator at 38.5°C so that it is at the correct temperature for administration. Alternatively it should be warmed to 38.5°C in hot water before use. See Table 3 for available fluids.

Transfusion pump
There are a number of different infusion pumps which can be programmed to transfuse the solution into the patient at a particular rate. They are fitted with an alarm which sounds if the transfusion stops.

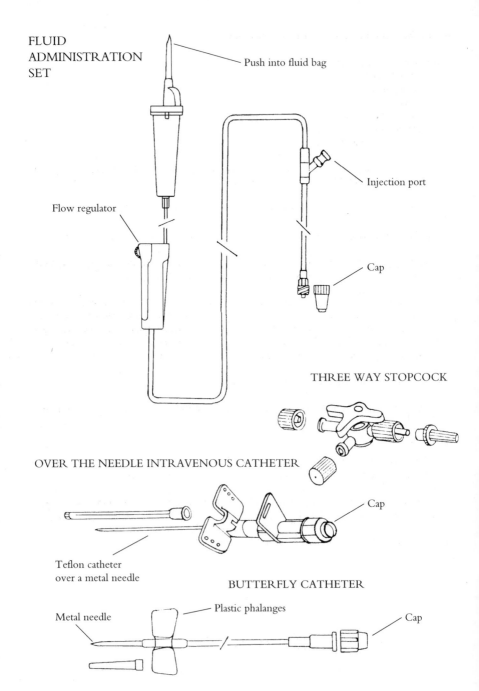

FLUID
ADMINISTRATION
SET

Push into fluid bag

Injection port

Flow regulator

Cap

THREE WAY STOPCOCK

OVER THE NEEDLE INTRAVENOUS CATHETER

Cap

Teflon catheter
over a metal needle

BUTTERFLY CATHETER

Metal needle

Plastic phalanges

Cap

Method for administration of intravenous fluids

1) Select all the equipment in advance:
   Suitable fluid
   Administration set
   Suitable catheter
   Tape and bandaging to secure the catheter in place
   2ml syringe with heparinised saline
   Intermittent injection cap

2) Set up the administration set and run fluid through it. The fluid chamber should not be more than half full and there should be no air bubbles present.

3) Clip the hair off over the administration site and prepare the site surgically.

4) Use digital pressure to occlude the vein. Do not touch the site of entry of the catheter.

5) A small skin incision adjacent to the vein being used facilitates visualisation, prevents catheters from bending, and reduces the risk of surface bacteria entering the vein.

6) Introduce the needle through the incision and into the vein. Do not push the needle through the skin until you are sure that you have identified the vein either by site or touch. Advance the needle into the vein and observe blood appearing at the end of the needle. If present, hold the needle still and advance the catheter up the vein. If no blood is present, redirect the needle. Do not withdraw the needle whilst there is still digital pressure on the vein.

7) Remove the stillette and leave the catheter in the vein.

8) Flush the catheter with heparinised saline and stop the end with an intermittent injection cap.

9) Tape the catheter into place.

10) Remove the cap and attach the giving set. The fluid should run steadily into the vein with the flow adjuster open. Check for evidence of the fluid running perivascularly.

11) If the fluid is running correctly, form a bend in the administration set then bandage the area and the administration set securely.

12) Set the fluid administration rate using the flow adjuster.

FLUID REQUIREMENTS

To calculate fluid requirements and rates, follow the following example:

1) **Calculate maintenance requirement**
   To calculate rate of maintenance fluid over 24 hours:
   Maintenance fluid requirement is 2ml/kg/hr
   Therefore :
   = 2ml x body weight (kg) x 24 hrs
   For example:
   A 20 kg dog
   = 2 x 20 x 24
   = **960 mls**

2) **Calculate deficits**
   To calculate fluid replacement rate in a dehydrated dog.
   For example a 20 kg dog that is 10% dehydrated:
   = 20 x 10%
   = 2 litres
   = **2000 mls**

3) **Consider ongoing losses**
   For animals which still have diarrhoea, vomiting, or renal loss. This information can be gleaned from close observation of the animals in the critical period.

4) **Calculate total fluid requirements in 24 hours**
   For example:
   2000 mls + 960 mls
   = 2960 mls

Acute losses can be administered more quickly than chronic losses. An example of replacement rate for chronic loss is given below:

Consider replacement in two 12 hour periods.
0 – 12 hrs –   50% replacement, 50% maintenance
12 – 24 hrs –   50% replacement, 50% maintenance

In this way, the total fluid requirement can be split into two equal halves making calculation easier. The next step is fluid administration rate.
1) Therefore, for the first 12 hours we need to supply our 20kg dog with approximately 1.5 litres of fluids.
2) Convert hours to minutes: 12 x 60 = 720
3) Calculate volume per minute: 1500mls / 720 minutes = 2mls
4) Calculate rate of flow to deliver required volume
   (The average giving set delivers 20 drops per ml)

Therefore drops per minute = 20 x 2 = **40 drops per minute over the first 12 hours.**

Alternatively programme the transfusion pump for the required volume to be delivered, the rate of delivery and activate it.

NOTES

1) If necessary, adjust for further fluid loss, e.g. diarrhoea.

2) *In all cases*, a piece of tape should be attached to the side of the bag and the expected volume to be reached should by marked off hourly. This allows a quick assessment of the progress of administration.

3) Measure urine production.

4) Assess the progress frequently. Feel the bandage to be sure that the fluid is going intravenously. Feel the leg for subcutaneous fluid accumulation.

5) The catheter should be checked daily and replaced every 48 - 72 hours. The bandage should be changed daily.

6) The central venous pressure should be monitored to assess the efficacy of treatment and prevent over hydration.

MONITORING FLUID THERAPY

Monitoring fluid therapy is of paramount importance. Not only because these animals are in need of critical care but to avoid consequences of overhydration which can be as disastrous as dehydration itself. In the oliguric animal, fluids accumulate in extravascular places, leading to tissue oedema (eg: pulmonary oedema). Techniques for monitoring fluid therapy can be simple or invasive and the need to use more sophisticated techniques depends on the individual case. These are summarised below.

1) **Central venous pressure**
   Central venous pressure (CVP) is a measure of the blood pressure in the right atrium and is a measure of venous return to the heart. A long catheter is placed in the cranial vena cava or right atrium and attached to a fluid manometer. The normal CVP in dogs is 0 - 5 cm water. The CVP can be used to indicate whether fluid therapy is required and how effective the therapy is.

2) **Blood pressure**
   Blood pressure can be measured non-invasively by recording the changes in a peripheral artery. Many methods are difficult to perform in small animals, require complicated equipment and a skilled operator. Direct pressure reading via the vena cava remains the most accurate method of assessing the effectiveness of fluid therapy.

3) **PCV**
   Packed cell volume can be easily and inexpensively monitored if a centifuge is present (see Laboratory techniques). PCV rises with increasing severity of dehydration, and as fluid therapy takes effect the results of haemodilution will cause the PCV to fall into the normal range. If normal urinary output is maintained, the PCV should not fall below normal (unless anaemia is concurrently present).

4) **Urinary output**

Urine output can be measured in one of two ways (active or passive),and is especially important in monitoring effects of fluid therapy in renal failure patients and those animals with oliguria. Passive monitoring is only of value in cases where the animal is able to ambulate easily and consciously urinate. This method is not adequate for severely ill patients. In these cases, a urinary catheter should be placed into the urethra with a collection system (fluid therapy line attached to an empty fluid bag). Urine production can the be continuously assessed.

5) More subjective means of assessing cardiac output are:
   capillary refill time
   colour of mucous membranes
   pulse strength
   rectal temperature.

OVERTRANSFUSION

Too much fluid leads to a dramatic increase in central venous pressure and congestive heart failure results, resulting in pulmonary oedema and respiratory compromise/collapse. Overtransfusion is most common in patients with pre-existing congestive heart failure, reduced urinary output (acute renal failure) or normovolaemic animals (anaemia).

Central venous pressure measurement, urine output, chest auscultation, respiratory rate, capillary refill time and jugular distention are extremely important monitoring tools.

Signs of overhydration
   Anxiety
   Depression
   Dyspnoea
   Collapse
   Soft cough
   Tachypnoea

BLOOD TRANSFUSIONS

Indications:
Acute haemorrhage or haemolysis with loss of more than 40% of PCV.
PVC of less that 10% with symptoms of hypoxia.

If surgical haemorrhage has occurred the blood loss can be estimated by weighing the swabs and assuming that 1g = 1ml blood.

The recipient's blood should be cross matched prior to transfusion to prevent a transfusion reaction to the donor blood. The A antigen is the most allergenic in dogs and ideally the donor dog should be A negative.

Blood must be collected into bags containing citrate as this anticoagulant prolongs the life of the red blood cells.

Collection of blood - from donor dogs:
1) Check the PCV of the donor before collecting the blood.
2) Weigh the dog. The blood volume of a healthy dog is 8% of its weight and it can donate 25% of its blood volume once a month.
3) Clip the hair over the jugular vein and prepare the area surgically.
4) Blood is collected through jugular venipuncture into a collection bag containing anticoagulant. These bags are made for the collection of 500mls of blood. If less blood is to be collected, remove the appropriate amount of anticoagulant from the bag.
5) Introduce the needle on the collection pack into the vein and collect the blood. Weigh the bag during the collection period so that the correct amount is collected. Mix the contents in the bag gently during collection to disperse the anticoagulant.

Storage
Blood can be stored for 3-4 weeks for Acid citrate dextrose and 6 weeks for Citrate phosphate dextrose adenine at 4.5°C.

Transfusion
Cross matching is not available so a small quantity of blood (1-2mls) is administered to the recipient who is then observed for 5-10 minutes for signs of a transfusion reaction. If this occurs, high dose hydrocortisone should be administered intravenously along with intravenous fluids such as 0.9% saline. If there is no reaction then the blood can be given over 20-30 minutes.

Signs of a transfusion reaction
1) Anxiety
2) Restlessness
3) Shivering
4) Vomiting
5) Tachycardia
6) Tachypnoea
7) Hypersalivation
8) Defaecation
* *If there are signs of a reaction stop the transfusion immediately*

FELINE BLOOD TRANSFUSIONS

Because cats tolerate severe anaemia better than dogs, and the risk of transfusion reactions is much greater, blood transfusion is an uncommon practice in in this species.

Blood types
Three major blood groups exist in cats - A, B and AB. A is the most common (80%), B (20%), and AB is rare (0.4%). The proportions of blood types vary greatly between breeds.

Donor
It should be obvious that the donor cat must be negative for the major retroviruses of cats - Feline Leukaemia Virus (FeLV) and Feline Immunodeficiency Virus (FIV), and also for Haemobartonella felis, the rickettsial blood parasite.

Collection
A healthy donor can donate 50 - 70mls of blood every three weeks. Sedation is occassionally required and is best achieved with ketamine and diazepam combination. Acepromazine should be avoided as it drops peripheral blood pressure. The blood must be collected from a jugular vein that has been surgically prepared.

Equipment
An 18-19 gauge butterfly needle attached to a 60 ml syringe containing 8 mls of Acid-citrate dextrose (ACD) or Citrate-phosphate-dextrose-adenine (CPDA). Gentle mixing of the blood as it is collected is recommended.

Collected blood should be stored at 4°C and used within 21 days of collection.

ADMINISTRATION OF BLOOD:

1) Attach a blood administration set to the collection bag.

2) Attach the administration set to the intravenous catheter.

3) Set the administration rate. In the event of circulatory collapse following haemorrhage, blood can be administered at a rate which will restore circulatory volume as soon as possible. If the circulatory volume is normal (CVP is normal) the blood should be administered at 2mls/kg/hour, or at a rate which will administer the whole volume over 8 hours.

4) Monitor the animal closely over the first half an hour for signs of a transfusion reaction.

Practical Veterinary Nursing

SHOCK

Shock describes a condition where severe impairment of effective capillary perfusion occurs resulting in deterioration of cell function. i.e.: blood flow is insufficient to provide adequate oxygen and nutrients to peripheral tissues and remove wastes, many of which are toxic.

Types of shock

Hypovolaemic shock: The direct acute loss of fluid volume due to haemorrhage (internal/external), plasma loss (burns/exudates), water and electrolyte loss (decreased intake/loss – vomiting or diarrhoea) or a combination of the above.

Vasculogenic shock: Results from a loss of vascular tone. Three main mechanisms are involved:
i) Septic and endotoxic shock from the release of endotoxins from gram negative organisms. Predisposing factors are poor nutrition, old age, dehydration, intravenous catheters, and immunosuppression.
ii) Anaphylactic reactions.
iii) CNS damage.

Cardiogenic shock: Mainly due to cardiac output failure resulting in poor tissue perfusion of peripheral tissues.

CLINICAL SIGNS OF SHOCK

Cardinal signs
Tachycardia
Weak pulse
Pale mucous membranes
Prolonged capillary refill time
Cold extremities
Low urine output

Hypovolaemic: Usually accompanied by a history of one of the inciting causes eg haemorrhage, trauma, vomiting, diarrhoea, along with the cardinal signs of shock.

Septic shock: May be accompanied by a history of known infection, abdominal surgery, immunosuppressive therapy or disease.

Cardiogenic shock: Along with cardinal signs, ascites, pleural effusion, pulmonary oedema may be present.

TREATMENT OF HYPOVOLAEMIC SHOCK

Once diagnosed, treatment of shock should not be delayed. After initiating treatment, the animal should be continually re-assessed. As hypovolaemic shock is due directly to fluid loss, therapy should be directed in this area.

1) **Volume replacement:** A polyionic infusion should be used until laboratory results return eg: Hartmann's.

2) **Oxygen therapy:** If hypoxia is present, O_2 via face mask, nasal tube, or oxygen cage.

3) **Vasodilators:** Except in early septic shock, venous constriction occurs in peripheral capillaries. Vasodilators should be used only when fluid therapy fails to result in vasodilation. Central venous pressure must be measured if vasodilators are to be used to avoid hypovolaemia.

4) **Glucocorticoids:** Best results in early shock and septic shock. *Never* an alternative to fluid replacement. Must be in high doses : e.g:
   Methylprednisolone succinate 30mg/kg
   Dexamethasone phosphate 4-6mg/kg
   Hydrocortisone 150mg/kg
   Beneficial effects – preserve vascular and lysosomal membrane stability, positive cardiac inotropy, decreased release of inflammatory mediators, increased regional blood flow, decreased intestinal absorption of endotoxin.

5) **Antibiotics:** Indicated prophylactically in severe shock and in septic shock.

6) **Bicarbonate:** If severe metabolic acidosis is present. Blood gases should be checked before addition of HCO3- to fluids.

7) **Anticoagulants:** To prevent Disseminated Intravascular Coagulation (DIC). Use of heparin is contraversial 100IU/kg every 4 hours given after the transfusion.

Fluids for shock

Speed of replacement is as important as the type of fluid which is used. A balanced electrolyte is generally the first choice e.g: Hartmann's. If platelets or red blood cells are required, then blood may be the first choice although the requirement for a rapid infusion speed may prevent this initially.

Plasma expanders or plasma, may be used if blood is unavailable, these increase osmotic pressure and are therefore very useful.

LABORATORY
TECHNIQUES

LABORATORY TECHNIQUES

The function of a laboratory is to provide a diagnostic service. Samples are analysed and the results help to confirm a diagnosis or improvement in the condition or reveal new abnormalities in the patient.

Laboratories vary in sophistication - some have equipment which can perform complicated analyses and some have very simple equipment which with skilled use, can reveal a lot of information.

It is most important that the equipment be kept clean and in perfect working order and that strict regimes are adhered to so that one can be sure that the results obtained are reliable and the equipment lasts as long as possible.

Sample collection and preparation is of vital importance so that the maximum amount of reliable information can be obtained from each sample.

It is essential that all samples are carefully labelled with the patient identification and the date as soon as they are collected and then recorded in a day book.

SAFETY

It is most important to adhere strictly to the safety procedures for collection of samples, their analysis and disposal whilst working in the laboratory to protect oneself from injury or contamination with infectious material.

1) No eating, drinking, biting fingernails, chewing the ends of pencils etc. or mouth pipetting.
2) Wear protective coats and protective gloves, masks etc. where necessary.
3) Wash hands.
4) Dispose of all material in the correct places.
5) Keep benches tidy and disinfected.
6) Know where the first aid kit is and what actions to take in the event of an accident – injuries from sharp objects, broken glass, spillage of corrosives and poisons, toxic fumes, eye contamination. Be familiar with the accident book routine.

LABORATORY APPARATUS

Microscope

The microscope visualises material which is too small to be seen with the naked eye. Its most important use is to look at blood smears, other tissue smears, skin, urine and faecal preparations. Most microscopes have an in-built light source which transmits light through a condenser and diaphragm below the sample, through the sample which is visualised through magnification lenses. There are two sets of lenses, one in the eyepiece and one in the objective stage. Combinations of these are used to achieve suitable magnification. The eyepiece lenses are usually 10X magnification and the objective lenses range from 10X to 100X. The magnification factors are multiplied together to get the total magnification. The 100X lens is usually used for oil immersion. Each microscope has a course and a fine focus and direction controls for moving the slide on the specimen stage.

To use the microscope

1) Place the slide onto the specimen stage.
2) Switch on the light and move the condenser up until it is 2mm below the slide.
3) Select the 10X eyepiece lens and 40X objective and use the course focus to bring the objective lens down to 4mm above the sample.
4) Use the fine focus to visualise the sample. If greater resolution is required the lenses on the objective stage can be exchanged.
5) If oil is to be used, place a drop on the sample and select the oil immersion lens.

It is important to use the correct magnification for the sample. Keep the lenses clean, dry and scratch free.

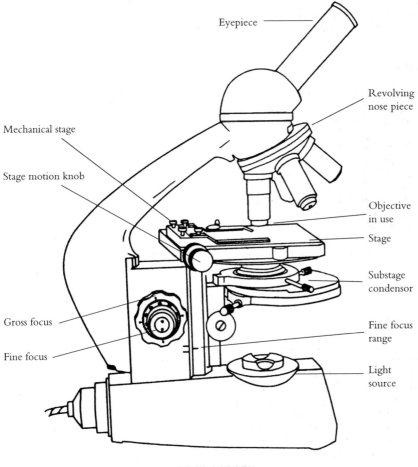

Eyepiece

Revolving nose piece

Mechanical stage

Stage motion knob

Objective in use

Stage

Substage condensor

Gross focus

Fine focus range

Fine focus

Light source

MICROSCOPE

Centrifuge

The centrifuge is used for the separation of blood samples into cells and plasma or serum and other fluids, e.g. faecal suspensions, into solid and liquid phases. Large centrifuges contain buckets which hold test tubes. Microcentrifuges are used to spin the capillary tubes used to measure the packed cell volume of blood. The most important point when using a centrifuge is to make sure that it is balanced. The diametrically opposite samples must have the same weight. Some centrifuges can be loaded with samples that are balanced by eye, but others are very sensitive and require the samples in the tubes to be weighed before they are loaded. If blanks are used to balance the centrifuge they should be loaded with a solution of similar density to the sample e.g. balance urine with water, balance faecal suspensions with the saturated solution.

To use the centrifuge

1) Load the samples.
2) Make sure that they are balanced.
3) Lock the secondary lid, if there is one, and then close the main lid. The machine will not run unless the main lid is properly closed.
4) Set the time and speed required and start the centrifuge.
5) If the machine starts to shake violently, stop it immediately as it is not balanced. Some centrifuges have a light to indicate this.

Most samples are spun for between 5 and 10 minutes at 2000 – 4000 revolutions per minute (rpm). Separate plasma and serum by spinning for 10 minutes at 2000 rpm. Microhaematocrit centrifuges have one speed and they should be set for 5 minutes.
Occasionally tubes break during centrifugation and if this happens the machine should be carefully cleaned.

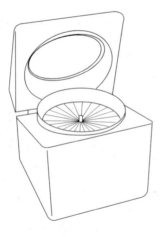

MICROCENTRIFUGE

CENTRIFUGE

Colorimeter, Spectrophotometer or Photometer

Instruments which measure the intensity of the colour of a solution by passing light of a known wavelength through the solution and measuring the absorbency of the light. They are used in biochemical tests where the end result is a coloured solution of unknown concentration. Blanks and solutions of known concentration are used to calibrate the machine which then reads the test samples. It is important that the cuvettes in which the samples are tested are clean or else this will affect the passage of light.

Wet and Dry Labs/Open and Closed Systems

Fluid biochemistry is carried out using chemical tests which result in a colour change in the test sample. A photometer quantifies the colour change. Some systems require the measurement and mixing of the various reagents for the reaction to be done by the operator and these are called wet laboratories, or open systems. A dry laboratory or closed system has the reagents premixed by the manufacturer, to which one simply adds the sample.

Refractometer

The refractometer measures the change in refractive index of a fluid due to the solutes dissolved in the fluid. It gives a measure of the specific gravity of the fluid. Refractometers can be used to measure the specific gravity of urine and the concentration of protein in serum.

To use the refractometer

1) Make sure that both the slide and prism surfaces are clean and dry.
2) Place the slide on the prism surface.
3) Using a pasteur pipette, allow a few drops of the sample to run down between the slide and prism and flood the entire surface of the prism.
4) Point the prism end at a light source, eg. a window, and look through the eyepiece.
5) Read the level of the relevant scale.

Some refractometers can measure both total protein and urine specific gravity and it is important to read the level using the correct scale.

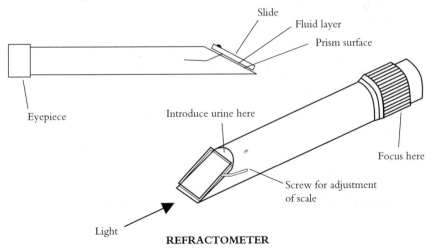

REFRACTOMETER

Incubator
A machine which keeps constant temperature.

Pipettes
There are two kinds of pipette – glass pipettes are used for measuring large quantities of fluid (>1cm), and automatic pipettes which measure very small quantities very accurately (1μl). Automatic pipette machines or rubber pipette bulbs are attached to the suction end of a glass pipette and fluid can be drawn in to the required level and expelled.

To use the pipette
1) An automatic pipette requires a tip to be fitted to the dispensing end. Use a new tip for each sample.
2) Set the pipette to the required volume, usually by twisting the plunger whilst looking at the counter.
3) Depress the plunger to the first stop. This displaces a volume of air equal to the volume of fluid required.
4) Insert the tip into the solution and release the plunger. Fluid will be drawn into the tip.
5) Insert the tip into the receiving receptacle and depress the plunger to the second stop. This releases all the fluid.

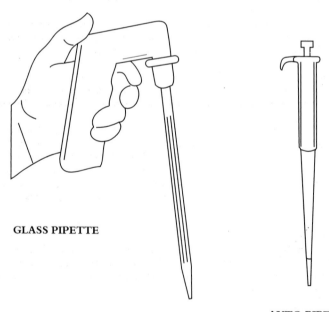

GLASS PIPETTE

AUTO PIPETTE

SAMPLE COLLECTION AND PREPARATION

The collection of specific samples is covered in the relevant section but in general it is most important that samples be collected correctly into the appropriate preservative and container. This prepares the sample for analysis and prevents sample deterioration. It is also important to label the sample and to analyse it as soon as possible to prevent deterioration and therefore inaccurate results.

Cerebrospinal Fluid

Cerebrospinal fluid is a clear ultra filtrate of plasma which bathes the central nervous system. General anaesthesia, and strict asepsis is required for the collection of CSF.

For cisternal puncture, the animal is anaesthetised and placed in lateral recumbency with the head flexed at 90 degrees to the spine. The point of insertion is the intersection of two imaginary lines between the lateral wings of the atlas and the occipital protuberance. The needle is inserted perpendicular to this to avoid the large venous sinuses running parallel to the midline. The CSF is allowed to drip into a sterile tube containing EDTA for cytology or heparin for bacteriology.

Synovial Fluid

Surgical preparation is required before beginning this procedure and sterile technique maintained. The point over the joint covered with least connective tissue should be used as the sight of entry and this varies from joint to joint.

Synovial fluid is an ultra filtrate of plasma with a very low cell count, and hyaluronate secreted by synovial B cells. It is highly viscous.

Most Joints can be entered with a 23-25 gauge 1" needle to obtain a sample. Only a small volume is required for cytology and this should be smeared as blood onto a glass slide and the excess placed into EDTA and heparin tubes for cytology and bacteriology respectively.

Abdominocentesis

Abdominocentesis is used to obtain samples of fluid which has accumulated within the peritoneal cavity. Fluid is not normally present, and the sample can be used to help establish a diagnosis of the underlying cause.

Abdominocentesis is a simple and safe procedure which is relatively non-painful. The area to be entered should be clipped and aseptically prepared. A 22-23 gauge, 1 inch needle is introduced in the midline or parallel to this, avoiding the left cranial abdomen to prevent entering the spleen. The area cranial to the umbilicus should be avoided as the falciform ligament and associated fat can obstruct fluid flow (a common problem). Specimens can be sent for cytology and bacteriology or more specific biochemical (e.g.: bilirubin, protein electrophoresis), or serological tests (eg Coronavirus titres).

Thoracocentesis

Describes the procedure of entering the pleural space to remove accumulated fluid. A very small amount of fluid is usually present in the pleural space to allow movement of the lungs within the thoracic cage. Where more fluid has collected thoracocentesis is performed for therapeutic (to allow easier respiration) and diagnostic purposes.

Dog: Between ribs 7 or 8 in the lower third of the thorax is the site of choice. Local anaesthesia may be required. Sedation should be avoided if possible as these patients are respiratory compromised. Samples are sent for cytology and bacteriology as described above.

Cat: EXTREME CARE is required in cats requiring thoracocentesis, as these animals are usually severely respiratory compromised by the time they present. No sedation or general anaesthetic should be required, and local anaesthesia is usually not necessary. Use as few handlers as possible. The cat may need to be stabilised first before this procedure e.g: oxygen therapy.

TISSUE SAMPLES, TUMOURS AND ORGANS

Biopsy samples

1) Tissue at edge of lesion should be selected.
2) Many samples should be taken.
3) Avoid crushing samples, overhandling, drying out.
4) Samples should be rapidly fixed.
5) Specimens for immunofluorescence should be frozen in liquid nitrogen.

Fixation

1) DILUTE 100% FORMALIN (40% Formaldehyde) 1 in 10 for fixation.
2) Add $CaCO_3$ chips to prevent formalin going off and staining tissue if infrequently used.
3) Wide necked plastic containers should be used for fixation.
4) Ratio of 10:1 Formalin to tissue volume should be used for fixation.
5) Large tissues may require 24 hours of fixation, or should be sectioned.
6) Brain requires at least 96 hours fixation before cutting.
7) Muscle, nerve, and small intestine should be gently pressed onto cardboard first to prevent contraction.
8) Small intestine – large samples can be tied at both ends, the lumen injected with formal-saline and placed into formal-saline.

SPECIMENS FOR PATHOLOGICAL EXAMINATION

If tissue samples are to be sent away for examination, it is important that they be preserved and packed in such a way as to ensure their arrival for analysis in perfect condition. If the samples have deteriorated *en route* the results will be meaningless.

SAMPLES

Blood and Tissue Fluids
Blood in the correct anticoagulant should be kept at 4°C and should be analysed within 24 hours. Blood samples for the collection of plasma should be centrifuged as soon as possible. If serum is required, blood should be centrifuged 2 hrs after taking and both plasma and serum should be stored at 4°C and analysed within 24 hrs. All tissue fluids should be collected in plain sterile containers or into EDTA to prevent clotting, stored at 4°C and analysed within 24 hrs.

Urine
Urine should be stored in a sterile container at 4°C and analysed within 6 hrs. Urine can be preserved with the addition of an equal volume of formal saline, boric acid or cytofix.

Faeces
Faeces should fill the container and should be stored at 4°C and be analysed within 6 hrs. Faeces can be preserved with the addition of twice the volume of formal saline.

Dermatology
Hairs for dermatophyte examination and culture should be placed in a sterile container. Coat brushings and skin scrapings should be mounted in liquid paraffin, a cover slip put in place and stored in a slide container.

Histopathology
Tissue samples should be preserved in 10 x their volume of formal saline.
It is important to mention a brief history, a description and the site of the lesion and the tests required on the laboratory request form

Post Mortem Samples
Organs and pieces of tissue should be fixed in a wide necked jar in 10 x their volume of formal saline. The time taken for the formal saline to fix the tissue depends on the size of the tissue and large organs should be cut in half to prevent autolysis occuring in the centre of the tissue. With fixing, the tissue becomes hard and if the neck of the container is too small it may be impossible to remove it without breaking the container.
It is important to mention a brief history, a tentative diagnosis, the cause of death and the tests required on the laboratory request form.

SPECIMENS FOR TOXICOLOGICAL EXAMINATION

To confirm a suspected poisoning, appropriate samples must be collected, preserved and analysed. These are usually samples of vomit, stomach contents or feed containing the suspected toxin.

1) Containers used should be clean and free of chemicals. Do not use metal screw cap lids.

2) Pack samples individually.

3) If preservation is required use 95% ethanol at 1ml per gram of tissue. Do not use formalin because it interferes with many tests. It is not necessary to preserve vomit as the low pH prevents bacterial growth. It may be necessary to pack samples in ice to prevent deterioration.

4) All samples should be clearly labelled with the identification of the case. A form should be included which records relevant history and if possible, states the suspected poison.

5) If legal action is a possibility the samples should be sealed in such a way that tampering can be detected, or the samples should be hand carried to the laboratory.

6) Include an empty container from the same batch as the ones containing the specimens.

7) If the a sample has been collected from bedding, include some normal bedding. This rules out the possibility of contamination.

DESPATCH OF PATHOLOGICAL OR TOXICOLOGICAL SAMPLES BY POST

Strict postal regulations are in force to protect the public and the postal workers from contamination from potentially deleterious material.

1) All samples must be in a primary container of not more than 50mls which is securely sealed. Special multi-specimen packs may be acceptable.

2) Each primary container should be wrapped in sufficient absorbant material to prevent any leakage in the case of damage.

3) All containers should be sealed in a leakproof plastic bag.

4) All plastic bags should be packed in a cardboard, plastic, metal or polystyrene box.

5) All boxes should be wrapped in brown paper or in a jiffy bag.

6) Include the laboratory request form.

7) All packages must be labelled **PATHOLOGICAL SPECIMEN** and **FRAGILE - HANDLE WITH CARE**. There should also be the name and address of the person to contact in the event of leakage.

8) All packages must be sent First Class Letter post or Data post.

9) If there is any possibility that the package will arrive on Saturday morning, keep it and post it on Monday.

INVESTIGATION OF BLOOD

Constituents of Blood

Cells:
Red blood cells (rbc) or erythrocytes.

White blood cells (wbc) or leukocytes; neutrophils, eosinophils, basophils, lymphocytes and monocytes.

Platelets or thrombocytes.

Plasma:
Water, proteins (albumin, globulin, clotting factors and enzymes, hormones), electrolytes and products of metabolism.

Serum:
The fluid component of blood from which the clotting factors have been removed following clotting of the sample.

COLLECTION OF BLOOD

It is important to use the correct site, equipment and procedures so that a representative sample is collected and prepared for analysis.

Site: Blood for haematology and biochemistry should be collected from the jugular vein. This vein provides easy access with practice and using the largest bore needle suitable provides a steady stream of blood with little turbulence and therefore minimal platelet clumping or haemolysis. Other veins used are the cephalic, saphenous (recurrent tarsal), where it crosses the gastrocnemius tendon and the femoral vein on the medial aspect of the thigh. Do not use these veins unless absolutely necessary, as they are used for intravenous catheters for fluid therapy and it is easy to create haematomas.

Equipment:

Syringe
Select a syringe of suitable size to collect enough blood to fill all the tubes.

Needle
A wide bore needle produces a steady stream of blood with minimal turbulence which cuts down on damage to the cells and platelets. Use a 21 or 23 gauge $^5/8$" needle for cats and small dogs and a 19, 20 or 21 gauge 1 -1$^1/2$" needle for giant to medium size dogs.

Containers

Blood normally clots within 10 - 20 seconds after contact with tissue, tissue fluid, glass or plastic. Prior to collection of the sample decide which tests are to be performed and therefore which blood tubes are required:

Serum: clotted sample
Plain tube - No anti-coagulant. Serum is required for biochemistry.

Plasma or Examination of Cells: unclotted sample

Anticoagulant	Uses
EDTA	Haematology - maintains the integrity of the cells
Heparin	Haematology and some hormones and electrolytes
Sodium citrate	Platelets and clotting parameters
Fluoride oxalate	Blood glucose level - fluoride oxalate prevents the rbc metabolising the glucose in the plasma

Vacutainers - plain and with anti-coagulants. Vacutainer tubes have a vacuum inside. Once the needle has pierced the vein, the tube is attached and blood drawn into the tube. There is no need to transfer blood to containers after collection. This reduces contamination and agitation which reduces platelet clumping and haemolysis. However, the vacuum can be too strong for small veins and cause them to collapse, which would cause platelet clumping. They are much more expensive.

Method:

1) Clip or cut the hair away over the vein if necessary and definitely if a sterile sample is required for culture. Swab the area with spirit - this helps to make the vein stand out and may reduce contamination with skin bacteria.
2) Restrain the animal firmly in the sitting position. Use digital pressure to occlude the vein so that the needle can be introduced into a distended vein.
3) Identify the position of the vein, introduce the needle and withdraw the blood into the syringe or attach the vacutainer tube.
4) Once the required blood has been collected remove the digital pressure on the vein and withdraw the needle and hold a swab over the exit site to reduce the chance of haematoma formation.
5) Remove the needle from the syringe.
6) Transfer the blood to the containers as quickly and with as little agitation as possible. Sodium citrate first, EDTA or heparin, Fluoride oxalate, plain last.
7) Invert the tubes which contain anticoagulant gently to mix.

PROBLEMS ASSOCIATED WITH BLOOD COLLECTION

Haemolysis is the rupture of red blood cells which leads to release of haemoglobin into the plasma or serum and stains it red. Haemolysis occurs if blood is added to a hyposmolar solution like distilled water. It can occur during the collection and processing of blood because the cells are very fragile. Turbulence, vigorous agitation, extremes of temperature and standing for long periods of time all cause haemolysis. The blood sample should be taken as quickly as possible from the largest vein through the largest bore needle. Remove the needle before gently releasing the blood into the tube. Invert the tube slowly if there is anticoagulant present, or allow to stand upright if it is a plain tube. Process as quickly as possible. Avoid extremes in temperature and do not allow samples to stand in the sun.

Clotting occurs when there is insufficient anticoagulant for the volume of blood, or when the sample is taken incorrectly and clotting occurs before anticoagulant is added. Always add the correct volume of blood to the anticoagulant in the tube, this is indicated on the tube. Take the sample as quickly as possible and if the vein is missed, use a new needle as the used needle may contain tissue factors which will initiate clotting.

Lipaemia is fat globules in the plasma or serum giving it a cloudy appearance and interfering with biochemistry. As feeding can affect the levels of certain substances in the blood, e.g. cholesterol, blood samples should always be taken 6-8 hours after feeding.

Haemolysis and lipaemia will affect serum biochemistry.

PREPARATION OF SAMPLES AND ANALYSIS

It is most important to process blood samples as soon as possible after collection. Standing, heat and light will all affect the condition of the cells and the constituents in the plasma or serum.

Plasma and serum should be stored temporarily at 4°C or frozen at -20°C.

Plasma is usually collected from samples containing sodium EDTA or heparin.
1) Centrifuge a sample containing anti-coagulant at 2000 RPM for 10 mins.
2) Use a pasteur pipette to remove the plasma from above the pellet of red blood cells and put it into a clean tube.
3) Examine the plasma to assess the colour and clarity.

Serum is collected from a sample which has been allowed to clot.
1) Allow a sample without anti-coagulant to stand for 2 hrs until the sample has clotted and the clot has retracted.
2) Centrifuge the sample at 2000 RPM for 10 mins.
3) Remove the serum from above the blood clot by pouring it out of the tube or by withdrawing it with a pasteur pipette into a clean tube.
4) Examine the serum to assess the colour and clarity.

Practical Veterinary Nursing

Total protein A drop of the plasma from a centrifuged capillary tube of blood is placed on a refractometer to assess the total protein concentration of the plasma.

Glucose There are a number of battery operated systems which are used in human medicine to measure blood glucose. These use dipsticks and a small photometer which quantifies the colour change.

Each biochemistry system has its own protocol and these should be strictly followed.

HAEMATOLOGY

Should be carried out on **EDTA** samples;

Red Blood Cell Count	Number of rbc per litre of blood
Haemoglobin (Hb)	Concentration of haemoglobin in g/100mls blood
Packed Cell Volume (PCV)	The volume of rbc expressed as a percentage of a volume of blood
Mean Cell Volume (MCV)	Average volume of a rbc in femtolitres (fl)
Mean Cell Haemoglobin Concentration(MCHC)	Concentration of haemoglobin in 100mls of packed rbc in g/l
Mean Cell Haemoglobin (MCH)	Average haemoglobin content of a rbc in picograms (pg)
Erythrocyte Sedimentation Rate (ESR)	Rate at which rbc sediment out when left to stand in mins
Reticulocytes	Immature rbc measured as the number of reticulocytes per 100 rbc counted
White Blood Cell Count	Number of wbc per litre of blood
Differential Count	Number of each of the wbc per 100 wbc counted

Carried out on **Sodium Citrate** samples;

Platelets	Number of platelets per litre of blood
Prothrombin Time (PT)	Time taken for blood to clot via extrinsic pathway in secs
Activated Partial Thromboplastin Time(APTT)	Time taken for blood to clot via intrinsic pathway in secs

HAEMATOLOGY

BLOOD SMEAR

1) Use a plain capillary tube to draw a small amount of blood from a well mixed sample of blood in EDTA.
2) Place a small drop at one end of a glass slide.
3) Hold another slide at an angle of 45° to the first and draw it backwards along the slide until it touches the drop of blood.
4) Allow the blood to spread across the slide and the push the slide forward firmly. The blood will be drawn out along the slide.

The glass slides must be clean and free of grease and dust or streaks and spots will appear in the smear. Use only a small drop of blood or the smear will be too thick.

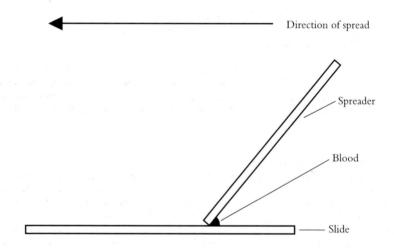

Direction of spread

Spreader

Blood

Slide

TO PREPARE A BLOOD SMEAR

PERIPHERAL BLOOD SMEARS

1) Swab the medial surface of the pinna with a spirit swab.
2) Prick the skin with a needle or lancet and wait for a spot of blood to appear.
3) Pick this spot up with a glass slide and make a smear on another glass slide in the manner described above.

A peripheral blood smear will reveal information about blood parasites and give a quick estimation of the number and condition of the rbc, wbc and platelets.

Practical Veterinary Nursing

To Stain the Smear

Leishman's stain:
1) Cover the smear with Leishman's stain and allow to fix for 2 mins.
2) Add twice the volume of buffered distilled water (pH6.8) to the slide and mix the solutions but avoid spillage. Allow to stand for approximately 15 mins when a metallic scum will be visible on the surface of the solution.
3) Wash with buffered distilled water (pH6.8) and allow to dry.

Giemsa stain:
1) Fix the slide in methanol for a few secs.
2) Place the slide in the stain bath, or flood the slide with stain and leave for 30 mins.
3) Wash the slide and allow to dry.

Diff-quik stain:
1) Fix the slide in the fixer for 5 secs
2) Place the slide in the red solution for 30 secs.
3) Remove and place the slide in the blue solution for 10 secs.
4) Wash the slide and allow to dry.

All of the above stains are Romanowsky stains which use two dyes; Haematoxylin which stains basic tissue blue, and Eosin, which stains acidic tissue, red. Leishman's stain is usually used by haematologists because it gives good cellular definition and is quicker than Giemsa stain. Giemsa stain is used to stain haemoparasites. Diff-quik is a very quick stain but gives poor cellular definition.

Examination of a Blood Smear

Examination of a blood smear will reveal a lot of information about the numbers and conditions of the cells in blood. It is important to have a well prepared smear so that the cells are one layer thick and not damaged. The smear should be examined under oil immersion. Red blood cells should be examined for the size, shape, colour and for intracellular inclusions.

Normal red blood cells are red, circular, biconcave discs which do not contain a nucleus. Sometimes during the processing the red cells are damaged or dehydrated and become crenated when they appear like stars. The changes that are seen in red cells usually occur because they have been released from the bone marrow before they are mature. These changes include; varying size of red cells called anisocytosis, different intensity of staining called polychromasia and understaining, called hypochromasia. Very immature red cells may contain a nucleus. Less immature red cells are called reticulocytes and they contain intracellular reticular material which stains blue. Intracellular parasites may be revealed.

Examine the "tail" of the smear to assess the numbers and character of the white blood cells. They are heavier and are swept to the end of the smear when it is prepared. Granulocytes are neutrophils, eosinophils and basophils and they have lobulated nuclei and granules in the cytoplasm. Lymphocytes have circular nuclei and monocytes have circular or bean shaped nuclei. The white blood cell differential count is the proportion of each of the different white blood cells in the blood and is calculated by counting the number of each type per 100 cells.

Examine the platelets to assess their number and look for platelet clumping which will explain a reduced number.

HAEMATOCRIT

The haematocrit or packed cell volume (PCV) is a quick and reasonably accurate measurement of the percentage of red cells in blood and it is used to assess anaemia or dehydration.

Centrifugation of blood in a capillary tube yields three layers; the red blood cells form a column at the bottom, the white blood cells form a very thin white band called the buffy coat above the red blood cells and the top layer is plasma. The plasma should be clear. Pink plasma indicates haemolysis. Yellow plasma indicates jaundice which has increased bilirubin in the blood. Cloudy plasma represents lipaemia. (NB. Cattle and horse plasma is normally yellow)

The PCV is calculated by measuring the height of the red cell column and expressing it as a percentage of the height of the whole column.

Method:

1) Blood from a sample in EDTA is drawn into a capillary tube by capillary action to fill about 3/4 of the length of the tube. Alternatively, a capillary tube containing heparin can be used to collect blood directly from a lancet prick through the skin.

2) One end of the tube is stopped up by inserting the end into a plastic sealing compound and twisting the tube as it is withdrawn.

3) Wipe the tube with a gauze swab and place in it the microcentrifuge with the plastic plug pointing outwards and fitted against the rim gasket.

4) Balance the centrifuge with a tube filled to the same level.

5) Screw the safety plate down and close the lid.

6) Centrifuge for 5 mins at 10 000 RPM.

7) Remove the tube and measure the PCV using a microhaematocrit reader. Place the tube in the groove on the reader and line up the top of the sealing plastic with the line at the bottom of the reader and the top of the serum with the diagonal line at the top of the reader. Move the slide so that it is in line with the top of the column of red blood cells and read off the measurement on the scale at the right hand side of the reader.

If a microhaematocrit reader is not available, measure the height of the blood cells and the height of the whole column and calculate the PCV

PCV =   Height of red cell column x 100%
         ─────────────────────────────────

         Total height of blood column

The PCV should always be considered in conjunction with the total protein of the plasma.

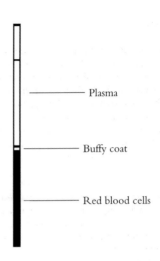

Plasma

Buffy coat

Red blood cells

CAPILLARY TUBE

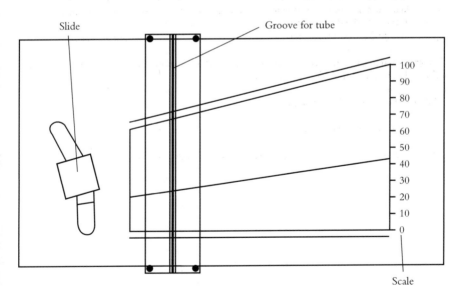

Slide

Groove for tube

100
90
80
70
60
50
40
30
20
10
0

Scale

MICROHAEMATOCRIT READER

RED BLOOD CELL COUNT

There are two methods of measuring the rbc count, one is using a cell counter and the other, manual. The cell counter works by counting the cells that pass through an aperture which is set according to the size of the cells. By the manual method, a very small quantity of blood is diluted and the cells are counted using a counting chamber called a Neubauer haemocytometer, a counting chamber which holds a known volume of diluted blood. Skill and accuracy are required to obtain reliable results.

Method:

To dilute the blood:
1) Pipette 20mls of red cell diluting fluid (Phosphate Buffered Saline) into a test tube.
2) Using an automatic pipette, add 100μl of blood from a well mixed sample of blood in EDTA. Seal the tube and invert several times to mix the solutions.

To fill the counting chamber:
1) Ensure that the counting chamber and cover slip are clean and dry.
2) Apply the cover slip to the counting chamber as shown in the diagram and if it is correctly applied "Newton's rings" which are small rainbow circles along the edges of the cover slip will be visible.
3) Fill a capillary tube with the solution and with the index finger over the top, transfer the tube to the counting chamber.
4) Hold the capillary tube at 45° to the cover slip and allow a small amount of fluid to be drawn into the counting chamber in one smooth flow. There must be no bubbles and no fluid in the grooves on either side of the counting chamber. If there are, start again. Fill both sides of the counting chamber.

To count the cells:
1) Keep the counting chamber horizontal and transfer to a microscope. Allow 2-3 mins for the cells to settle.
2) Count the cells in five of the squares in the central area using the 40X objective. (See Diagram)

Calculation: Number of cells in 5 squares divided by 100
                = rbc x 10^{12}/l

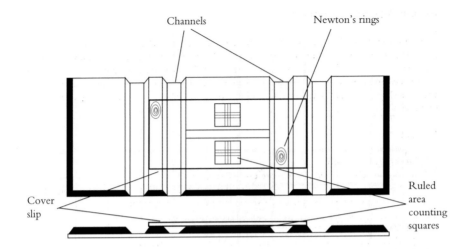

IMPROVED NEUBAUER HAEMOCYTOMETER

Channels

Newton's rings

Ruled area counting squares

Cover slip

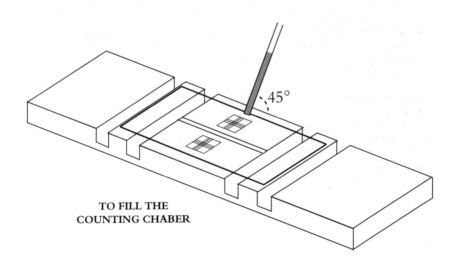

45°

TO FILL THE COUNTING CHABER

TO PREPARE A RED OR WHITE BLOOD CELL COUNT

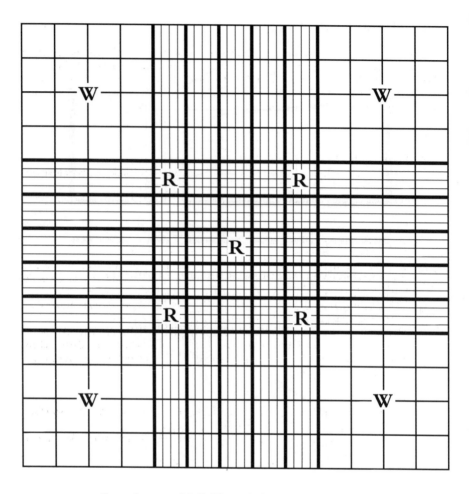

Count the squares labelled **R** to calculate a red blood cell count

Count the squares labelled **W** to calculate a white blood cell count

COUNTING SQUARES

TO PREPARE A RED OR WHITE BLOOD CELL COUNT

WHITE BLOOD CELL COUNT

The wbc count can be measured using a cell counter or a manual method. The cell counter counts the cells that pass through an aperture and the size of the aperture depends on the cells that are being counted. By the manual method, a very small quantity of blood is diluted and the cells are counted using a counting chamber called an improved Neubauer haemocytometer, which holds a known volume of diluted blood. Skill and accuracy are required to obtain reliable results

Method:

To dilute the blood:
1) Use a 2ml automatic pipette and pipette 2ml of white blood cell diluting fluid (Phosphate Buffered Saline, Acetic Acid, Gentian Violet) into a receptacle.
2) Add 100µl of blood from a well mixed sample of blood in EDTA. Depress the plunger several times to mix the solutions.

To fill the counting chamber:
1) Ensure that the counting chamber and cover slip are clean and dry.
2) Apply the cover slip to the counting chamber as shown in the diagram and if it is correctly applied "Newton's rings" which are small rainbow circles along the edges of the cover slip will be visible.
3) Fill a capillary tube with the solution and with the index finger over the top, transfer the tube to the counting chamber.
4) Hold the capillary tube at 45° to the cover slip and allow a small amount of fluid to be drawn into the counting chamber in one smooth flow. There must be no bubbles and no fluid in the grooves on either side of the counting chamber. If there are, start again. Fill both sides of the counting chamber.

To count the cells:
1) Keep the counting chamber horizontal and transfer to a microscope. Allow 2-3 mins for the cells to settle.
2) Count the cells in the four large squares on the outside using the 40X objective. (See Diagram)

Calculation: Number of cells in 4 squares divided by 20
                  = wbc x 10^9/l

RETICULOCYTE COUNT

Reticulocytes are immature rbc that are released early by the bone marrow in anaemia. They contain remnants of endoplasmic reticulum which stains up as dark blue strands in the cytoplasm. They are stained using a supra vital technique. Their presence is used to quantify the response of the bone marrow to the anaemia.

Method 1:
1) Place 2 mls brilliant cresyl blue or new methylene blue stain into a centrifuge tube and add 4-5 drops of blood
2) Mix and place the tube in the incubator at 37°C for 30 mins.
3) Spin the centrifuge tube at 1000 rpm for a minute and remove the supernatant.
4) Resuspend the cells at the bottom of the test tube and prepare a slide as for a blood smear.

Method 2:
1) Prepare a 0.3% solution of brilliant cresyl blue.
2) Make thin films of the stain on coverslips and allow to dry.
3) Place a drop of blood on one coverslip, sandwich with another one, draw them apart and allow to dry.

To count the cells:
The number of reticulocytes per 1000 rbc are counted.

To calculate:

$$\text{Reticulocyte count} = \frac{\text{number of reticulocytes x 100\%}}{\text{the number of cells scanned}}$$

In order to accurately assess the responsiveness of the bone marrow, this count must be corrected for the PCV of the patient.

To calculate:

$$\text{Corrected reticulocyte count} = \frac{\text{reticulocyte count x patients PCV}}{\text{normal PCV for the species.}}$$

HAEMOGLOBIN

The haemoglobin concentration of blood can be measured manually or by using an electronic counter. It is used in conjunction with the red blood cell count and the PCV to assess the degree of anaemia present.

ERYTHROCYTE SEDIMENTATION RATE

The ESR measures the rate at which rbc settle out in unclotted blood. This is a completely non-specific test and is seldom used.

RED CELL INDICES

MCV =

$$\frac{\text{PCV} \times 1000}{\text{rbc count}}$$

= mean volume of a rbc in fl

MCHC =

$$\frac{\text{Haemoglobin g/dl}}{\text{PCV}}$$

= % haemoglobin in 100ml of packed rbc

MCH =

$$\frac{\text{Haemoglobin g/dl} \times 10}{\text{rbc count}}$$

= concentration of haemoglobin in a rbc in pg

These indices give information about the size of the red cells and the amount of haemoglobin that they contain. This information can be used to establish whether the cells are being produced and released into the bloodstream normally.

HAEMATOLOGY

INTERPRETATION OF RESULTS

TEST	INCREASE	DECREASE	NORMAL DOG	NORMAL CAT
RBC	DEHYDRATION POLYCYTHAEMIA	ANAEMIA	5.5-8.5 x10^{12}/l	5-10 x 10^{12}/l
HAEMOGLOBIN		ANAEMIA IRON DEFICIENCY	12-18g/dl	8-15g/dl
PVC	DEHYDRATION	ANAEMIA	0.37-0.55l/l	0.30-0.45l/l
MCV	REGENERATIVE ANAEMIA	LIVER DISEASE	60-77fl	39-55fl
MCHC		IRON DEFICIENCY	32-36 g/dl	30-36 g/dl
RETICULOCUTES	REGENERATIVE ANAEMIA		1% rbc's	1.5-11% rbc's
NUCLEATED RBC	REGENERATIVE ANAEMIA		0	0
PLATELETS		DESSEMINATED INTRAVASCULAR COAGULATION AUTOIMMUNE DISEASE VASCULITIS	200-500 x10^9/l	300-700 x10^9/l
PARTIAL THROMBOPLASTIN& ACTIVATED PROTHROMBIN TIME	CLOTTING DEFICIENCIES		<95 secs	<90 secs
WBC COUNT	BACTERIAL INFECTION STRESS NEOPLASIA	ACUTE BACTERIAL INFECTION VIRAL INFECTION IMMUNOSUPPRESSION	6-17 x10^9/l	5.5-19.5 x10^9/l
NEUTROPHILS	INFECTION (L-SHIFT) STRESS	ACUTE BACTERIAL INFECTION VIRAL INFECTION AUTOIMMUNE CONDITIONS BONE MARROW NEOPLASIA	3-11.5 x10^9/l	2.5-12.5 x10^9/l
LYMPHOCYTES	CHRONIC INFECTION NEOPLASIA	ACUTE INFECTION STEROID ADMINISTRATION STRESS	1-4.8 x10^9/l	1.5-7 x10^9/l
EOSINOPHILS	ALLERGY PARASITISM	STRESS	0.1-1.25 x10^9/l	0.1-1.5 x10^9/l
MONOCYTES	CHRONIC INFECTION		0.15-1.35 x10^9/l	0.1-0.85 x10^9/l
BASOPHILS			0	0

Practical Veterinary Nursing

DEFINITIONS

ANAEMIA	Decrease in the number of red blood cells in the blood
POLYCYTHAEMIA	Increase in the number of rbc in the blood
ANISOCYTOSIS	Variation in the size of rbc
POLYCHROMASIA	Variation in the staining of rbc
HYPOCHROMASIA	Poor staining of rbc
NORMOCHROMIC	Normal staining of rbc
MICROCYTOSIS	Average rbc size smaller than normal
MACROCYTOSIS	Average rbc size larger than normal
CRENATION	Wrinkling of the rbc membrane during processing, contact with a hyperosmolar solution or in the event of dehydration of the red cell
RETICULOCYTE	An immature rbc containing remnants of endoplasmic reticulum which stains darkly.
NORMOBLAST	A nucleated red blood cell
NUCLEATED RED BLOOD CELL	An immature rbc which still contains a nucleus
HOWELL JOLLY BODIES	Remnants of nuclear material in the rbc seen as dark staining fragments
LEUCOPAENIA	Decrease number of wbc in the blood
PANLEUCOPAENIA	Decrease of every different wbc in the blood
LEUCOCYTOSIS	Increased number of wbc in the blood
NEUTROPAENIA	Decreased number of neutrophils in the blood
NEUTROPHILIA	Increased number of neutrophils in the blood
LEFT SHIFT	Increased number of neutrophils in the blood with an increase in immature neutrophils
EOSINOPAENIA	Decreased number of eosinophils in the blood
EOSINOPHILIA	Increased number of eosinophils in the blood
MONOCYTOSIS	Increased number of monocytes in the blood
BASOPHILIA	Increased number of basophils in the blood
ROULEAUX	The formation of stacks of red cells when blood is allowed to stand
SUPRA VITAL STAINING	The staining of live cells by incubating them with the stain in vitro. Used to stain reticulocytes.

BIOCHEMISTRY

INTERPRETATION OF RESULTS

SUBSTANCE	INCREASE	DECREASE	NORMAL DOG	CAT
TOTAL PLASMA PROTEIN	DEHYDRATION	HAEMORRHAGE	55-77g/l	58-80 g/l
ALBUMIN		MALNUTRITION DECREASED SYNTHESIS e.g. LIVER DISEASE INCREASED LOSS e.g. BURNS, HAEMORRHAGE GASTROINTESTINAL AND KIDNEY DISEASE	25-40 g/l	25-40 g/l
GLOBULIN	CHRONIC INFECTION NEOPLASIA	HAEMORRHAGE IMMUNOSUPPRESSION	25-45 g/l	28-55 g/l
CHOLESTEROL	HYPOTHYROIDISM DIABETES MELLITIS HIGH FAT DIET	GASTROINTESTINAL DISEASE	2.5-8 mmol/l	2-6.5 mmol/l
CREATININE	REDUCED RENAL PERFUSION RENAL DISEASE		40-130 μmol/l	40-130 μmol/l
UREA	RENAL DISEASE GASTROINTESTINAL HAEMORRHAGE HIGH PROTEIN DIET	LIVER DISEASE	2.5-7 mmol/l	5-11 mmol/l
BILIRUBIN UNCONJUGATED CONJUGATED	HAEMOLYSIS OR LIVER DISEASE BILE STASIS		1.7-10 μmol/l	2-5 μmol/l
BILE ACIDS	IMPAIRED LIVER FUNCTION		1-10 μmol/l	<2 μmol/l
ENZYMES				
ALANINE AMINOTRANSFERASE	LIVER DISEASE		NORMAL VALUES FOR ENZYMES DEPEND ON THE TEST USED - REFER TO YOUR SPECIALIST LABORATORY OR OWN REFERENCE GUIDES	
ALKALINE PHOSPHATE (SAP)	LIVER DISEASE BONE GROWTH AND DISEASE CORTICOSTEROID TREATMENT		N/A	
CREATINE PHOSPHOKINASE (CPK)	MUSCLE DAMAGE		N/A	

Practical Veterinary Nursing

BIOCHEMISTRY

INTERPRETATION OF RESULTS

SUBSTANCE	INCREASE	DECREASE	NORMAL	
			DOG	CAT
ELECTROLYTES				
SODIUM	GASTROINTESTINAL DISEASE KIDNEY DISEASE	GASTROINTESTINAL DISEASE ADDISON'S DISEASE	140-155 mmol/l	145-157mmol/l
POTASSIUM	ADDISON'S DISEASE KIDNEY DISEASE	GASTROINTESTINAL DISEASE	3.6-5.8 mmol/l	3.6-5.5 mmol/l
CALCIUM	NEOPLASIA HYPERPARATHYROIDISM	ECLAMPSIA	2-3 mmol/l	1.8-3 mmol/l
PHOSPHATE (Carried out on plasma; collected in fluoride oxalate)	KIDNEY DISEASE YOUNG ANIMALS	HYPERPARATHYROIDISM	0.8-1.6 mmol/l	1.3-2.6 mmol/l
GLUCOSE	DIABETES MELLITUS STRESS	INSULIN OVERDOSE SEPTICAEMIA	3.3-6 mmol/l	3.3-6 mmol/l

EXAMINATION OF FAECES

Examination of the faeces gives us information on the health of the gastrointestinal tract and how well it is functioning.

METHODS OF COLLECTION

Faeces can be collected in two ways

1. From the ground following defaecation. This is not ideal as the sample may be contaminated with grass, bacteria and worm larvae etc. The sample should be collected as soon as it is produced.

2. By insertion of a gloved finger through the anus into the rectum and withdrawal of faeces from the rectum.

The sample should be examined within two hours, but if this is impossible it should be placed in a container of suitable size so that it fills the container and stored in the fridge. There should be as little air in the container as possible to prevent parasite eggs from hatching. Alternatively, twice the volume of 10% formal saline can be added to preserve the faeces and prevent parasite eggs from hatching.

GENERAL OBSERVATIONS

1)	CONSISTENCY	Hard (constipation), firm (normal), watery (diarrhoea).
2)	COLOUR	Brown (normal), black (changed blood), yellow or white (malassimilation).
3)	SMELL	Normal, rancid (malassimilation).
4)	ABNORMAL MATERIAL	Blood (originating caudal to caecocolic junction) Mucus (inflammation of the colon) Undigested food particles (maldigestion) Round worms or tapeworm segments Sand, string, grass (depraved appetite) Hair, bones.

PREPARATION OF A FAECAL SMEAR

1) Place a few drops of water or saline on a clean microscope slide.

2) Mix a small quantity of faeces into the fluid using a spatula.

3) Use a coverslip to cover the preparation.

4) View under x40 objective.

This is a quick and easy method for screening faeces but is purely qualitative. It is possible to detect parasite eggs and protozoa if the infection is heavy enough.

5) Add a drop of iodine before applying the coverslip.

Starch granules will stain dark blue/black.
This will stain undigested muscle fibres, whose striations and nuclei can be clearly seen.

6) Add a drop of sudan red before applying the coverslip.

This will stain fat globules red.

The presence of undigested food particles in the faeces is suggestive of digestive enzyme deficiency, e.g. pancreatic insufficiency.

DETECTION OF PARASITIC OVA

It is necessary to identify the ova and count the ova per gram of faeces. This is done by flotation in a saturated solution of salt, glucose or zinc sulphate state to using a known quantity of faeces and counting the ova found in a counting chamber which holds a known volume, called a McMaster slide.

1) Thoroughly mix 3g of faeces with 42 mls of water. If necessary, pass the solution through a strainer. Pour the filtrate into a 15ml test tube.

2) Leave the solution to settle for 15mins or centrifuge at 1500rpm for 3mins.

3) Discard the supernatent and fill the test tube with saturated salt solution.

4) Invert the tube to mix the solution and withdraw a sample with a pasteur pipette and flood both sides of the counting chamber. Avoid introducing bubbles.

5) Examine the slide under the x40 objective. Count the total number of eggs within the lined areas of both chambers. If more than one species of eggs is detected, each must be counted separately.

6) To calculate the faecal egg count per gram of faeces (FEC)
FEC = total no. of eggs x 50.

Round worm eggs float to the surface of the solution in the McMaster chamber and by bringing the markings into focus, the eggs can be visualised. Coccidia oocysts float more slowly so it is necessary to wait 10 mins before counting. Tapeworm segments don't float and the faeces should be examined microscopically for gravid segments.

COMMON INTESTINAL PARASITES OF DOGS AND CATS

NEMATODES – ROUND WORMS

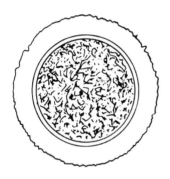

Toxocara canis

Toxocara cati

Toxascaris leonina

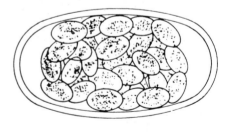

Uncincaria stenocephala
Hookworm

Practical Veterinary Nursing

Trichuris vulpis
Whipworm

TAPEWORMS

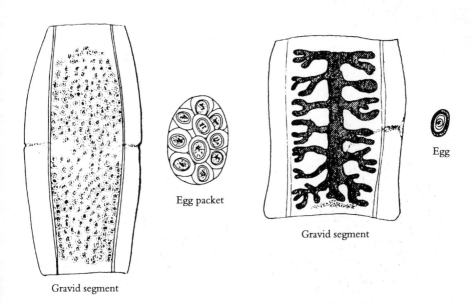

Gravid segment

Egg packet

Gravid segment

Egg

Dipyllidium caninum

Taenia spp

TUBE-TEST FOR PANCREATIC TRYPSIN

In dogs the test for faecal trypsin has been replaced by the serum TLI (trypsin-like immunoreactivity) test which is much more accurate. However there is no similar test for cats and the tube-test for pancreatic trypsin is performed to diagnose pancreatic insufficiency in the cat.

Method:
1) Measure 9ml of 5% NaCO3 and add enough faeces to make a final volume of 10ml. Mix well.
2) Add 1ml of the faecal suspension to 2ml of 7.5% gelatin solution at 37°C.
3) Incubate for 1 hour at 37°C or 2.5 hours at room temperature.
4) Refrigerate for 20 minutes and observe.

The presence of trypsin is indicated by failure of the solution to solidify. This test should be repeated and the results should be compared with examination of a faecal smear for undigested food components.

BACTERIAL CULTURE

In the event that a bacterial culture is required, the sample must be collected using sterile gloves, from the rectum, and placed in a sterile container. The sample should be sent for culture as soon as possible to prevent overgrowth by normal flora. Strict hygiene must be employed to protect against contamination with potentially pathogenic bacteria.

INVESTIGATION OF URINE

Methods of Collection

Urine can be collected in three main ways:

1) Free flow sample
2) Catheterisation
3) Cystocentesis.

The method of collection should always be stated on laboratory correspondence.

Methods of Catheterisation

DOG
1) Standing or lateral recumbancy
2) Extrude penis by holding prepuce and aseptically introduce catheter
3) Lubrication is necessary (Xylocaine jelly)
4) Sedation may be required
5) Midflow sample
6) Do not insert too far into the bladder, stop introducing when urine beigns to flow.

BITCH
1) Standing position
2) Rarely requires sedation
3) Vaginal speculum required to identify urethral papilla

MALE CAT
1) General anaesthesia or heavy sedation usually required
2) Lateral recumbency

QUEEN
1) Catheter passed blind into urethra
2) Heavy sedation or general anaesthesia often required.

Cystocentesis

Easily performed in cats, and is the method of choice for collection of urine samples in this species. Minimal and gentle restraint is generally all that is required. Cats can be restrained in lateral or dorsal recumbency. A 1 - 1^1/2" 23 - 25 gauge needle is attached to a 5 - 10 ml syringe. Once the bladder is fixed in position against the abdominal wall, the needle should be inserted into the lumen. Once inside the lumen the angle of the needle should not be altered to avoid lacerating the bladder mucosa.

The procedure is the same for dogs, although in large dogs, the preferred position is generally in dorsal recumbency. In these animals it may be impossible to hold the bladder in position and a 'blind' technique is adopted.

ADVANTAGES AND DISADVANTAGES URINE COLLECTION METHODS

	ADVANTAGES	DISADVANTAGES
MIDFLOW	EASY TO PERFORM	CONTAMINATION FROM URETHRA
	NON-TRAUMATIC	CONTAMINATION FROM COLLECTION CHAMBER eg litter tray
	GOOD SAMPLE FOR HAEMATURIA INVESTIGATION AS NO IATROGENESIS	PATIENT NON-COMPLIANCE
	QUITE STERILE IN CATS MIDFLOW	BLADDER RUPTURE OR HAEMATURIA WITH MANUAL EXPRESSION
CATHETER-ISATION	RELATIVELY STERILE	MAY REQUIRE SEDATION OR GENERAL ANAESTHETIC - ESPECIALLY CATS
		IATROGENIC INFECTION
		EXPERIENCE REQUIRED IN BITCHES
		INCREASED COST
		IATROGENIC HAEMATURIA
CYSTOCENT-ESIS	QUICK	MORE EXPERIENCE REQUIRED
	RELATIVELY NON-PAINFUL	CONTRAINDICATED IN EXTREME BLADDER DISTENSION
	STERILE	
	LITTLE IATROGENIC HAEMATURIA	
	NO URETHRAL CONTAMINATION	
	EASY TO PERFORM - ESPECIALLY IN CATS	
	IATROGENIC INFECTION UNCOMMON	

ANALYSIS

Urine should be analysed within 30 minutes or stored in the refrigerator.

URINE PRESERVATIVES

BORIC ACID - 200 mg/15 ml urine, NOT for bacteriology
'CYTOFIX'
FORMALIN

GROSS EXAMINATION

Colour of Urine

Ranges from light transparent yellow to slightly turbid dark yellow-brown. Varies according to diet (food colourings), and concentration. One can normally 'read' text through a urine sample. Turbidity can be increased by protein, pus, blood, crystals, or a highly concentrated urine. Brown urine can be a result of old 'changed' blood, haemoglobin, or myoglobin.

Odour

Ranges from slightly sweet to pungent and ammoniacal.

URINE DIPSTICK TESTING

Multiple reagent dipsticks provide rapid and reasonably accurate information. The sticks contain enzymes and chemicals which (after quite complex reactions) produce a colour change which can give a qualitative analysis. It is important to ensure that the strips are kept dry and that only the end of the test strip is touched. The stick should be placed in a urine specimen which is less than 4 hrs old so that all squares are moistened and then the strip should be taken out of the sample and gently tapped on the urine container to remove excess. Read colour changes at appropriate times. Timing is very important in interpretation.

The following test are available on commercial dipsticks

1) Glucose
2) Ketones
3) Specific gravity   The accuracy of these strips and
4) Blood   relative limitations are discussed
5) pH   under the appropriate sections in
6) Protein   the text.
7) Nitrites
8) Leucocytes.

Always check that the dipsticks are "in date" and have been stored correctly.

SPECIFIC GRAVITY

Specific gravity is an estimation of the concentrating ability of the kidney and is important in the assessment of renal function. No conclusions can be made about renal failure without the measurement of urine specific gravity.

Specific gravity varies from hour to hour in any animal according to water and salt intake and the hydration status of the patient. The specific gravity of urine should always be interpreted in the light of these facts, along with measurements of blood urea nitrogen and creatinine. A specific gravity of 1.010 - 1.050 can be normal. Extreme readings at either end of this scale should be repeated before being considered clinically significant.

The two main methods of assessing specific gravity are by refractometer and dipstick. The refractometer provides a reliable and quick estimation of specific gravity. Dipsticks are reportedly unreliable as far as specific gravity is concerned and do not show concentrations of greater than 1.030 - which is considered to be below the normal range for cats.

METHOD FOR USING A REFRACTOMETER

Refractometers provide a cheap and easy way of determining urine specific gravity and are the most accurate method available.

1) Ensure glass prism is clean
2) The refractometer can be calibrated with distilled water which should be a specific gravity of 1.000.
3) Place plastic cover over glass
4) Using a pipette (glass/plastic) place 1 - 2 drops of urine under the plastic cover to ensure that the entire glass surface is covered.
5) Hold refractometer to light and read specific gravity off the division between the light and dark portions.

INTERPRETATIONS OF URINE SPECIFIC GRAVITY

1)	> 1.045	Dogs - Normal concentrating ability, usually with mild dehydration. Cats - Within normal limits in most cats but may indicate abnormal renal function if azotaemic.
2)	1.030 - 1.045	Dogs - Considered normal if not azotaemic or dehydrated. Cats - Normal cats should have specific gravities of > 1.035. If dehydrated or azotaemic, specific gravity of 1.035 could be clinically significant.
3)	1.013 - 1.029	Some concentrating ability. If azotaemic or dehydrated indicates imparied renal function. May warrant investigation, especially in cats.
4)	1.008 - 1.012	ISOSTHENURIA: No concentration has occurred. Clinically significant if azotaemaic/dehydrated, NEVER normal in cats.
5)	< 1.008	HYPOSTHENURIA: Able to dilute urine. Normal if patient has to excrete water load, eg Primary polydipsia, Diabetes insipidus (renal/central). Usually associated with profound polydipsia/polyuria or fluid therapy. Clinically significant if dehydrated/azotaemic.

pH

pH varies according to diet and time of feeding. There is no pH which can be considered absolutely normal, although it is usually in the range of 5 - 7.

Values greater than 7.0 may be due to

a) Post-prandial sampling

b) Staphlococcus or Proteus infection

c) Struvite urolithiasis

d) Renal tubular acidosis (RARE)

Values significantly less than 7.0 may indicate acidosis.

GLUCOSE

Normal urine should have no glucose present.
Clinistrips are specific and reliable for glucose. (False positives occur in the presence of hydrogen peroxide or chloride.)
If positive, a blood glucose measurement should be taken. Diabetes mellitus should not be an instant diagnosis in these cases as cats can exceed urine thresholds for glucose during stress, and renal tubular disorders can result in glycosuria - eg Fanconi's syndrome of Basenjis.

KETONURIA
Clinistrips are very sensitive to ketones.
Always abnormal.
CAUSES: Diabetes mellitus, starvation, catabolic disease, pyrexia, liver disease, hypoglycaemia.

BILIRUBINURIA
Can be normal in dogs in small amounts, but are not normally present in cats. Indicates an increased serum level of conjugated bilirubin, eg biliary obstruction, cholestasis, and occasionally in haemolytic jaundice.

BILE SALTS
Sodium salts of glycocholic acid and taurocholic acid, absent in normal animals, found in similar conditions to the above.

BLOOD

Strip tests are very sensitive to red blood cells, haem pigments or myoglobin. If positive, microscopic examination should be carried out on a fresh sample to confirm intact or lysed red blood cells.

CAUSES: HAEMATURIA   - bleeding from any part of the urinary tract, neoplasia, coagulopathies.

             HAEMOGLOBINURIA   - haemolytic anaemias, blood transfusion cross reactions.

PROTEIN

Small amounts of protein in urine are considered normal because of the presence of small filtered proteins & protein formed within the urinary tract itself (Tamm Horsfall Protein).
Protein can be assessed by dipstick or precipitation of salicyl-sulphonic acid. Since the colour change on dipstick is the most difficult to interpret, the precipitation method is more accurate. Both of these tests are qualitative only and quantitative analysis should also be carried out if a considerable amount of protein is discovered in the urine.

PRECIPITATION METHOD

1) Spin sample for 2000 rpm for 5 mins
2) Place 2 ml of salicyl-sulphonic acid in a test tube
3) Carefully place urine supernatant on top using pipette and wait for precipitate to form (immediate)
4) Record as trace - ++++

NB: Interpretation of the result should take into account the specific gravity of the sample.

CAUSES OF PROTEINURIA

1) Haematuria
2) Pyuria
3) Cystitis
4) Prostatitis
5) Urethritis - depending on method of collection
6) Glomerulonephritis - SEVERE proteinuria
7) Decreased tubular resorption (Rare) - MILD proteinuria
8) Chronic interstitial nephritis - MILD proteinuria
9) Increased glomerular filtration pressure, eg right-sided congestive heart failure, ascites, caudal vena cava obstruction.

QUANTITATIVE ANALYSIS

Protein can be measured by most laboratories, however, a 24-hour collection is required to take into account changes in specific gravity (estimation of urine produced produces only a crude assessment). Normal protein excretion over 24 hours are as follows:

Dogs - 0 - 30 g/l
Cats - 0 - 20 g/l

Proteinuria can be evaluated on a one off urine sample by assessing how much protein is in the urine compared to creatinine. This is referred to as the PROTEIN:CREATININE RATIO and is useful in the diagnosis of glomerulonephritis.

Normal values are as follows:

Dogs:- GRAVIMETRIC UNITS (Both protein and creatinine measured in mg/dl)

> < 0.5 Normal, > 1-5 Abnormal, > 5 Glomerular disease, > 13 Severe glomerular disease or renal amyloidosis.

> SI UNITS (Protein in g/l, creatinine in mmol/l)

> < 0.06 Normal, > 0.11 - 0.57 Abnormal, > 0.57 Glomerular disease, > 1.47 Severe glomerular disease or amyloidosis.

Cats:- GRAVIMETRIC UNITS

> < 0.5 Normal
> SI UNITS
> > 0.06 Abnormal

MICROSCOPIC EXAMINATION

Wet and dry preparations are required for full microscopic examination.

Wet Preparation
1) Centrifuge at 2000 rpm for 5 mins
2) Remove most of the supernatant
3) Shake test tube to resuspend deposit in the small amount of urine
4) Pipette a small drop onto a slide
5) Place cover slip over preparation and examine under x 10 and x 40 for casts, crystals, strands.

Dry Preparation
1) Repeat 1,2 3 and 4
2) Spread film thinly over slide as blood smear
3) Dry in air
4) Stain with Leishman's stain
5) Observe under x 100 for epithelial cells, white blood cells, red blood cells, and bacteria.

INTERPRETATION

CASTS

Formed by the sticking together of albumin and other substances within kidney tubules.
a) Hyaline   Consist entirely of protein. Transparent. Normal in small numbers.
b) Cellular   More acute renal disease, can be RBC's, WBC's or epithelial.
c) Granular   Degenerated cellular casts. Longer standing renal disease.
d) Waxy   Dull and opaque. Nephroses. Uncommon. Amyloidosis.

MUCOUS STRANDS

From mucous glands in urinary tract
Very long and irregular
Normal in small numbers, increased amounts suggest inflammation, or bitches in heat.

SPERMATOZOA
Normal in small numbers in males.

CRYSTALS
Can help to type stones in urolithiasis. Many types. See Table.

BACTERIA
Significant especially if in high numbers and/or accompanied by WBC's.

EPITHELIAL CELLS
Small numbers are normal. Large numbers indicate inflammation or trauma usually of the bladder.

WHITE BLOOD CELLS
Small numbers are normal. Large numbers indicate inflammation, often bacterial infection.

RED BLOOD CELLS
Bleeding from any part of the urinary tract or contamination from the reproductive tract in females eg from vaginal polyps, bitch in season.

BACTERIA
Depends on method of collection
Large numbers indicate infection.

CRYSTAL/ CASTS	APPEARANCE
CALCIUM OXALATE CRYSTALS	
URIC ACID CRYSTALS	
TRIPLE PHOSPHATE OR STRUVITE CRYSTALS	
CYSTINE CRYSTALS	
AMMONIUM BIURATE CRYSTALS	
BILIRUBIN CRYSTALS	
HYALINE CASTS	
CELLULAR CASTS	
GRANULAR CASTS	
WAXY CASTS	

EXAMINATION OF THE SKIN

COAT BRUSHING

A flea comb is brushed through the coat to collect superficial debris and hair. The hair can then be examined under a hand lens or microscope for evidence of parasites, their eggs or fungal arthrospores.

Fleas
If the brushing is collected onto a moist piece of paper flea dirt will dissolve into red 'bloody' deposits. When dry, flea dirt appears as black gritty specks. Flea eggs are white and oval but are rarely found on the coat of an animal. Larvae are white and segmented, and are also an uncommon finding on coat brushing. Adults are reddish-brown and laterally compressed, they are highly mobile and because the adult spends only a small time on the host, an adult flea does not have to be seen to diagnose a flea related problem.

Lice
Lice and their eggs attached to hair shafts can be readily seen with microscopic examination.

SKIN SCRAPING

The type of scraping performed depends on the suspicion of infection. Suitable areas for scraping should be gently clipped before scraping is begun.

Demodectic Mites
Dog:
Demodex canis
These mites are found deep within hair follicles and the scraping must therefore be deep. Squeeze a fold of skin between thumb and forefinger to extrude material from hair follicles. A drop of mineral oil on the skin/ scalpel blade facilitates removal of material. Scrape till capillary ooze appears. The material should be gently smeared onto a glass slide and a cover slip placed on top. A few dead adults can be considered normal but many mites and the presence of immature forms confirms infection.
Cat:
Demodex cati
Rare. Two forms.

Sarcoptes
Dog:
Sarcoptes scabei
Multiple (15-20) deep scrapings, especially in areas such as the ears and elbows are often required to find this mite which lives in deep epidermal burrows. Excoriated skin should be avoided, clipping the hair to reveal small raised papules is helpful as these areas are the sites of choice. One mite is diagnostic. Place skin scraping on slide and mix with KOH 10%, leave for 20 minutes to help digest keratin and aid examination.
Cat:
Notoedres cati
Much easier to find than the canine form so deep scrapings are not required.
Eyes, ears and face usually affected.

Cheyletiella

Very large and can be seen with the naked eye in heavy infestations as 'walking dandruff'. Clip coat gently then use small amount of mineral oil to obtain very superficial scrapings.
An acetate strip, sellotape, or coat brushing can be more useful in cats.
Hair pluckings to look for *Cheyletiella* eggs - smaller and more loosely attached than louse eggs.

Otodectes

Dog and cat affected.
Mites visible with naked eye.
Not only ears, but can also become generalised.
Superficial scrapings, waxy impression smears of ear swabs, or acetate strips can be used.

See end of chapter for life cycles and diagrams of ectoparasites.

EAR WAX EXAMINATION

Can be collected via cotton swab or metal loop and mixed with mineral oil on a glass slide to facilitate visualisation.
Can be air dried or stained with 'Diff-Quick' for detection of bacteria yeasts and fungi.

PUSTULE EXAMINATION

Pustules are very delicate and are easily ruptured. This primary skin lesion can be rare to see as the animal's movements and scratching will naturally burst these structures.
Hair should be gently clipped over a suspected region to identify intact pustules.
Needle aspiration can be carried out on large pustules and the fluid sent for bacterial culture and cytology.
Impression smears of pustules gently pricked with an hypodermic needle can be transferred to glass slides for cytology.

DERMATOPHYTE INVESTIGATION

REMEMBER DERMATOPHYTES ARE ZOONOTIC WEAR GLOVES.

Mc KENZIE BRUSH TECHNIQUE

Mc Kenzie Brush Technique is used to identify asymptomatic dermatophyte carriers. The cat is brushed all over paying particular attention to the feet, and face with a sterile (new toothbrush in wrapper) toothbrush, which is sent directly to the laboratory, or inoculated into culture medium.

WOOD'S LAMP

A Wood's lamp is an ultraviolet lamp used for the detection of ringworm.

Important Points:

Should be warmed up for 5-10 mins

Dark room

Microsporum canis – yellow-green/'apple-green' fluorescence. Not all strains of *M. canis* fluoresce.

Iodine prevents fluorescence, other substances can cause false positive results.

A negative Wood's test does not rule out fungal infection. A positive fluorescence is suggestive of infection.

DERMATOPHYTE CULTURE

The best hairs to choose are those that fluoresce or those at the periphery of a lesion. Hairs in sterile container to laboratory or for in-house dermatophyte culture.

MICROSCOPY

Mount affected hairs in 10% KOH and examine for fungal hyphae or arthrospores - small, spherical, refractile bodies around the hair. Lactophenol or Indian Ink can enhance detection.

PARASITE	Ctenocephalides Fleas	Dipteron Flies	Lignognathus Louse	Trichodectes Louse	Cheyletiella Mite
APPEARANCE AND EGGS	Small, brown laterally compressed white eggs	Many forms	Sucking lice with typical fixed piercing mouth parts. Eggs are small white and attached to hair follicles – 'nits'	Biting louse. Typical chewing mouthparts, on ventral side of broad head	Large white mites that can be seen with naked eye or magnifying glass. 'Walking dandruff' Eggs are attached loosely to hair
HOST SPECIFICITY	No	No	Yes	Yes	No
ZOONOTIC	Yes	Yes	No	No	Yes
TEMP/ PERMANENT	Temp	Temp	Perm	Perm	Perm
CLINICAL SIGNS	Acute signs such as wheals, and erythema, and more chronic signs such as seborrhoea, lichenification and alopecia	Local wheal, may be severe 'fly blown' signs	Variable:- asymptomatic carrier to papules, crusts, seb. sicca	Miliary dermatitis in cats and similar signs as described for suckling lice	Mild, non-suppurative dermatitis. A symptomatic carriers
DISTRIBUTION	DOGS: Particularly dorsum, lumbo-sacral area and ventrum CATS: Typically presents as miliary dermatitis, or eosinophilic granuloma complex	Anus and genitalia, wounds, etc	Under matted hair, around orifices		Diffuse. More dorsal in cats

PARASITE	*Ixodes* Ticks	*Sarcoptes* Scabies	*Otodectes* Ear mites	*Notoedres* Feline Scabies	*Demodex* Mite
APPEARANCE AND EGGS	Flattened ovoid yellow–white to reddish-brown	Round bodied microscopic mite	Visible as white dots with naked eye	Resembles *Sarcoptes*	Small cigar shaped mites. 4 Stages of lifecycle on scrapings
HOST SPECIFICITY	No	No (Rarely)	No	No	Yes
ZOONOTIC	Yes	Yes	Occasionally	Yes	No
TEMP/ PERMANENT	Temp	Perm	Perm	Perm	Perm
CLINICAL SIGNS	Asymptomatic to local irritation	INTENSE PRURITUS. Alopecia, scales and crusts	Otitis externa. Occasionally generalised and may mimic flea bite hypersensitivity	PRURITUS Lichenification crusting alopecia	Mild erythema to pruritis. Alopecia
DISTRIBUTION	Ears, face and ventral body	Ventrum, ears and elbows	Ears Occasionally generalised	Head, Ears and neck. Can be generalised	Localised, or generalised

LIFE CYCLE OF *CTENOCEPHALIDES SPP*

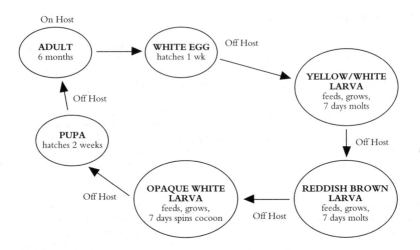

PARASITE APPEARANCE

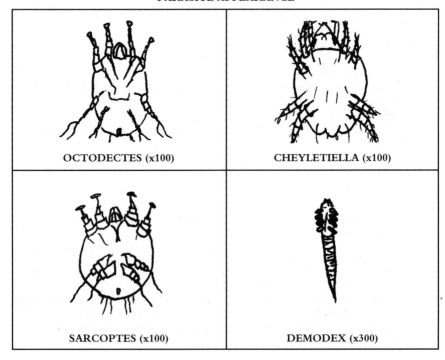

BACTERIOLOGY AND VIROLOGY

SAMPLE COLLECTION

A variety of reasons may arise when specimens for bacteriology may be required by the veterinary surgeon. A suspicion of bacterial infection in the skin, body cavity (thorax,abdomen), or organ (bladder, colon, intestine) requires samples to be sent for culture (to detect what type of organism is present) and sensitivity (to determine the choice of antibiotic to use).

The sample is usually collected on to a sterile swab from the lesion (eg: pustule on the skin surface, abscess), or from fluid collected from a body cavity. Samples should be sent immediately to the laboratory or chilled in the refridgerator until they can be plated out. For organisms with specific requirements, such as mycoplasmas, and chlamydia, special transport media should be inoculated with the swab before being sent to the laboratory. This is paramount for the detection of these organisms.

Failure to recover bacteria from a suspicious site does not always rule out infection. Delays in transport, incorrect methods of swabbing, incorrect culture medium, or inhibitory substances (such as current use of antibiotics) can lead to a negative culture. Contamination from normal environmental organisms is also a common problem but with sterile technique this can be avoided.

Because of the specialist techniques involved in recognising, and growing bacteria and other micro-organisms, and the risk to public health, detailed bacterial examination is carried out in specialist laboratories.

Laboratory Techniques

Laboratories will carry out the following tests:-
1) Smears and staining of samples to examine microscopically for bacteria, protozoa, and fungi.
2) Culture of sample to detect type of organisms present.
3) Sensitivity testing to allow the clinician to choose the most appropriate antibiotic and detect resistance.
4) Carry out virus isolation to confirm serological tests (eg: Feline Leukaemia Virus, Feline Immunodeficiency Virus).

Swabbing of Lesions

1) Take care to remove the cotton tipped swab from the container in a sterile manner. Avoid the neck of the tube.
2) If lesion is exposed, no preparation of the skin is necessary, if the lesion is not exposed, surgical preparation should be carried out to prevent surface contamination.
3) Rub the tip into the lesion and collect as much material as possible, especially from the periphery of the lesion, as central parts of abscesses can be sterile.
4) Place the swab aseptically into the tube and send to laboratory without delay, or place into transport medium. This is particularly important for organisms with specific reqirements such as anaerobes and *Chlamydia*. If you are unsure as to the best way of preparing a sample telephone the laboratory.

STAINING

Glass slides can be prepared for staining by :-
   a)   Gently rolling a swab over the slide and quickly air drying.
   b)   Making a smeared preparation from fluid samples similar to that described for making a blood smear. The slides can be stained in the veterinary clinic for rapid detection of microbials or to determine the types of inflammatorty cells present.

GRAM'S STAIN

   1)   Place slide on horizontal rack.
   2)   Flood slide with 0.5% aqueous crystal violet - WAIT 60 seconds.
   3)   Rinse carefully with distilled water.
   4)   Wash with Lugol's iodine, flood slide with Lugol's iodine, and WAIT 60 seconds.
   5)   Rinse with distilled water.
   6)   Rinse with methylated spirits 2-3 times. Not too prolonged or vigorous as violet stain will be removed.
   7)   Rinse with distilled water.
   8)   Flood slide with dilute carbol fuchsin WAIT 2 MINUTES.
   9)   Rinse with distilled water.
   10) Pour off water and stand on edge to drain.
   11) Examine under oil immersion.

Used to detect most bacteria and identify predominant inflammatory cell types. Bacteria staining Gram+ve are deep blue/purple. Bacteria staining Gram-ve are red. If no bacteria are seen in the presence of many inflammatory cells, specialised stains should be employed to check for mycobacteria (eg: Ziehl-Neelsen acid fast stain).

METHYLENE BLUE STAIN

   1)   Place slide horizontally in rack.
   2)   Flood slide with 1% aqueous methylene blue for 2 MINUTES.
   3)   Gently wash with distilled water.
   4)   Pour off water and stand on edge till dry.
   5)   Examine under oil immersion.
For the detection of bacteria in the veterinary practice.

VIROLOGY

Virology is used for the detection of viral infections in small animals. It is useful not only for the individual animal, but has important implications for other animals in the household. Exposure to a virus can be demonstrated in two ways :-
a)   VIRUS ISOLATION - The demonstration of the virus itself.
b)   SEROLOGY - The detection of virus particles or antibodies to the virus.
Obviously, virus isolation confirms the presence of the virus in the animal at that point in time, whereas serology only provides the clinician with the fact that at a point in time, the animal was exposed to the virus. Because of the variable length of time antibodies remain detectable in the blood stream, serology has limitations.

VIRUS	SAMPLE IN LIVE ANIMAL	SAMPLE IN LIVE ANIMAL	INTERPRETATION OF RESULTS
CANINE DISTEMPER	Extremely difficult. Paired blood samples 5mls of clotted blood two weeks apart to demonstrate a rising titre. 5mls of blood to detect if vaccination has been effective.	Difficult. Based on histopathology of fixed organs. Brain, lung, lymph nodes, kidney.	Antibodies to the virus last for prolonged periods therefore **not indicative of recent exposure**. Low titres are usually present in dogs that are not going to recover from infection. Titres are of greatest use in vaccinated dogs to check for immunity.
CANINE PARVOVIRUS	Faeces (5mls) and serum (5mls). 5mls post vaccination.	Histopathology of intestines and lymph nodes.	Infected dogs usually have titres of virus much higher than vaccinated dogs. ie: >2048 compared to around 60-600.
CANINE HEPATITIS	2 serum samples (5mls), 2 weeks apart.	Liver for histopathology, along with liver 1cm cube in viral transport medium.	
KENNEL COUGH	Nasal and tonsillar swabs in virus transport medium for virus isolation of adenovirus, parainfluenza virus and herpesvirus. Paired blood samples for adenovirus and parainfluenza serology 2-3 weeks apart.		Adenovirus – Vaccinated animals less than 4096, infected animals have very high titres in the 10,000+ range. Parainfluenza – Highest titres in natural infection (2000-16,000), vaccination by intranasal route generally produces titres <4000.

VIRUS	SAMPLE IN LIVE ANIMAL	SAMPLE FROM POST-MORTEM	INTERPRETATION OF RESULTS
FELINE RESPRATORY VIRUS	Calcivirus and herpesvirus grow readily in cell culture. Tonsillar and nasopharyngeal swabs immediately into culture medium. Thorough swabbing is necessary in some cases.		A positive isolation indicates infection. Acute or chronic.
FELINE PANLEU-COPANIA	Serology for antibodies in 1-2mls of serum.	Same as for canine parvovirus.	
FELINE INFECTIOUS PERITONITIS	Antibody titres in serum (1-2mls), or ascitic fluid.	Histopathology of affected organs	Because this test does not distinguish between coronaviruses which cause enteritis and the F.I.P. form this test is notoriously unreliable. High titres have been found in F.I.P.-ve animals, and low titres in cats suffering from the F.I.P. form of the disease. Full regard to clinical signs is required. Histology of affected organs is the **only** definative test.
FELINE LEUKAEMIA VIRUS	Antigens of FeLV are tested for in serum. A paired sample **3 months** apart must be positive. If these are positive virus isolation on 1-2mls of heparinised blood is necessary to confirm infection.		Very reliable if -ve, false positives are common where the virus has a low prevalence. Positive antigen tests should always be confirmed by virus isolation.
FELINE IMMUNO-DEFICIENCY VIRUS	Serology to detect antibody to the virus. 1-2mls of heparinised blood.		Good accuracy.

REFERENCES AND FURTHER READING

BUSH B. (1991) *Interpretation of Laboratory Results for Small Animal Clinicians*, Blackwells Scientific, London.

BUSH B. (1993) Examination of Geriatric Animals. In: *Practice*, Vol 15 (3) pp 139 - 145.

BUSH B. (1975) *Veterinary Laboratory Manual*, Gresham Press.

CULLEN L. (1989) *Veterinary Anaeshesia*. Murdoch University Pub. Perth Western Australia.

DOXEY D.L. and NATHAN M.B.F. (ed) (1989) *Manual Of Laboratory Techniques*. British Small Animal Veterinary Association, Gloustershire.

GEORGI J.R. and GEORGI M.E. (1990) *Parasitology For Veterinarians*, 5th Ed. WB Saunders and Co., Philadelphia.

GRANT D.I. (1986) *Skin Diseases In The Dog and Cat*, Blackwell Scientific Publications London.

HARVEY LOCKE P. (Ed) (1993) British Small Animal Veterinary Association's *Manual Of Small Animal Dermatology*. BSAVA Publications, Gloucestershire.

KIRK R.W. (Ed)(1989) *Current Veterinary Therapy X*. WB Saunders Co. Philadelphia.

KIRK R.W., BISTNER S.I. and FORD R.B. (1990) *Hanbook of Veterinary Emergency Procedures and Treatment*, 5th Edition. WB Saunders and Co., Philadelphia.

LANE D.R. (Ed) (1989) *Jones's Animal Nursing* 5th Edition. Pergamon Press, Oxford.

LORENZ M.D. and CORNELIUS L.M. (1987) *Small Animal Medical Diagnosis*, J.B. Lippincott Co., Philadelphia.

MAFF (1984): *Manual of Veterinary Investigation*, Volumes 1 and 2.

MICHELL A.R., BYWATER R.J., CLARKE K.W., HALL L.W. and WATERMAN A.E. (1989) *Veterinary Fluid Therapy*, Blackwell Scientific Publications, Oxford.

MULLER G.H., KIRK R.W. and SCOTT D.W. (1989) *Small Animal Dermatology*, 4th Edition. W.B. Saunders and Co., Philadelphia.

WILLARD M.D., TWEDTON H. and Turnwald G. (1989) *Small Animal Clinical Diagnosis*, W.B. Saunders and Co., Philadelhia.

MEDICAL
NURSING

ROUTINE CARE OF PATIENTS

Routine care is the day to day, hour by hour provision of essential needs for patients supervision.

DAILY ROUTINE

For basic nursing care of in-patients a daily routine is essential in every veterinary establishment. Routine should include:-

1) Observation of kennel and patient on arrival, prior to disturbance, assess:-
   a) Demeanour; depressed, bright, crying, etc.
   b) Any urine or faeces passed; colour, amount, consistency, smell, presence of blood etc.
   c) Presence of vomit; nature and amount.
   d) Presence of blood.

2) Temperature, Pulse and Respiration (TPR) see Table One. Preferably before exercise.
   a) Respiration at rest. Record rate, depth and manner.
   b) Temperature and pulse rate simultaneously to save time. Record both.
      Note rate, strength, rhythm and character of pulse,
   eg. Rectal T.38.5°C, P.84 regular and full, R.20 regular and deep.

3) Check ears, eyes, nose, mouth, for: abnormalities, discharge, crusting.
   Clean as required. Use plain water generally unless a particular product/antiseptic/cleaning agent is specifically indicated eg Sebumol to soften ear wax.

4) Disinfection of kennels.
   It is extremely important kennels are cleaned prior to disinfection, many disinfectants are prevented from effective performance in the presence of organic matter. Use a detergent and elbow grease!

5) Exercise.
   Observe and record:
   a) ambulation: manner, any difficulty or abnormality.
   b) urination: manner, any dysuria (difficulty), straining, colour, amount, smell of urine.
   c) faeces: nature, colour, presence of worms, blood, discomfort.
   d) any change in respiration, demeanour etc.

6) Provide fresh food and water. Note instructions for feeding: prescription diets, tube feeding, liquid food only, feed from a height, chicken and rice etc.

7) Targeted checks of wounds, dressings, drips, indwelling catheters (urinary & intravenous) etc.

8) Administration of medicines.

9) Change of dressing.

10) Physiotherapy.

11) Preparation for procedures planned eg. enemas, starvation, introduction of intravenous catheters etc.

ONGOING OBSERVATIONS

To detect or check:-

1) Any deterioration/change in alertness, medical condition, ambulation, attitude etc.

2) Intravenous fluids are running at correct rate, temperature and no catheter displacement has occured.

3) Patient can reach fresh water and food easily.

4) No interferance with wounds/dressings.

5) Urine collection bags do not require emptying etc.

6) Presence of pain/discomfort, agitation.

TABLE 1

TEMPERATURE, PULSE AND RESPIRATION VALUES
FOR SMALL ANIMALS KEPT AS PETS

Species	Temperature °C	Temperature °F	Heart/Pulse Rate per minute	Respiratory Rate per minute
DOG	38.3 - 38.7	100.9 - 101.7	60 - 120	15 - 30
CAT	38.0 - 38.5	100.4 - 101.6	100 - 140	20 - 30
RABBIT	37.0 - 39.4	99 - 103	220	38 - 65
GUINEA PIG	39 - 40	102.2 - 104.2	130 - 190	90 - 150
HAMSTER	36 - 38	98 - 101	300 - 600★	33 - 127
MOUSE	37.4	99.5	500 - 600★	100 - 250
RAT	37.5 - 38	99.8 - 100.5	260 - 450★	70 - 150
GERBIL	38 - 39	100.4 - 102.2	450 - 500★	80 - 140
CHINCHILLA	38 - 39	100.4 - 102.2	100 - 150	40 - 80
FERRET	37.8 - 40	100 - 104.2	300 - 400★	30 - 40

REPTILES

Reptiles are poikilothermic ("cold blooded"), this means they are unable to regulate their own body temperature and as a result are dependent on environmental temperature. All reptiles have preferred body temperatures (PBT) which will vary between species, seasons and the time of the day. The PBT of a species is therefore the optimum temperature in which that species should be housed. Maintenance at these PBT's enables all other body systems (especially the gastrointestinal tract) to work at their most efficient levels.

★ For information only (no-one can count this quickly!!)

DISINFECTANTS

IDEAL PROPERTIES

1) Rapidly toxic to a wide range of micro-organisms at room temperature.

2) Unaffected by environmental factors eg. organic matter, soaps, pH, temperature.

3) Non toxic.

4) Non corrosive.

5) Capacity to penetrate, preferably with detergent action.

6) Stable in concentrated and dilute form.

7) Soluble in water.

8) Unaffected by hard water.

9) Odourless or a mild, pleasant odour.

10) Readily available and cheap.

Manufacturers directions for *any* disinfectants *must* be followed. Metered pumps, fitted to tops of containers, make this an efficient, less laborious task. Many disinfectants cause mild skin irritation in some people, wearing gloves may help, although a change of disinfectant may be necessary. When disinfectants are used in higher concentrations (post hospitalisation of an infectious disease) or in spray form, ensure adequate ventilation, to prevent possible development of transient but uncomfortable respiratory, ocular or olfactory reactions in users.

There are many medical as well as veterinary disinfectants on the market. Table 2 is simply a sample list of those commonly used in veterinary practice at present.

Practical Veterinary Nursing

TABLE 2

COMMONLY USED DISINFECTANTS

Active substance	Product example	Presentation	Uses
Alcohol *Ethyl alcohol*	**alcohol**	70% solution	Skin disinfection or general surfaces
Halogen *Hypochlorite*	**bleach (various) names)**	Liquid	General Rinse thoroughly
Aldehyde *Formaldehyde*	**Formula H** B.K. Vet	Concentrate Spray Wipes	Multipurpose; floors tables etc. Broad spectrum disinfectant kills viruses, bacteria, skin fungal organisms
Halogen *Sodium Tosychloramide*	**Halamid** Solvay Duphar	powder (to make up) solution)	General disinfection
Diguanides *Chlorhexidine gluconate*	**Hibiscrub Vet** Pitman-Moore	Liquid concentrate	General disinfection Skin disinfection
Phenol	**Jeyes Fluid**	Liquid	General. Rinse very thoroughly. NOT FOR CAT HOUSING
Benzalkonium chloride	**Marinol Blue** B.K. Vet	Solution	General, pre-op instruments and when diluted topically
Aldehyde *Glutaraldehyde* *Q.A.C.*	**Parvocide** Solvay Duphar	Liquid concentrate	Broad spectrum disinfection for all animal contact areas
Iodophors	**Pevidine** B.K. Vet	Liquid	Skin disinfection
Iodine	**Iodine Aqueous Solution** B.P. Animalcare	Liquid	Surfaces, stains some surfaces after minimal time contact
Tri-n-butytinbenzoate formaldehyde Isopropyl	**Vet-cide** Millpledge	Liquid	General disinfection
Oxidising agents *Peroxide*	**Virkon** Animalcare	Powder concentration	Broad spectrum, virucidal, bactericidal and fungicidal

ADMINISTRATION OF MEDICINES

Administration of medicines should always follow the manufacturers directions or those of the prescribing Veterinary Surgeon.

Parenteral routes   Oral   Topical   Enteral
/ | | \
s/c i/m i/p i/v

PARENTERAL ROUTES

1) **Subcutaneous (s/c)** – Injection beneath the skin but not into muscle.

Sites
a) Caudal neck
b) Various: 'loose' skin areas on trunk.

Method
a) Select 21-25 gauge needles, to encourage slow administration and avoid 'needle shy' patients. Avoid multiple administrations.
b) Restrain patient.
c) 'Tent up' skin in area of choice, part hair, swab skin unless contraindicated and insert needle. Draw back on barrel of syringe prior to injection to ensure no inadvertent puncture of a blood vessel.
d) Inject smoothly.
e) After injection, massage area to encourage dispersal of medication/fluid.

Complications
Infection/abscessation, due to contaminated needle or drugs.

   ★ Do NOT assume all drugs can be administered s/c. Read instructions on packaging.
   ★ Do NOT give large volumes of fluids by this route (20-40mls maximum for a dog).

2) Intramuscular (i/m) – Injection into one of the large skeletal muscle groups of the body.

Sites (see Figure 1)
a) Quadriceps femoris   cranial aspect of femur.
b) Hamstring   caudal aspect of the stifle.
c) Lumbar   either side of lumbar spine.
d) Neck   base of caudal neck (rarely used).

Method
a) Select short 5/8ths" length needles, 21-25 gauge.
b) Restrain patient.
c) Part hair, swab skin at chosen site.
d) Feel for muscle mass and insert needle directly into muscle.
e) Draw back on barrel of syringe.
f) Inject at a steady speed.
g) Massage muscle to aid dispersal.

Complications
a) Pain, especially if volumes larger than 2-4 mls are injected. Good, gentle restraint is required.
b) Nerve trauma, can be permanent eg damage to the sciatic nerve.

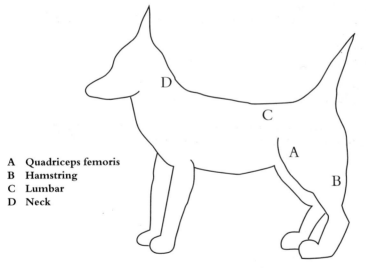

A **Quadriceps femoris**
B **Hamstring**
C **Lumbar**
D **Neck**

FIGURE 1
SITES FOR INTRAMUSCULAR ADMINISTRATION OF MEDICINES

3) Intravenous (i/v) – Positioning needle into lumen of a vein.

Sites
a) Cephalic.
b) Lateral saphenous.
c) Femoral – medial thigh.
d) Jugular (rarely used for administration of medicines).
e) Ear vein – rabbits/small mammals.
f) Tail vein – rats/mice.

Method
a) Select suitable needle (will vary but most useful sizes are listed).

18 gauge – 1 inch	large dog
21 gauge – 1 inch	med/lge dog
22 gauge – 1 inch	med/large dog
22 gauge – 1/2 inch	medium dog
22 gauge – 5/8 inch	small dog
23 gauge – 5/8 inch	cat
25 gauge – 5/8 inch	cat

b) Restrain patient – technique will vary depending on site chosen.
c) Clip injection site.
d) Assistant raises vein by applying pressure over the vein closer to the heart than the injection site, thus preventing venous return and providing engorgement of the vein.
e) Swab injection site *gently* with alcohol/skin prep. (**Do NOT scrub skin**, this results in soreness and irritation).
f) Insert needle through skin into vein.
g) Slide needle up lumen of vein until hub is 'flush' with the skin.
h) Draw back until venous blood appears, this ensures correct needle position.
i) Inject medication slowly (read manufacturers instructions regarding speed of injection).
j) Remove needle and apply digital pressure over entry point, preferably with gauze/cottonwool swab.

Complications
a) Haematoma formation.
b) Needle occlusion.
c) Collapsed vein.
d) Infection
e) Perivascular injection of drugs. (this can cause serious irritation with some drugs).

> *★ Some drugs especially those which may cause perivascular irritation are best given via an intravenous catheter.*

4) Intraperitoneal (i/p) – Injection into peritoneal cavity, rarely used for drug administration except in small mammals. May be used for administratation of fluids.

Site
Level of umbilicus right or left of midline on ventral aspect of the abdomen.

Method
a) Select needle 18-22 gauge 1 inch (11/2 - 2 inch if very fat) for a dog. Smaller gauge shorter needles in small mammals
b) Firm patient restraint.
c) Clip area.
d) Prepare using full aseptic surgical preparation technique.
e) Insert needle perpendicular to skin, into peritoneal cavity, needle hub should touch skin surface.
f) *Do NOT aspirate* – fat etc may block needle.
g) Inject slowly.
h) Withdraw needle quickly.

Complications
a) Infection and possible peritonitis. ASEPSIS IS ESSENTIAL.

* Large volumes should be warmed to body temperature, prior to administration.

TOPICAL

Application of drugs directly to the body surface.

Sites	**Types**
a) eye	a) creams
b) ear	b) ointments
c) skin	c) lotions
	d) soaps/solutions
	e) shampoos

Method
Apply in accordance with veterinary surgeon's guidelines.

Complications
a) Excessive application may result in absorption of toxic quantities of a drug.
b) Access to the site of application eg. ear canals.
c) Accurate dosage.

PER OS (P/O) (By mouth)

Types
a) tablet
b) capsule/spansule
c) liquids

Methods A and B
Administration of p/o medicines to dogs is usually a one person job, cats may require assistance.

DOG:
There are many variations, this is one! (see Figure 2).
If right handed,
a) Grasp maxilla with thumb and forefinger of left hand behind canine teeth.
b) Lift head, nose pointing to the ceiling. Mandible will drop slightly.
c) Open lower jaw with right hand 3rd & 4th fingers.
d) With tab/capsule between thumb and forefinger, place over base of the tongue.
e) Remove hand, close mouth keeping head raised until patient swallows.

CAT:
As above, except, thumb and forefinger grasps the cats head under the zygomatic arches.
Tablets are dropped over the base of the tongue.
The key to success is quick, correct placement, keeping the mouth closed and head upright until swallowing occurs.

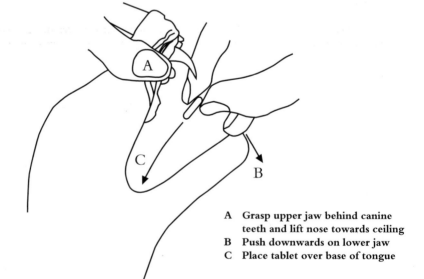

A Grasp upper jaw behind canine
   teeth and lift nose towards ceiling
B Push downwards on lower jaw
C Place tablet over base of tongue

FIGURE 2
PER OS ADMINISTRATION OF TABLETS IN THE DOG

Method C
When giving liquids hold muzzle in a natural position.
Administer by means of a syringe, placing the hub between the premolar teeth.
Allow the patient to swallow of its own accord.

Complications
a) Aspiration of fluid.
b) 'Spat' out tablets! Try again with a dry one, or 'cheat' by giving in food, helpful when tempers are frayed and injury may be a risk.
c) Attempted bites, scratches. These become less frequent as your technique and skill improves, if in doubt ask for help.

ENTERAL

Administration of drugs directly into the gastro-intestinal tract ie. tube feeding.

Types
a) oesophageal
b) stomach
c) pharyngostomy
d) naso-pharyngeal
e) naso-oesophageal
f) naso-gastric
g) gastrostomy
h) jejunostomy

Any tablet/capsule can be crushed/opened and dissolved/suspended in sterile water, thereby allowing administration by the above routes. Ensure adequate flushing of the tube after use in this way.

ISOLATION

ISOLATE: to place apart/alone, free from combination with all others.

Isolation is necessary whenever a patient is believed/proven to be suffering from a contagious disease (see Table 3).

TABLE 3

COMMON INFECTIOUS DISEASES REQUIRING ISOLATION IN THE DOG AND CAT.

DOGS	CATS
Canine distemper	Dermatomycosis (ringworm)
Canine infections hepatitis	Feline infections peritonitis (FIP)
Canine parvovirus enteritis	Feline immunodeficiency virus (FIV)
Dermatomycosis (ringworm)	Feline leukaemia virus infection (FeLV)
Leptospirosis	Feline Panleukopenia
Parainfluenza and other respiratory infections	Notoedric mange
Salmonellosis	Salmonellosis
Sarcoptic mange	Toxoplasmosis
	Upper respiratory infections ('cat flu' and alike)

A) Purpose built. (see Figure 3)

Will include: areas for cages, runs, sink, treatment table, medical supplies and changing/shower facilities for personnel. It will be a totally separate unit, self sufficient, with all requirements available. Entry to the unit will be via changing rooms and foot baths.
Clean protective clothing should be worn at all times and discarded prior to leaving the isolated facility. Surgical masks are rarely required except in the case of birds with psitticosis (this zoonotic disease can be transmitted by inhalation of aerosol organisms).

B) 'Home made' (see Figure 4).

'Home made' isolation areas can be very effective if managed correctly, with co-operation from all staff. The following are essential requirements for an effective isolation area.

1) Kennel patient as far from other inpatients as possible, leave neighbouring kennels empty.
2) Handle only when necessary, doing all required procedures at one time.
3) Wear protective clothing, gloves and full length, long arm waterproof gown (a calving gown does nicely with long large animal rectal gloves!!).

4) Footdips available on approach to kennel or plastic shoe covers that are discarded on leaving the isolated area.
5) Exercise in a designated area .
6) Disinfect any surface having contact with the patient before re-use.
   ★ check disinfectant is active against isolated disease!
7) Separate food/water bowls, lead, blankets etc.
8) Label area **CLEARLY** (eg.striped tape on the floor). Inform **ALL** staff.
9) All required equipment should be selected and kept within the area.
10) All waste must be bagged separately in the isolated area and go directly for incineration.

On discharge inform clients of any risk to other pets. Advise on continued house / garden isolation at home. These patients should generally have limited contact with other pets for a reasonable period of time.

FIGURE 3
PURPOSE BUILT
ISOLATION UNIT

A   Sink
B   Worktops with storage below
C   Examination table
D   Dog kennels
E   Cat kennels
F   Female changing
G   Male changing
H   Independant exit to isolated walking area
I   Footdip

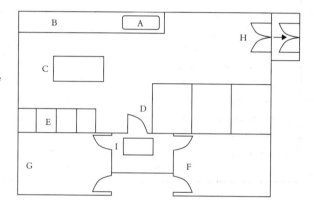

FIGURE 4
'HOME MADE'
ISOLATION UNIT

A   Isolated kennel
B   Notice to indicate isolation
C   Clinical waste bin
D   Marked lead for individual use
E   Protective clothing
F   Boots
G   Footdip
H   Individual food/water bowls
I   Line to indicate isolated area
J   Box of consumables

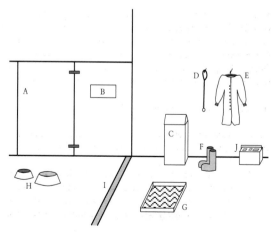

1) THE CARDIAC PATIENT

Congenital defects

Nursing congenital defects concentrates on limited exercise, monitoring of pulse and respiration. Surgical intervention may correct defect eg. patent ductus arteriosis, or medical treatment may be prescribed.

Cardiac failure

1) Restricted exercise (compromised circulation),which needs to be frequent if diuretics are administered.
2) Monitor pulse and respiration on arrival, followed by regular checks at rest and following exercise, enabling rapid detection of any changes.
3) Patients may be inappetent. Prescription low sodium diets may, as a result, be refused.
   *** Do NOT force feed unless instructed by a veterinary surgeon, it causes considerable stress.**
   Practical suggestion – Offer freshly cooked warm food of high biological value (chicken), little then needs to be eaten to achieve daily protein requirement. Hand feed if necessary.
4) Keep patient warm (peripheral circulation may be compromised).
5) Avoid excitement.
6) *Cardiac drugs are potentially dangerous if given in excess or at incorrect time intervals.*
   Double check: tablet size
                   name of drug
                   time of last treatment
                   dose required
7) Observe after medication for signs of toxicity eg. vomiting.

Cardiac patients are often depressed, placing them outside (when warm) or spending time hand feeding may help mental attitude.

2) THE RENAL PATIENT

1) *NEVER withdraw water.*
   If patient is vomiting, an intravenous drip can be placed to supply fluid requirements.
2) Feed low protein diets:
           prescription diets eg.   Hills k/d★
                              Waltham Low Protein ★
        Chicken and rice
        Cottage cheese
        Spaghetti rings (tinned with tomatoes!)
   ★ these are often unpalatable for already inappetant patients, hand feeding, warming and liquidising them may help if the other options are unavailable.
3) Regular blood samples may be required to measure blood urea and creatinine levels.
4) Measure fluid intake (renal cases are usually polydipsic).
5) Record urination. If polydipsia is present then polyurea results, therefore frequent walks are required to prevent soiling and ensure that fluid drunk/given is being expelled.
   Report any failure to urinate IMMEDIATELY.

3) THE JAUNDICED PATIENT

As for the 'Renal Patient' excepting:-
  a) Feed very low protein diets eg. Hills u/d.
  b) Generally drip rates are higher, therefore more frequent walks and additional care in respect to avoiding soiling.
  c) Note mucous membrane colour.

4) THE RECUMBENT PATIENT

Causes
1) Spinal trauma, eg. disc protrusion.
2) Fractures eg. pelvis, limbs.
3) Collapse eg. head injuries, electrolyte imbalance.
4) Weakness eg. Cushings syndrome, cardiac cases.

Nursing
1) Bed on thick waterproof covered foam mattress.
2) Use 'Vet bed' or similar, for comfort and prevention of urine scalding.
3) Incontinent: catheterise (preferably indwelling).
4) Continent: a) Take out to urinate/defaecate.
  b) If possible encourage limb movement by use of slings, towels etc. This may take 2-3 people with larger patients.
5) Check regularly for any decubitus ulcers forming, especially on bony prominences. Clip, dry and treat quickly when redness is seen, use 'Vasaline', 'Dermisol' or similar.
  * *Hardening of areas prone to decubitus ulcers with spirit is NOT to be recommended.*
6) Ensure water and food are within reach, hand feed if necessary.
7) Passive physiotherapy: To help maintain and improve peripheral circulation.
  MINIMUM of 4-6 times daily for 10-15 minutes
  a) Massage. Direction: feet to body
  b) Turn every two hours if in lateral recumbency, to prevent hypostatic pneumonia and decubitus ulcers. Encourage (or provide the means for) sternal recumbency.
  c) Supported exercise.
  d) Hydrotherapy (swimming!).
8) Stimulate alertness with games, placing patients in active area etc.

5) THE COMATOSE PATIENT

If the coma is long term the patient will require all nursing listed for the recumbent patient (except exercise) plus:
1) Keep airway patent – endotracheal tube, pull tongue forward.
2) Avoid secretions building up in oral cavity, swab, suck or lay with head lowered.
3) Monitor every 15 minutes:
   temperature
   pulse
   respiration
   mucous membrane colour
   capillary refill time
   urine output (an indwelling catheter should be placed and rate be at least 1ml/kg/hour)
   drip rate
4) Constant, 24 hour observation ie. intensive care.

6) PATIENTS WITH VOMITING AND/OR DIARRHOEA

Causes are many, varied and individual cases require differing approaches. There are, however some basic rules for nursing these patients.

1) STARVE for 24 hours, offer small amounts of water FREQUENTLY. Do not withdraw water, offer little and often.(100-200mls).
2) The only exception to (1) is where water intake induces vomiting, intravenous fluids should be utilised to supply fluid requirements.

If vomiting/diarrhoea ceases:
   a) After 24-48 hours re-introduce bland, low fat hypo-allergenic food little and often. Prescription diets can be used eg. Hills i/d, Waltham Selected Protein, or offer chicken/fish in small amounts with rice.
   b) Over 48-72 hours increase quantity of food offered.
   c) Over the following 3-7 days re-introduce the patients normal diet (unless a change is indicated, eg. food allergies, or puppies that have diarrhoea when fed on certain brands of food).

If vomiting/diarrhoea continues:
   a) Treatment or other action will be required, proceed as directed by the veterinary surgeon.
   b) Treatment is not given orally in the vomiting patient! An intravenous catheter may be required for either i/v fluid or drugs.

3) Note and report:
   a) Any inpatient vomiting and diarrhoea.
   b) Colour, consistency, amount and frequency.
4) Clean immediately – kennel and patient, bath if necessary.
5) If necessary keep sample for veterinary surgeon to inspect.
   * Any unexpected vomiting or diarrhoea must be reported immediately.

7) THE DYSPNOEIC PATIENT

Management
1) Keep patient calm and quiet.
2) Avoid any stress, unnecessary handling.
3) Have oxygen available in case cyanosis develops or respiratory arrest occurs.
4) *Do NOT force acceptance of an oxygen mask*, this results in struggling and deterioration of the patient.
5) If available, place in an oxygen tent.
6) Have a pre-prepared CARDIAC ARREST ★ box available in case of an emergency.
7) Endotracheal tubes, tracheotomy tubes and sucking equipment should also be ready for use if required.

Monitoring

Temperature:	These patients often over heat.
Respiration:	Usually increased, shallow and laboured.
Pulse:	Usually increased, may be weak and thready.
Mucous membranes:	Note colour, may be cyanosed.

Collapse may result in prolonged dypsnoea just prior to respiratory arrest, watch for ataxia, disorientation and lack of response to stimuli.

★ See "Intensive Care" for contents.

8. THE CONVULSING PATIENT

Stabilised epileptics
1) Identify and inform all members of staff.
2) Ensure an anti-convulsant drug is readily available if required eg. Diazepam (Diazemuls, Dumex).
3) Give prescribed drugs at correct times (these are nearly always SPECIFIC).

Action if patient found Convulsing
It is wise to place an intravenous (i/v) catheter in any animal likely to convulse, whether due to medical condition or procedure being performed. Trying to give i/v drugs to a convulsing patient is both difficult and dangerous.

1) Give i/v diazepam (under veterinary instruction).
   Do NOT risk injury to yourself.
2) Place blankets around patient
   a) To protect patient, eg head injury.
   b) To soak up any voided urine.

After convulsion
1) Gently clean away saliva and ensure a patent airway.
2) Place in a cool (NOT cold), padded, darkened kennel.
3) Avoid any unnecessary stimulation (noise, touch, vibration).
4) Observe frequently.

9) THE DIABETIC PATIENT

1) Use an 'easy to read' record chart (see Figure 5).
2) Identify patient as a diabetic (notice on kennel), inform all staff.
3) Daily urine samples. Check, with dipstick, for presence of glucose and ketones.
4) Measure fluid intake – this will decrease as stabilisation is achieved.
5) Daily blood samples for blood glucose levels (take at same times each day).*See note A.
6) Insulin administration.
   Always get a colleague to check insulin dose drawn up.
   a) Sub-cutaneous administration
   b) At precise time(s) determined by veterinary surgeon.
   c) Intravenous administration; soluble insulin is given in an intravenous saline drip.
7) Feeding.
   a) Accurate weighed amounts.
   b) No titbits.
   c) Feeding times are specified and will be at least twice daily. Either before, at same time or after insulin injection, according to veterinary surgeons preference.
8) Exercise: constant length of time and distance to ensure equal energy utilisation each day.
9) Signs of ataxia, collapse, shaking, fits could indicate HYPO-GLYCAEMIA.
   a) Feed immediately (if conscious).
   b) Call for assistance.
   c) If (a) is impossible, draw up 10mls 20–50% dextrose solution for intravenous administration.
   d) The patients life is at risk if not treated promptly.

Note A

The availability of 'cheap' glucometers (Ames Ltd) requiring only a drop of blood, make frequent blood glucose monitoring possible and economic. This is especially useful during stabilisation and quick checks during routine outpatient clinics. It also has the advantage of showing if hypoglycaemia is present before clinical signs develop.

FIGURE 5

DIABETIC CHART

PATIENT NAME ....

WEIGHT ....

Date	Urine sample result	Fluid intake	Insulin dose and time	Food and time	Blood glucose

10) THE GERIATRIC PATIENT

1) Ensure water is available at **all** times. **Never** advise water removal more th
   to surgery. It is unnecessary in ALL patients but more significant in geriatr
   of water intake may result in renal compromise, many geriatrics being in cc
   chronic renal failure.
2) House in a warm, draught free kennel.
3) Use soft bedding.
4) Feed small meals twice daily (many geriatrics are obese, institute diets whilst hospitalised
   and discharge with strict written diet sheet).
5) Follow patients home feeding, walking routine, if possible.
6) Allow own bedding, may help to reassure and enable easier handling.
7) Remember many geriatrics are blind, deaf, arthritic (in any combination) refer to owners
   regarding individual degrees of sight, hearing, ambulation.
8) Short frequent walks, adapt speed and length to each individual.

11) THE OBSTETRICAL PATIENT

Prior to whelping
1) Disturb as little as possible.
2) Provide blankets etc to allow bed making activities or use a whelping box.
3) Feed small amounts 4-6 times daily. Food may be refused just prior to whelping.
4) Provide warm (20-22°C) ambient temperature, avoid extremes and draughts.
5) Exercise little and often to allow urination.
6) Observe for signs of imminent whelping eg. straining, waterbag at vulva, unsettled behaviour.

Whelping
1) Record: strength and frequency of contractions.
               time of each arrival
2) Check mother cleans mucous etc from face of neonate and breathing commences.
3) Only observe bitch/queen UNLESS
   a) Failure of first to second stage labour.★
   b) Prolonged visible straining with no resulting birth eg. obstructed birth canal.★
   c) When a bitch (rarely queen) is known to prefer human company during whelping.
   ★ *Require veterinary surgeon assistance before action is taken.*

Post whelping
1) Count placentas, ensure ALL have been expelled.
2) Remove dirty bedding.
3) Offer mother food and water.
4) Ensure ALL neonates are suckling.
5) Provide ambient temperature of 22-24°C.
★ *Use infra-red lamps with care, they can result in overheating of confined areas.*

) CARE OF THE NEW BORN

In most cases leave to the mother.

Exceptions:
1) If pup fails to breath.
2) Mother (especially highly strung primiporous animals) fails to bite umbilicus or clear membranes from face of neonate.

Action:
1) Clamp umbilicus one inch from the body, detach from placenta.
2) Clear membranes/mucous from head, nostrils, mouth, body.
3) Rub with a warm towel to dry, stimulate breathing.
4) If not breathing, administer respiratory stimulant lingually eg. 'Dopram V'(Doxapram Hydrochloride, Willows Francis)
5) Cup neonate in hands, head down. Ensuring neck is well supported swing gently to allow fluids to exit airway by means of gravity.
6) Return to mother as soon as possible.

13) HAND REARING PUPPIES/KITTENS

Reasons
orphaned
weak/premature
large litters
rejection
lack of milk production

Temperature

1-7 days	26.6-29.4°C (80-85°F)
8-14 days	21.1-26.6°C (70-80°F)
14-56 days	21.1°C (70°F)

This needs to be the *ambient* level not just immediately below the lamp or next to the heat source. Ideally an incubator is used.

Feeding
Colostrum from mother if possible.

1-7 days	feed every 2 hours, 24 hours/day.
8-14 days	feed every 2 hours during the day and every 4 hours at night.
until weaned	every 3-4 hours, 24 hours/day.

Substitute milk is best provided by proprietary products. Welpi and Cimicat (Hoechst Ltd) Equipment: Catac feeders (Cat Accessories Ltd.), syringe and teat.
REMEMBER, neonates can sometimes be transferred to other lactating bitches / queens successfully.

Toileting
After every feed, wipe genital/anal areas with damp cottonwool.
Neonates may be prone to infection, especially if colostrum is not consumed. High levels of hygiene are essential.

TABLE 4

OBSTETRICAL DATA

NAME	OESTRUS *OESTRUS CYCLE*	BREEDING SEASON	GESTATION (DAYS)
DOG	3-21 days (Average 9) *Two oestral periods per year*	Continuous	63
CAT	4-6 days Ovulate after coitus *14 days*	May be continuous or seasonal (spring/summer)	63
RABBIT	Ovulate at coitus *12 hours recurring every 4-5 days*	Continuous although less active in winter	31-32
GUINEA PIG	4-6 days *13-20 days*	Continuous	59-72
HAMSTER	4-24 hours *polyoestrus all year*	Continuous	Golden 15-16 Chinese 20-21
MOUSE	4-5 days *12 hours every 4 days*	Continuous	19-21
RAT	4-5 days *12 hours every 4 days*	Continuous	21-23
GERBIL	4-6 days *4-6 days*	Continuous	24
CHINCHILLA	30-40 days *30-50 days*	November-May	106-118
FERRET	Ovulate 30 hours after coitus	March-August	42

URINARY CATHETERIZATION

Reasons to catheterise
Obtain sterile urine sample.
Empty bladder.
Introduction of contrast agents.
Incontinence – indwelling catheter placement.
Recumbency – to prevent soiling.
Maintain patent urethra – eg. male cats.
Measure urine production – eg. intensive care.

Types of catheter (see Figure 5)
Dog catheter (can be used in the bitch).
Foley catheter (bitch, indwelling).
Dowes (bitch indwelling).
Tieman's (bitch).
Cat catheter (queen and tom).
Jackson cat catheter (tom).
Metal bitch catheters – used less frequently than in the past.

FIGURE 5
TYPES OF CATHETERS

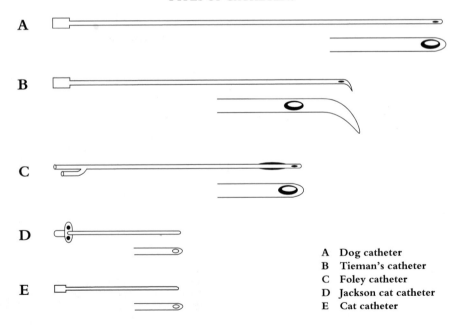

A Dog catheter
B Tieman's catheter
C Foley catheter
D Jackson cat catheter
E Cat catheter

Practical Veterinary Nursing

Complications associated with catheterization
1) **Infection.**
   Use aseptic technique:-
   a) New, or re-sterilised catheters (ethylene oxid/formaldehyde).
   b) Sterile gloves or use 'no touch technique'.
   c) Sterile lubricants.
   d) Clean penis/vulva thoroughly before catheterization.
   e) Ensure antibiotics are prescribed.

2) **Cystitis post catheterization** – especially associated with indwelling catheters
   a) Covering antibiosis.
   b) Plenty of water intake, encourage drinking and/or add water to food.
   c) Provide plenty of opportunities to urinate.

3) **Urethral damage** – more likely in the male.
   Never use force. If difficulty occurs apply more lubrication to catheter, at point of resistance gently move catheter back and forwards in a rocking action. *If resistance remains stop.*

4) **Blockage of indwelling catheters.**
   Check indwelling catheters frequently, record amount collected.
   Dogs and cats should produce at least 1ml/kg/day.
   If blockage suspected flush with sterile saline or water.
   If required remove catheter and replace.

5) **Failure to catheterise urethra**
   More likely in the bitch where it is occasionally possible to catheterize the cervix.
   Rare occurrence. No urine will flow from catheter.

6) **Patient resistance.**
   Sedate or in extreme cases general anaesthesia.

7) **Removal of indwelling catheters by patient.**
   Place Elizabethan collar.

DOG CATHETERIZATION

1) Prepare equipment:
   catheter
   lubricant (xylocaine gel/KY jelly)
   swabs – for cleaning
   syringe to speed urine collection (+/- 3-way-stopcock)
   sample pot (if required)

   If catheter is to be indwelling
   suture material
   tape

2) Position patient, standing or lateral recumbency.

3) Wash hands

4) Assistant extrudes penis.

5) Wearing gloves (protective multi-pack type) remove catheter from outer wrapping, cut a feeding sleeve from the inner sterile packaging (see Figure 6). This allows easy feeding of the catheter from the packaging into the urethra by the 'no touch technique', ie sterile gloves not required because catheter is not touched.

6) Lubricate catheter tip. Insert into urethra.

7) Resistance may occur in the region of the os penis and at the perineal area where the urethra curves back into the caudal abdomen.

8) Drain bladder/collect sample.

9) Indwelling:
   a) place a zinc tape butterfly around the catheter near to the prepuce.
   b) Stitch to prepuce (see Figure 7).
   c) OR stick catheter to prepuce with tape alone.
   Neither of these choices is ideal because dog catheters are not designed to be indwelling.

FIGURE 6
PRODUCING A FEEDING SLEEVE FOR A DOG CATHETER

A   Feeding sleeve
B   Outer packaging
C   Catheter

FIGURE 7
CREATING AN INDWELLING MALE URINARY CATHETER

A   Zinc tape butterfly
B   Leur tip catheter
C   Suture
D   Penis
E   Prepuce
F   Catheter in urethra

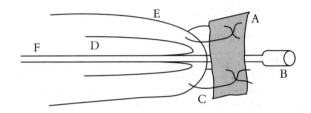

BITCH CATHETERIZATION

Methods:

A Viewed in dorsal recumbency.　　Good method for beginners!!
B Viewed standing.　　　　　　　Useful in the large, strong, difficult patient.
C Digital (standing or lateral).　　Less equipment, quicker, but needs practice to be slick!!

Method A:
Equipment:
speculum (+/- light source) or the like eg; auroscope or cut syringe case
alternative light source if not on speculum
catheter (Tiemans, Foley, Dowes, Dog catheter)
gloves (+/- sterile)
swabs for cleaning
lubricant
If Foley catheter used:
stylet (see Figure 8)
water to inflate cuff (see Figure 8)
urine bag

Method
1) Wash hands, put on gloves.
2) Position in dorsal recumbency, usually need two assistants.
3) Remove catheter from outer packing, expose tip only from inner sleeve.
4) Foley – place stylet along side of catheter and insert into tip, NOT up the middle.
5) Draw hindlegs cranially, immobilise tail .
6) Clean vulva.
7) Place speculum blades between vulval lips as caudally as possible (to avoid clitoral fossa).
8) Insert vertically into the vestibule and turn handles cranially.
9) Open blades of speculum. The urethral opening lies on the cranial side of the vertically orientated vestibule, approximately half way between the vulva and cervix.
10) Insert tip, bring hindlegs caudally, push catheter into the bladder.
11) Collect sample etc.
12) If Foley used: inflate balloon, withdraw stylet, attach bag, place Elizabethan collar.

FIGURE 8
FOLEY CATHETER

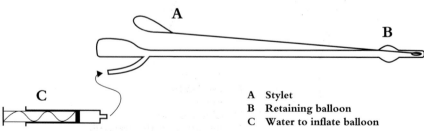

A Stylet
B Retaining balloon
C Water to inflate balloon

　　　　　　　　　　　　　　Practical Veterinary Nursing

Method B:
　Equipment and method as for A.
　　Only one assistant is needed, patient standing.
　　1)　Place speculum horizontally into vulva at the most dorsal point (to avoid clitoral fossa).
　　2)　Identify urethral opening on ventral aspect of vestibule.
　　3)　Place catheter tip in urethral orifice and insert ventrally to follow line of urethra.

Method C:
　Equipment: no speculum or light source required, otherwise as in A.
　　1)　Restrain in preferred position (in conscious dog standing is generally better tolerated).
　　2)　Wash hands, put on sterile gloves, by open gloving technique.
　　3)　Ask assistant to wash vulva, open outer packing of catheter.
　　4)　Holding sterile part of packing (place stylet if necessary) lubricate first finger of non-writing hand.
　　5)　Place finger into vestibule and feel along ventral surface for a raised pimple (area of urethral orifice).
　　6)　Place tip of finger just cranial to this area (see Figure 9).
　　7)　Raising hand and finger dorsally, guide catheter, tipped slightly ventrally, with finger, until tip enters urethral orifice. The catheter will run past the finger if the orifice is missed.
　　　　Continue as for **A**

FIGURE 9
DIGITAL CATHETERIZATION

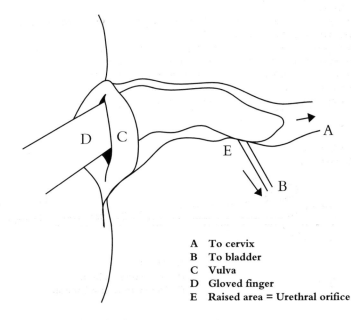

A　To cervix
B　To bladder
C　Vulva
D　Gloved finger
E　Raised area = Urethral orifice

TOM CAT CATHETERIZATION

1) Prepare equipment, as for dog catheterization.

2) Restrain patient and raise tail.

3) With one hand extrude penis by applying gentle pressure each side of the prepuce with two fingers (see Figure 10).

4) Prepare feeding sleeve as for dog catheter. Lubricate tip and introduce into the urethra.

5) If a Jackson catheter is used to be indwelling, stitch flange to prepuce.
   A collection bag may be attatched (old giving set and bag), the catheter bunged and drained periodically or left to drain freely (latter less desirable due to soiling).

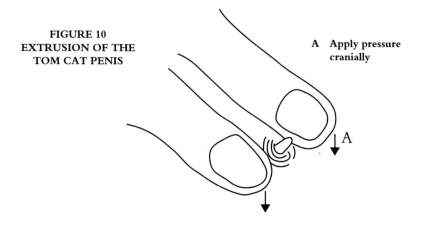

**FIGURE 10
EXTRUSION OF THE
TOM CAT PENIS**

**A   Apply pressure
cranially**

↓A

QUEEN CATHETERIZATION

Rarely performed.
Steps 1 & 2 as for tom catheterization, using a plain cat catheter.

3) The catheter is placed between the vulval lips and 'blindly' introduced to the urethra.
   Angle catheter ventrally, placing gentle pressure until the catheter slips into the urethra.

4) The catheter is not designed to be indwelling.

MANAGEMENT OF INTENSIVE CARE FACILITY

Intensive care is 24 hour constant monitoring/nursing of critically ill patients (surgical or medical) whose lives would be severely endangered if constant care was unavailable.

★ Intensive care continues at home time
(ie there has to be a staff shift system to cover every 24 hours)

An intensive care facility SHOULD be ready for use at ALL times. Make weekly checks on all equipment and drugs.

Location
1) Should not interfere with the normal running of practice/hospital.
2) Situated so help can be called for quickly and easily without leaving the patient.

Basic minimum requirements

The room
1) Good lighting
2) Adequate heating, ventilation.
3) Table/trolley at waist height (kennels at floor level are not ideal).
4) Comfortable seating for personnel.
5) Telephone/intercom.
6) Storage trolley/cupboard.

Equipment
1) Endotracheal tubes/masks.
2) Oxygen supply with appropriate circuit.
3) Stethoscope.
4) Thermometer.
5) Drip stand.
6) Cardiac arrest box★
7) Warming aids eg.blankets, 'safe and warm', heated pads (use with care, can cause burns).
8) Electrocardiogram (ECG) monitor, preferable, not essential.
9) Microhaematocrit for Packed Cell Volume (PCV).
10) Non-invasive blood pressure and carbon dioxide monitoring if available!
11) Ideally laboratory facilities for sodium, potassium, blood urea, creatinine, calcium and glucose estimations.

Consumables
1) Syringes
2) Needles
3) Catheters, intravenous/urinary.
4) Fluids, crystalloids/colloids.
5) Giving sets.
6) Bandaging materials.
7) Manometer sets – for Central Venous Pressure (CVP) monitoring, (can use extension sets and 3-way-taps).

★ See following page.

8) Basic drugs,
    sedatives
    antibiotics
    analgesics
    diuretics
    local anaesthetics
    cardiac drugs
9) Record sheets (see Table 5).

Monitoring
RECORD (at least every 15 minutes)
1) Temperature, pulse, respiration.
2) Capillary refill time.
3) Colour of mucous membranes
4) Urine output
5) Response to drug therapy
6) Other paramemters eg. blood pressure, electrolyte levels, PCV as required.
7) CVP (if set up)
8) Cleaning of tracheotomy tubes (1-2 hourly).

* Downward trends or worrying results should be brought to a veterinary surgeon's attention immediately.

Nursing
All basic care applies as in 'Routine Care', also refer to 'The Recumbant Patient'.

* CONTENTS OF A CARDIAC ARREST BOX (minimal essentials)
Endotracheal tubes, laryngoscope.
Saline.
Syringes (2ml - 20ml)
Needles (23 x $5/8$, 21 x 1, 19 x $1^1/2$, 20 x 2inch).
Catheters (12 - 22 gauge)
Three way taps
Electro-cardiogram needles (ECG) if machine available.
Dog catheter to facilitate the administration of intra-tracheal drugs ie adrenaline.
Drugs: adrenaline, atropine, sodium bicarbonate, calcium chloride, lignocaine, dobutamine hydrochloride.
Other useful additional drugs: dexamethasone, frusemide, sodium nitroprusside, verapamil.

Before deciding to provide intensive care the following should be considered

1) Staffing: Are there adequate personnel to give 24 hour cover ?
2) Space: Is there an area that can be used for intensive care ?
3) Finance: Can clients/practice afford an intensive care facility, where patients may need to remain for days ?

These factors will not be a nurses decision, BUT if you are asked for an opinion these three points should be discussed.

Practical Veterinary Nursing

TABLE 5

INTENSIVE CARE RECORD

Date/time	Temp °C	Pulse/min	Resp/min	CRT	M.M. colour	Urine output	Fluids (state route)	Drugs	Other comments

FIRST AID

FIRST AID OBJECTIVES

a) To preserve life
b) To reduce pain and discomfort
c) To prevent further damage and promote recovery

THE ROLE OF THE VETERINARY NURSE

In all cases the veterinary surgeon should be contacted immediately.
In the absence of, or in conjunction with a veterinary surgeon, the role of the nurse is to:

1) Advise owners/persons in charge of ill or injured animals regarding:
    a) emergency treatment
    b) restraint and transport
2) Record all necessary information
3) Carry out emergency examination/assessment
4) Prepare for/carry out first aid measures
5) Monitor the patients response/progress

1) ADVICE TO OWNERS/PERSONS IN CHARGE OF ILL OR INJURED ANIMALS

This is most usually given over the telephone. It is essential that the nurse assesses the problems encountered correctly. This is best achieved by the use of the correct attitude and questioning of the owner.
All instructions must be clearly given, repeating important points. Asking the owner to repeat back instructions to check understanding may be useful in some cases.

a) Emergency treatment
Instructions/advice regarding immediate first aid that is within the capabilities of the owner/handler should be given as per suspected injuries. The objective is to stabilise and prevent further damage to the animal for immediate transport to the surgery. (See specific first aid situations/problems commonly encountered).

b) Movement and restraint
Usually animals requiring the most urgent attention require the least restraint, though any restraint carried out should be sufficient and suitable to each animal and their condition.

Major injury – animal conscious
Animal will be frightened, possibly aggressive – approach calmly, cautiously and move slowly, watching the animal very closely. Dogs are usually easier to restrain if control of the head is established. This is usually achieved with the use of a slip lead that can be made into a noose, and slipped over the dogs head without the handlers hands being at risk of being bitten. Where possible, muzzle dogs unless there is injury to the nose or jaw, or the animal is experiencing difficulty in breathing. Once under control, the animal can be moved according to its suspected injures.

Non ambulatory animals

Suspect spinal injury, fractures, abdominal or thoracic injury:

Use a ridged stretcher or board. A removable trolley top may be used at the practice, as this can then be lifted onto the trolley for ease of transport. The animals position should be disturbed as little as possible. Care should be taken not to twist the animal at all, keeping the spine as straight as possible. Two or more people should be involved in moving the animal. If the animal is on its side, the skin should be grasped along the back at several points, ie above the scapula, midway along the back and above the pelvis. The animal is then pulled onto the stretcher or board.

Where the above injures are not suspected:

Small dogs and cats can be carried in the arms with one hand under the sternum the other holding the scruff. Slightly larger dogs can be carried with one hand under the sternum and the other around the back of the pelvis supporting the trunk against the carrier's body.

Where the dog is large enough to require two persons to carry it and it is not a suitable case to be safely transported by a stretcher, it can be carried as follows:

One person should be positioned at the shoulder of the dog with one arm curled around the dogs neck, holding the dogs head against the handlers shoulder. The second arm is passed under the thorax, just behind the front legs. The second person should be positioned at the hind quarters with one arm placed under the abdomen, just in front of the hind legs, the other arm is curled around the hind quarters of the dog supporting the pelvis.

Boxes and baskets

If available, these should be recommended for use. The use of a box or basket is the safest way to transport small dogs and cats which are fairly active and/or frightened and aggressive.

Unconfined animals in transit to the surgery

Owners should be advised to ensure that animals are restrained during transit. This will ensure that they do not move around, disturb temporary dressings or slide off a car seat if the vehicle brakes or stops suddenly.

Unconscious animals

Where spinal injury, fractures, abdominal or thoracic injuries are not suspected but the animal is unconscious, a non ridged stretcher can be used. Owners can be advised that improvised stretchers can be made of blankets, sacks, coats etc.

It is important that the airway is kept clear by pulling the tongue forward and keeping the head and neck out straight during transit.

Practical Veterinary Nursing

2) RECORD ALL NECESSARY INFORMATION

The veterinary nurse may often take the history of the emergency case while a veterinary surgeon attends to the patient. Where a veterinary surgeon is not immediately available, the nurse will attend to the patient while the receptionist records all necessary information. It is essential that a standard brief format is used to record essential information in the shortest possible time.

A suggested format would be:

Presenting complaint – what happened (if known), description of symptoms.

When was the patient last normal – or if an accident the approximate time it occurred.

Course of the condition – since the onset of the condition is the problem better, worse or the same.

Other questions regarding the animals condition – further specific questions asked will depend on the case and the answers already given by the owner/person in charge of the animal.

* This information should be made available to the veterinary surgeon as soon as possible to assist with immediate first aid treatment.

General information

The usual owner and patient details should be recorded.

ACTION CHART FOR FIRST AID

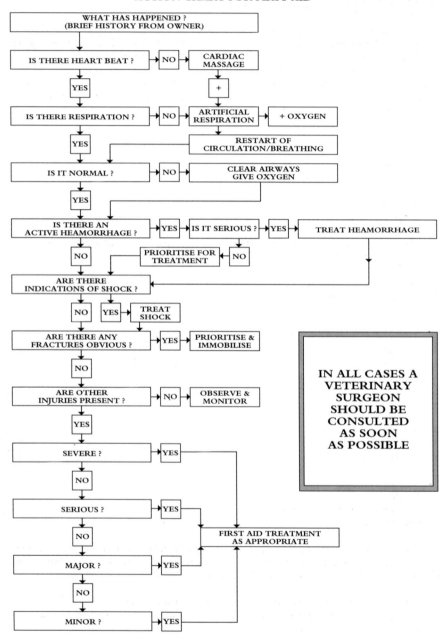

Practical Veterinary Nursing

3) EMERGENCY EXAMINATION/ASSESSMENT

a) Practice emergency routine

It is essential that the practice should have a specific routine for dealing with all emergency patients which are presented at the surgery. All staff should be aware of the action that must be taken and their specifically allocated tasks when working as a team.

It is useful to have a priority list for the evaluation of critically ill patients at the practice, and an emergency treatment area with immediate access to essential equipment once the emergency examination/assessment has been carried out.

An example of a priority list is as follows:

Very severe
Action must be taken immediately
Cardiac arrest
Airway obstruction
Respiratory arrest
Severe arterial or venous haemorrhage
These are immediate life threatening conditions and only prompt first aid measures will prevent the loss of life.

Severe
Multiple deep lacerations with hypovolaemia
Shock (from any cause)
Penetrating wounds of the thorax and abdomen
Any loss of consciousness (particularly head injures)
Respiratory distress
Spinal trauma with obvious neurological deficits
Poisoning
Anaphlaxis (acute, life threatening allergic reaction)

Serious
Multiple deep lacerations
Blunt trauma with moderate shock
Compound fractures/massive musculosceletal injuries
Acute overwhelming infection

Major
Fractures of limb bones or pelvis
Deep puncture wounds

All of the above conditions should be dealt with as soon as possible by a veterinary surgeon, or in their absence appropriate first aid measures taken. This list is useful where an animal is presented with several of the above conditions, to enable the conditions to be dealt with in order of priority.

In addition to the above, conditions that require urgent attention include:
Prolapsed organs, urethral obstruction, burns, heat stroke, profuse diarrhoea and/or vomiting, gastric dilation, large open wounds.

b) Arrival of the emergency case at the surgery
Once at the surgery the animal will be admitted to an area where emergency procedures can take place (restrained and transported as described above).

c) Immediate action that must be taken on arrival
Immediately upon a patient arriving at the surgery it must be evaluated. A decision is then made as to any immediate first aid measures to be taken.

d) Initial examination
★ Rapid examination of the animal should be carried out to ensure there is a presence of heart beat and respiration. A brief account of what has happened (if this is known) should be obtained.

e) Immediate action

Ensure breathing and circulation
Where an animal displays widely dilated pupils which do not respond to light this is an indication of poor oxygenation of brain cells. The prognosis in these cases is very poor. When the brain is deprived of oxygen for longer than 3-4 mins irreversible damage takes place. Prompt action in all cases of respiratory/cardiac arrest is therefore of the utmost urgency.

Cardiac arrest – cardiac massage & provide oxygen - see page 209.

Respiratory arrest – intubate & artificial respiration - see page 210.

Laboured or dubious breathing – clear airways. Check that the collar or anything else around the neck is loosened. Check for any obstruction of the airway ie nothing at the back of the throat or nostrils (may be a toy – particularly a small ball, a bone, broken teeth). If present, remove with fingers, artery forceps etc. If blood, vomit or mucus is present wipe or aspirate the liquid materials away. Keep animal still and give oxygen (without distressing the patient).
If unconscious – pull the tongue forward and extend neck. Check for/remove obstructions, intubate the animal and provide oxygen. Check for any wounds that may have penetrated the chest (usually identifiable by blood stained froth in wound/nose and mouth. Often the animal will cough.

Haemorrhage – identification and control of active haemorrhage. The type and source of any haemorrhage should be identified and immediate action taken to control any active haemorrhage.

Shock – mucous membranes. The colour of the mucous membranes and capillary refill time should be assessed, any deviation from pink being abnormal and with capillary refill time of more than 2 Sec or less than 1/2 to 1 Sec being abnormal. Pulse – the pulse taken, with a rate of less than 60 or more than 200 beats per min being considered abnormal dependant on the size and breed of the animal.

Fractures – the presence and priority status of any fractures.

Other conditions/injuries – all other conditions/injuries should be assessed and appropriate action taken.

Road traffic accident – specific injuries (Fractures and prolapses prioritised and then dealt with in order of priority).

Practical Veterinary Nursing

4) PREPARE FOR/CARRY OUT FIRST AID MEASURES

The veterinary nurse should carry out any necessary first aid measures or assist if a veterinary surgeon is present. The nurse should also make preparations for the attending veterinary surgeon to administer further necessary treatment by preparing any medication, materials and instruments for immediate use.

SPECIFIC FIRST AID SITUATIONS/PROBLEMS AND FIRST AID ACTIONS

CARDIAC ARREST - REQUIRING CARDIAC MASSAGE

Signs – The animal will be in flaccid collapse, with cyanosis of the mucous membranes. The pupils will be dilated (N.B. widely dilated pupils that do not respond to light indicates poor oxygenation of the brain cells, the prognosis in these cases is very poor).
A heart beat is not detectable or there may be ventricular fibrillation. Usually, the heartbeat is detected by using a stethoscope between 5th and 6th ribs on the left side of the animal. If no stethoscope is available then with the animal on the left side, flex the elbow and place flat fingers between two ribs on the area immediately behind the point of the elbow.
If there is no heart beat, the time scale is 3 minutes before there is irreparable damage to the brain due to lack of oxygen.

Action – When an animal is in cardiac arrest cardiac massage is carried out:

One person method:
a) The palm of a hand should be placed over the heart area of the dogs chest (ribs 3-4) 15 cardiac compressions should be given with $^1/_2$ second intervals between each.
b) Two breaths as for artificial respiration
c) Repeat and check for heartbeat at 60 second intervals.

Two person method:
a) 1st person– compresses heart 5 times with $^1/_2$ second intervals, while the second person administers two breaths as for artificial respiration.
b) Repeat and check for heartbeat at 60 second intervals.

In large dogs the thorax should be supported by foam pads or the equivalent.
It is important to control any haemorrhage in severely injured animals.

RESPIRATORY ARREST - REQUIRING ARTIFICIAL RESPIRATION

Signs – Animal will be in flaccid collapse with cyanosis of the mucous membranes becoming rapidly evident. No visible respiration. (Check using mirror or equivalent in front of the nose).

Action – If respiration has stopped for one minute then artificial respiration should be undertaken:

Animal not intubated
a)   Extend head and pull the tongue forward
b)   Place the animal on its right side
c)   Pull forelegs forward to give optimum access to thoracic wall
d)   In the case of a drowning accident, the animal should be on a sloping surface with the head sloping downwards.
e)   Apply intermittent pressure with the palm/palms of the hands to the thoracic wall immediately behind the scapula.This should be done suddenly to expel air from the lungs, and then suddenly released to allow the chest to expand and draw in air.
f)   This should be repeated at one to two second intervals in smaller animals and up to five seconds for larger dogs to allow oxygen to diffuse into the blood stream.

* This method should not be used in cases where there is damage to the thoracic wall as fractured ribs are likely to cause serious damage to the lungs or heart.

Animal intubated
With intubated animals great care should be taken during artificial respiration not to over-inflate the lungs. This is particularly easy to do in small and very young animals.
a)   Blow down the tube intermittently, watching the lungs gently inflate and deflate. The lungs should be inflated at the same intervals as above.
b)   If oxygen is available then the animal should be attached to an anaesthetic machine (supplying oxygen only). The rebreathing bag should be compressed to gently inflate the lungs.

Practical Veterinary Nursing

SHOCK

Shock is a condition where there is inadequate blood flow to the body tissues. This leads to lack of oxygen, an accumulation of acids, and ultimately death of the cells.

Shock is present or threatened in most first aid situations. The understanding of first aid treatment for shock is therefore of paramount importance in treating and promoting the recovery of emergency cases.

Signs – In all first aid situations some degree of shock should be expected.
Indications that an animal is in shock include:

a) Pale mucous membranes
b) Shivering and reduction in body temperature
c) Skin cold and clammy to the touch
d) Breathing – rapid and shallow
e) Pulse – rapid and weak
f) Pupils dilated
g) Apathy and weakness

Action –

a) Attend to any problems with breathing and/or haemorrhage
b) Keep the animal still and in a horizontal position if possible to ensure effective circulation.
c) Keep warm and dry – cover with light weight blankets or similar to conserve body heat. A hot water bottle can be used but should not exceed the normal body temperature of the animal. Direct heating with fires or heated pads should be avoided as overheating of the skin surface of the animal in shock is contraindicated.
d) Don't move or handle the animal needlessly, keep as still and quiet as possible.
e) If not contraindicated by other conditions, after consultation with a veterinary surgeon the animal may be given a small amount of fluid warmed to body temperature. On no account should alcohol ever be given.
f) Fluid therapy is widely prescribed in cases of shock. The fluids of choice are usually crystalloid solutions, lactated Ringers solution being widely used. The aim is to maintain the P.C.V. between 20-60%. Where there has been acute haemorrhage blood transfusion may be necessary.
g) The veterinary surgeon may administer drug therapy. Some drugs used include corticosteroids in aqueous solution, vasoactive drugs, sodium bicarbonate and antibiotics.

HAEMORRHAGE

Signs/definition
a) Bleeding from any part of the body due to injury or disease.
b) Arterial – Most serious, forceful, red and spurting. Usually bleeding point can be detected.
c) Venous – Darker colour, steady stream (force dependent on size of vessel), definite bleeding point can be detected.
d) Capillary – oozes with little force, multiple pin-point sources.
e) Mixed – usually profuse bleeding from all types of vessel, sources of individual vessels bleeding may be difficult to locate

Haemorrhage may be: External – escaping from the body from any source
or Internal – blood lost into tissues or body cavity

Action –
a) Direct digital pressure.
Pressure is applied directly to the wound site over the bleeding point. This method can be used for temporary control of haemorrhage in a small wound. Ensure the wound is free from any foreign bodies (if present, direct pressure may push them further into the wound). Care should be taken where fractures are present that pressure does not displace bone fragments.

Method
Sterile swabs and/or clean hands are used to apply pressure to a bleeding point. The edges of the wound are pinched together if possible.

b) Pressure bandage.
Direct pressure is applied to a wound by a pad and firmly applied bandage. This method is widely used to control haemorrhage from limbs, and can be used where the bandage is not likely to impede functions such as breathing.

Method
A dressing is placed directly over the wound, with a thick pad of cotton wool placed on top. A bandage is then applied firmly. If blood seeps through, an additional dressing should be applied on top of the first and firmly bandaged in place. As with direct digital pressure, care should be taken to avoid pushing a foreign body deeper into a wound or displacing fracture fragments. To prevent this occurring, a ring pad can be used to apply pressure to the wound while avoiding direct pressure to any foreign bodies etc.

Practical Veterinary Nursing

c) **Pressure points**

Pressure points are sites where it is possible to prevent blood loss from a damaged artery. At certain sites in the body it is possible to press an artery against a bone to stop blood flow.

Method

i) **To assist in arresting haemorrhage below the elbow:**

Apply pressure to the **Brachial artery** situated $1-1^1/_2$" above the elbow at the medial aspect of the lower third of the humerus.

ii) **To assist in arresting haemorrhage below the stifle:**

Apply pressure to the **Femoral artery** situated on the medial aspect of the thigh (where the pulse can be taken).

iii) **To assist in arresting haemorrhage from the tail:**

Apply pressure to the **Coccygeal artery** situated on the underside of the tail.

d) **Tourniquet**

A tourniquet is only used if other methods of haemorrhage control fail, for example, where limbs have been severed. It stops all circulation below the area where it is applied and is used only on the limbs and tail.

Method

The most common tourniquet is a flat stretchable band with a fastening clip. Other items can be used in a emergency such as a length of rubber tubing or a length of strong bandage; not string or rope as this is damaging to the application area.

a) Fix the band around the limb a few inches above the wound and tighten.

b) The pressure should be adjusted to stop the haemorrhage.

c) Never leave in place for more than 15 mins (time exactly when it was applied).

d) Slacken off slowly after 15 mins, and attempt temporary control of haemorrhage by a pressure bandage. The tourniquet must be released for at least one minute to allow blood to circulate and revive tissues.

e) If haemorrhage cannot be successfully controlled by a pressure bandage, the tourniquet can be re-applied to a different area. The same area of application should never be used as the tissues here will be badly damaged as a result.

CONVULSIONS

Some causes include:
a) Poisoning,
b) Metabolic problems such as low glucose or calcium levels or high ammonia levels
c) Some forms of structural or developmental abnormalities
d) Some infectious diseases
e) Epilepsy
f) Head injures

Signs – May vary in severity from a few seconds of head shaking or facial twitching to a spastic (rigid) unconscious collapse. The later is most likely to involve the veterinary nurse in a first aid situation. Most fits last between 1-2 mins with the animal falling to its side and displaying violent involuntary muscular spasms causing the limbs to "paddle". This is accompanied by a increased respiratory rate and salivation. The animal may urinate and defecate involuntarily. Continuous or rapidly repeating seizures require attention as soon as possible, as a serious metabolic problem or poisoning may be responsible for the convulsion.

Action – It is generally recommended to interfere with the animal as little as possible during a fit. The animal should be removed from areas where it may damage itself.
It should have minimal external stimulation ie be in a quiet darkened area. Take a rapid history to try to establish the likely cause. Specific treatment will be determined by the veterinary surgeon dependent on the cause. It is therefore essential that the veterinary nurse takes a rapid but full history, including questioning regarding whether the patient is lactating. Access to poisons such as strychnine, metaldehyde, orgarophosphorous compounds or alphachloralose etc should be ascertained. The animal should be monitored and all signs noted. Provide general supportive therapy ensuring that the animal does not become hypo or hyper-thermic. Ensure all drugs that may be necessary are made available, eg Diazepam or pentobarbitone to control the convulsion or specific treatments where indicated, eg intravenous calcium solution for cases of suspected eclampsia in lactating bitches or specific antidotes for poisoning.

ELECTROCUTION

Signs – This most commonly occurs when puppies chew through electric cables. The dog may be unconscious, both heart and respiration may have stopped and there may be burns to the mouth.

Action – * *Ensure the current is switched off before handling the animal.*
If this is not immediately possible, with **low voltage supplies** a long non conducting object may be used to push or pull the animal from the source of current. Once there is no danger to the handler if the dog's heart has stopped along with its breathing then cardiac massage and artificial respiration should be carried out immediately. Once heart beat and breathing has re-commenced constant monitoring is necessary for 12-24 hours following the incident. Any burns should be treated as for thermal burns.

Practical Veterinary Nursing

POISONING

a) **Poisoning through ingestion**
   Signs – Owner may have found the animal eating a poison or discovered a empty/partly consumed poison container with the animal. Signs are usually sudden and varied, depending upon the toxic agent concerned.

   Common signs of poisoning include;-
      violent vomiting and/or diarrhoea
      incoordination and/or convulsions
      profuse salivation
      collapse and unconsciousness – death

   These signs may relate to conditions other than poisoning. When a history of a patient suggests access, or possible access to toxic agents and where no known existing condition can account for the above signs, then poisoning may be suspected by the attending veterinary surgeon.

   Action – Identify type of poison if possible and assess the condition of the patient. Contact a veterinary surgeon/carry out necessary first aid treatment as instructed eg administration of an emetic.
   Keep animal warm and monitor until arrival of the attending veterinary surgeon.
   * Emetics must never be given in cases of caustic poisoning or where the animal has reduced consciousness or where a suspected corrosive agent has been ingested.

b) **Poisoning through skin absorption**
   Causes – creosote, paint thinners etc. jeyes fluid, oil, tar, some disinfectants and parasite control products eg flea sprays.

   Signs – symptoms of poisoning as above. Presence of and/or odour of toxic materials on the animal's coat.

   Action – treat for shock and remove any remaining materials from the coat, taking care to keep the animal warm if a large area of the animal requires to be wet in this process. The veterinary surgeon may prescribe an antidote.

c) **Poisoning by inhalation**
   Causes – carbon monoxide/smoke inhalation

   Signs – case history of exposure, respiratory difficulties/failure, red mucous membranes and coughing.

   Action – remove from source, give oxygen and artificial respiration if necessary.

INSULIN OVERDOSE

Signs – A diabetic patient routinely receiving insulin displaying signs of hypoglycaemia (ie, weakness, in-coordination, shaking, collapse).

Action – If the animal is conscious and able to swallow then some form of sugar should be given preferably glucose tablets. Honey, sugar lumps, chocolate etc will also produce the desired effect. This treatment should produce a rapid improvement in the animals condition. If the animal is unconscious then immediate steps should be taken to administer an intra venous glucose solution. This should produce a very rapid improvement. The veterinary surgeon will then decide on further action to prevent recurrence.

GASTRIC DILATION/VOLVULUS

Accumulation of gas and a failure of the pyloris to empty the stomach results in gastric distension. Volvulus may occur (the stomach twists either partly or completely occluding the oesophagus).

Signs – This is most commonly seen in large deep chested dogs. The abdomen is obviously distended with the animal usually distressed and considerably shocked.
Action – This is a life threatening situation with the primary objective being to decompress the stomach as soon as possible.

If a veterinary surgeon is not immediately available:
a)   The passing of a stomach tube may be attempted. Resistance at the cardia suggests volvulus has occurred. In some cases forceful blowing down the tube may allow passage of the tube or
b)   If this fails or is not attempted, prepare for a emergency gastrotomy (clip up etc) and attempt to relieve the gas pressure by inserting an 18 gauge needle through the left abdominal wall.

General first aid treatment for shock should be given, including preparation for the animal to receive fluid therapy.

HEAT STROKE

Signs – There is usually a history of the animal being confined in an over heated area or having undergone considerable exercise in hot or humid weather. The animal is usually distressed, panting, salivating, restless and unsteady on its feet. In severe cases the animal may be collapsed and may develop blueish purple mucous membranes. The animal's body will feel hot with a very high rectal temperature (frequently off the scale of the thermometer).

Action – The animal should undergo body cooling treatment as soon as possible with the body temperature being constantly monitored (every 5 mins). The cooling should be ceased when the body temperature is within 1°F of the normal range.

Cooling can be achieved by:
a) Wrapping in blankets soaked in cold water
b) Ice packs applied particularly around the neck of the animal
c) Immersion in a cold bath
d) Dousing with a hose of cold running water
e) Dousing with buckets of water

At all times the animal must be observed and its airway maintained, if a animal has collapsed or appears at all cyanosed oxygen should be given immediately. Once the temperature has been satisfactorily reduced it should be monitored every 10 mins to ensure its stability.

INSECT STING

Signs –
a) Owner may have seen the insect, usually a bee or wasp.
b) Sting visible in mouth, lips or occasionally on the feet. Stings in mouth can cause considerable swelling, salivation and discomfort, the animal may paw at its mouth.
c) In some cases animals may develop a very severe allergic reaction leading to collapse.

Action – Where the sting has just occurred and is not in a area likely to cause severe problems, then the sting can be removed if visible. Take care not to squeeze the poison sack. The sting area can be bathed with vinegar to neutralise a wasp sting or bicarbonate of soda to neutralise a bee sting. In the event of severe allergic reaction/collapse, or where stings are in the mouth/throat, a veterinary surgeon should be contacted and preparation made for the administration of appropriate medication (antihistamines etc). Oxygen should be available and the animal treated for shock.

SNAKE BITE

Snake bites are generally uncommon in Britain, the only venomous snake being the Adder. In some upland areas particularly in Scotland, however, dogs are quite commonly bitten. The owner will rarely see the snake but may be aware of the dog being interested in something in the grass and reeling back suddenly.

Signs – The marks of two fangs may be seen immediately after the bite, usually on the head or limbs. The tissues swell rapidly with the area of the bite becoming painful. Bites on the head, mouth, and throat area may rapidly lead to breathing difficulties. The dog will often become lethargic and depressed or very distressed, collapse may occur.

Action – The animal should be kept quiet and still, and a cold compress applied to the area. The veterinary surgeon should be contacted and preparations made for the administration of appropriate drugs. Oxygen should be available and the animal treated for shock.

BURNS AND SCALDS

Signs – Burns – dry heat, scalds – hot liquid. Both classed as thermal burns, produce shock, and are painful.

Action – Immediate action – douse any flames, apply cold water to the affected area by spraying, pouring or sponging. Remove any constrictions eg collar, but material that has adhered to the skin should not be removed in a first aid situation. Any surplus material should be cut to within 3-4" away from the skin surface. Apply general first aid treatment for shock. Make preparations for the animal to receive fluid therapy to replace fluid losses and relieve pain. Prepare for the cleaning and irrigation of the site and application of antibacterial preparations, non adherent dressings etc.

PENETRATING WOUNDS OF THE THORAX

Signs – Air can be heard being sucked into the thoracic cavity when the animal inhales or a foreign body may be seen protruding from the wound.

Action – Remove any superficial foreign bodies and dirt from the wound (deeply penetrating foreign bodies should be left in place for surgical removal). Cleanse the wound with well wrung out swabs to ensure that no antiseptic enters the thoracic cavity. Seal the wound by folding any torn tissue and skin over the wound and bandage gently in place.

PROTRUSION OF ABDOMINAL ORGANS

Signs – When the abdominal wall is damaged, the contents particularly the intestines protrude.

Action – The animal should be restrained on its back if not contra indicated by other injuries, in which case it should be restrained on its side. The protruding organs should be rinsed with warm sterile saline to remove any dirt and debris. The protruding organs should be covered with a large piece of sterile gauze or similar soaked in saline and bandaged in place. The animal should be kept quiet and still until the veterinary surgeon is available.

PROLAPSE OF THE EYEBALL

Signs – The eye ball may be partly or completely prolapsed by a blow or other trauma. It is commonly associated with dogs that have prominent protruding eyes due to their conformation.

Action – Keep the eyeball moist with either "Optrex", liquid paraffin, olive oil or if available "false tears", while in transit to the surgery. If none of the above are available then advise a cold water pad be held over the eye while in transit. Moisten the eye with warm saline once at the surgery, and gently attempt to draw the lids over the eye and ease back into the socket. If the eye cannot be easily replaced then keep the eye constantly moist and the animal comfortable until the veterinary surgeon is available.

R.T.A. OR OTHER ACCIDENTAL TRAUMA

The occurrence of road traffic accidents and other accidental trauma are the most common emergences involving dogs and cats.

Signs – A variety of injuries can result depending on the exact nature of the accident.
Road traffic accident – A road traffic accident victim may be identified by;
a) The owner/handler witnessing the accident.
b) The animal may be at the scene of the accident or found later with wounds missing hair or frayed claws and oil and dirt on the coat.
Other traumatic injuries can be caused by falls, fights or contact/entanglement with sharp or constricting objects/materials.

Action – For multiple injuries an immediate assessment should be carried out and the principles described earlier used to prioritise the actions taken.

FRACTURES

The most common road accident fractures in the dog are the femur, radius & ulna, with the pelvis, tibia, and fibula being the next common. The most common fractures in the cat are the femur, pelvis, coccygeal-vertebrae and mandible.

Signs – Pain at the site of the fracture with possible swelling and loss of function. An unnatural degree of movement, deformity and crepitus may also be present.

Action – Movement of the fracture should be restricted by immobilisation. Restrain the animal to prevent from moving unnecessarily. Support/immobilise affected part by bandaging to body or splinting where possible.

ND RECORD THE PATIENTS RESPONSE/PROGRESS

patients are continually monitored, particularly patients in shock situations.

oring includes:

Tem, e
Pulse rate and character
Respiratory rate and character
Colour of mucous membranes and capillary refill time
Urinary output

Check –

Haemorrhage remains under control,
Endotracheal tubes are in place and patent,
Drips – i) Intravenous cannulas are in place and patent,
       ii) The giving set is functioning normally
      iii) The drip rate is correct

General Nursing care

In addition to the general nursing care given to the patients, such as keeping the animal comfortable, warm and constantly monitored to prevent self mutilation, the animals owner should not be forgotten. The owner/handler of an animal presented in a serious condition is usually in a highly emotional state. The veterinary nurse should therefore be comforting and sympathetic to both the patient and the owner/handler.

REFERENCES

KIRK, R.W. and BISTNER S.I. (1985). *Handbook of Veterinary Procedures and Emergency Treatment* (4th edn) WB Saunders and Co., Philadelphia.

LANE D.R. (1985). *Jones's Animal Nursing*, (4th Edn). Pergamon Press.

WILLIAMS (1989). A Practical Approach To Acute Trauma Care in Small Animals, Technical Paper, *BVNA Journal*.

PHARMACY

LEGISLATION

MISUSE OF DRUGS ACT 1971 AND MISUSE OF DRUGS REGULATIONS 1985
1) These acts together control 'dangerous or otherwise harmful drugs'.
   ie. 'controlled drugs'.
2) Veterinary surgeons have authority to possess, prescribe and administer these drugs.
3) Controlled drugs are prescription only medicines (POM's).
4) Controlled drugs are placed in five schedules, numbered in decreasing order of severity of control.

Schedule 1
1) Includes cannabis and hallucinogenic drugs such as LSD.
2) These drugs normally have no therapeutic use.
3) Veterinary surgeons have no general authority to possess and use them.
4) Available on special licences only, mainly for research purposes.

Schedule 2
1) Includes opium, morphine, diamorphine, cocaine, pethidine and major stimulants.
2) Available on prescription only to the public.
3) Records must be kept in a controlled drugs register. Only one register per premises.
4) Drugs must be kept in a locked receptacle which can be opened by the veterinary surgeon or a person authorised by him.
5) Unwanted stocks must be destroyed by an authorised person.

Schedule 3
1) Includes butobarbitone, pentobarbitone, phenobarbitone, buprenorphine and pentazocine.
2) Special prescription and requisition requirements.
3) Transactions do not have to be recorded in the controlled drugs register.
4) Except for diethylpropion and buprenorphine, they do not have to be kept in a locked receptacle.
5) Unwanted stocks do not have to be destroyed.

Schedule 4
1) Including the benzodiazepines eg. diazepam.
2) Exempted from any restrictions as controlled drugs when used in normal veterinary practice.

Schedule 5
1) Includes certain preparations of cocaine, opium or morphine in which less than a specified amount of the drug is present.

Purchase of controlled drugs
Schedule 2 and 3 controlled drugs may be obtained for professional use from a pharmacist, wholesaler or manufacturer providing the following is in writing:
1) Signature of veterinary surgeon.
2) His name, address and profession.
3) Purpose for which the drug is required.
4) Total quantity required.

Controlled Drugs Register

1) Veterinarians must record the purchase and administration or supply of all Schedule 2 drugs in a register within 24 hours.
2) Only one register for each premises.
3) A separate part of the register must be kept for each class of drugs.
4) Class of drug to which the entries relate must be at the top of each page.
5) Entries must be made in chronological order.
6) Entries must be indelible.
7) Entries must not be cancelled, obliterated or altered.
8) The register must be kept for a period of two years from the date of the last entry.

THE MEDICINES ACT 1968

The manufacture, importation and distribution of medicines is controlled by the "Medicines Act 1968" through a licensing system. Medicinal products are classified into three main categories under Part III of the Medicines Act:

1) **General sale list products (GSL's)**
   This consists of medicinal products which may be sold without any restriction as to the seller.

2) **Pharmacy medicines (P's)**
   Pharmacy medicines are medicinal products which are not prescription only medicines or medicinal products on a general sale list. There are no formal prescription requirements for pharmacy medicines when prescribed by veterinary surgeons.

3) **Pharmacy and merchants list (PML)**
   Permits a specified range of non-general sale list licensed veterinary drugs to be sold by product licence holders, specially authorised persons and agricultural merchants who are registered with the Royal Pharmaceutical Society or with the Department of Health in Northern Ireland. A veterinary surgeon can supply PML products but only for use "in animals under his care".

4) **Prescription only medicines (POM's)**
   These are medicinal products which may be sold or supplied only under the authority of a veterinary surgeon, for use in "animals under his care". Veterinary drugs controlled under the Misuse of Drugs Act 1971 (controlled drugs) are also classified as POM's, as are medicinal products intended for parenteral administration regardless of whether or not they contain prescription only substances.
   Legal restrictions require the prescribing veterinary surgeon to prescribe a product licenced for the species and condition under treatment wherever this is available.

THE PREMISES
Premises in which medicinal products are stored and dispensed should be:
1) A building, or part of a building of a permanent nature.
2) Capable of being secured so as to exclude the public and deter unlawful entry.
3) Vermin proof and in a good state of repair.
4) Divided into areas for public and for staff only.

There must be no smoking, eating or storage of food for human consumption in areas where medicinal products are stored or dispensed.

STORAGE OF DRUGS
1) Well designed shelving and fittings should be installed to reduce the possibility of breakage, spillage or stock misplacement.
2) Stocks of veterinary medicinal products to be supplied to clients must not be stored in toilets, laboratories or places where animals are kept such as kennels. This is to avoid contamination.
3) Ensure old stock is issued before new stock.
4) Remove packs with damaged or defaced labels or those that have passed the expiry date.
5) Medicinal products should be stored in accordance with manufacturers' instructions and be protected from the adverse effects of extremes of environmental conditions eg. light, temperature and humidity. Certain preparations may need to be refrigerated eg. vaccines, insulin.
6) Ventilation must be adequate.

RECORDS
Under prospective EC legislation detailed records of medicines entering and leaving the dispensary will be needed. An annual audit will also be needed. Records must be kept for three years and made available to any statutory enforcement authority.

DISPENSING OF MEDICINAL PRODUCTS

All medicines sold or supplied by a veterinarian are by definition ' dispensed medicines' and as such must be labelled in accordance with the requirements given below.

1) The name of the person who has possession or control of the animal, and the address of the premises where the animal is kept.
2) Name and address of the veterinary surgeon.
3) Date of dispensing.
4) The words **'For animal treatment only'** unless the container or package is too small.
5) The words **'Keep out of the reach of children'** or words with similar meaning.
6) The words **'For external use only'** for medicines which are only for topical use.

When writing a prescription the veterinary surgeon may request that it be labelled with any of the following particulars.

1) The name of the product, size and strength.
2) Directions for use.
3) Warnings relating to the use of the product.
4) Name or description of animals to be treated.

Example

Essential	**For animal treatment only** **Mrs Smith** **23 Flowerpot Lane** **Surrey**
Optional	20 x 250 mg Synulox tablets 1 tablet every 12 hours
Essential	**Keep all medicines out of reach of children** **P. Yam MRCVS** **Veterinary surgeon** **R(D)SVS Summerhall Edinburgh**

Associated responsibilities when dispensing to the public

1) Only sufficient quantities of the medicinal products are prescribed or supplied to the owner for the individual animal being treated.
2) Once stock has been dispensed, it should not be accepted back into the dispensary.
3) It is the duty of the veterinary surgeons to report all suspected adverse reactions in humans as well as animals.
4) Qualified Veterinary Nurses may only supply P.O.M. products on the authority of the prescribing veterinary surgeon.

Common abbreviations used in the pharmacy

1) Names of drugs to be included in the prescription should not be abbreviated but should be written out in full to avoid possible errors.

2) Abbreviations of Latin words are commonly used in writing a prescription because they save time and are readily understood by the pharmacist.

Commonly used abbreviations are[1]:

Abbreviation	Latin	Meaning
ad lib	ad libitum	freely as wanted
aa	ana	of each
a	ante	before
a.c.	ante cibum	before meals
aq	aqua	water
b.i.d.	bis in die	twice a day
cap.	capula	capsule
c	cum	with
div	divide	divide
dos	dosis	a dose
eq. pts.	equalis partis	equal parts
h.	hora	hour
M.	misce	mix
o.d.	omne die	every day
p.c.	post cibum	after meals
q.s.	quantum sufficiat	a sufficient quantity
q4h	quoque 4 hora	every 4 hours
q6h	quoque 6 hora	every 6 hours
q.i.d.	quater in die	four times a day
s.i.d.	semel in die	once a day
sol.	solutio	solution
t.i.d.	ter in die	three times a day

Practical Veterinary Nursing

CONTAINERS

When medicines are repacked from bulk or when they are prepared extemporaneously in a veterinary practice, the containers used should be those recommended in the British Pharmacopoeia (Veterinary) and by the the RPSGB as follows.

1) **Coloured fluted bottles**
   For all external applications
   eg. shampoos, soaps, solutions for external use.

2) **Plain glass bottles**
   For linctuses, cough mixtures, tonics.

3) **Wide mouthed jars (plastic or glass)**
   Creams, dusting powders, granules, ointments, powders, suppositories.

4) **Paper board cartons and/or wallets**
   Sachets and manufacturers strip or blister packed medicines.

5) **Child resistant containers**
   For all oral formulations (tablets and capsules).
   Containers should protect tablets from breakage, crushing, moisture, contamination and deterioration.

★ *Paper envelopes and plastic bags are unacceptable as the sole container for veterinary medicinal products.*
★ *Medicines sensitive to light should be dispensed in an opaque or coloured appropriate container.*

Safe handling of drugs

1) Handle drug preparations with clean hands to avoid contamination of tablets.
2) Avoid smoking, eating or rubbing eyes when handling drugs.
3) Wear gloves when handling cytotoxic drugs and prostaglandins.
4) Wear face mask if handling powders.

WEIGHTS AND MEASURES USED IN DISPENSING MEDICINES

1) Metrology is the study of weights and measures used in prescription writing.
2) The metric system has replaced the two Imperial systems of weights (Avoirdupois and the Apothecaries). (see Table 1)

TABLE 1

THE METRIC SYSTEM

Weight	1 picogram=10-12g 1,000 picograms = 1 nanogram (ng) or 10^{-9} g 1,000 nanograms = 1 microgram (g) or 10^{-6} g 1,000 micrograms= 1milligram (mg) or 10^{-3} g 1000 milligrams =1 gram (g) 1,000 grams = 1 kilogram (kg)
Volume	1,000 millilitres (ml)= 1 litre (L)

CALCULATION OF PERCENTAGE SOLUTIONS

1 ml of water weighs 1g at 4°C

This makes the calculation of percentage solutions and doses of drugs relatively simple. A 1% solution is produced by either:

1) 1 gram of a solid in a total volume of 100ml (this applies to a solid dissolved in a liquid and is called a weight/volume solution, w/v), or
2) 1 ml of a liquid in a total volume of 100 ml (this applies to a liquid dissolved in another liquid, and is called a volume/volume, v/v solution).

From the definition of a 1% weight/volume solution it can be deduced that:

$$\% \text{ solution} = \frac{\text{weight (g) x 100}}{\text{vol. of solution (ml)}}$$

$$\text{weight (g)} = \frac{\text{Vol. of solution (ml) x \% solution}}{100}$$

If it is a volume/volume solution, with a liquid A dissolved in another liquid B, the above formula can be applied by substituting the volume of liquid A (ml) for the weight (g).

Examples

1) How much dextrose is required to prepare 250 ml of a 5 % dextrose solution?

$$\text{Weight of dextrose (g)} = \frac{\text{Vol of sol (ml) x \% sol}}{100}$$

$$= \frac{250 \times 5}{100}$$

$$= \mathbf{12.5\ g}$$

2) What % solution would be obtained by dissolving 12g of dextrose in 300 ml of water?

$$\% \text{ sol} = \frac{\text{weight (g) x 100}}{\text{vol of sol (ml)}}$$

$$= \frac{12 \times 100}{300}$$

$$= \mathbf{4\%}$$

Calculation of doses

Information required before drug doses can be calculated:
1) Mass of dog (kilograms or pounds: 1 kg = 2.2 lb and 1lb = 0.45 kg).
2) A calculated total daily dose. This may need to be divided over the day.
3) 'Concentration' of each tablet.

Examples

1) **Question**

A 20 kg dog needs to be anaesthetised with a 2.5% solution of thiopentone at a dose of 5 mg/kg. What volume of thiopentone should be injected?

Answer

A 1 kg dog requires 5 mg of thiopentone. A 20 kg dog requires 5 x 20 mg = 100 mg

$$\text{Volume of solution (ml)} = \frac{\text{weight (g) x 100}}{\% \text{ solution}}$$

$$= \frac{0.1\text{(g) x 100}}{2.5}$$

$$= \frac{10}{2.5}$$

$$= \mathbf{4\ ml}$$

2) Question

A dog weighing 10 kg (22 lb) requires to be given cimetidine by mouth as tablets for 14 days. The recommended dose is 5 mg/kg every 6 hours. The tablets are 200mg each. How many tablets should be dispensed?

Answer

A 1 kg dog requires 5 mg every 6 hours.

A 10 kg dog requires 50 mg every 6 hours. Therefore a quarter of a tablet should be given four times a day. ie.1 tablet will be required daily.

Since 1 x 200 mg tablet is required per day for 14 days, 14 tablets should be dispensed.

DRUG DOSAGE BY SURFACE AREA

Certain drug dosage is based on body surface area rather than on body weight (see Table 2).

Example

Question

The dose for digoxin for dogs weighing more than 22 Kg is 0.22 mg/m^2 every 12 hours. For a dog weighing 25 kg, what is the dosage of digoxin?

Answer

From the table, 25 kg   =   0.85 m^2

Dose of digoxin   =   0.22 mg/m^2 every 12h

                      =   0.22 x 0.85 every 12h

                      =   0.187 mg every 12 h

TABLE 2
CONVERSION TABLE OF WEIGHT TO BODY SURFACE AREA FOR DOGS

kg	m^2	kg	m^2	kg	m^2
0.5	0.06	18.0	0.69	36.0	1.09
1.0	0.10	19.0	0.71	37.0	1.11
2.0	0.15	20.0	0.74	38.0	1.13
3.0	0.20	21.0	0.76	39.0	1.15
4.0	0.25	22.0	0.78	40.0	1.17
5.0	0.29	23.0	0.81	41.0	1.19
6.0	0.33	24.0	0.83	42.0	1.21
7.0	0.36	25.0	0.85	43.0	1.23
8.0	0.40	26.0	0.88	44.0	1.25
9.0	0.43	27.0	0.90	45.0	1.26
10.0	0.46	28.0	0.92	46.0	1.28
11.0	0.49	29.0	0.94	47.0	1.30
12.0	0.52	30.0	0.96	48.0	1.32
13.0	0.55	31.0	0.99	49.0	1.34
14.0	0.58	32.0	1.01	50.0	1.36
15.0	0.60	33.0	1.03		
16.0	0.63	34.0	1.05		
17.0	0.66	35.0	1.07		

TYPES OF PREPARATIONS

Local or topical
ie. drug applied directly to the affected part of the body if this is at the surface or communicates with the surface.

Systemic
ie. drug required to act on an internal organ or throught the whole body.
Drug may be given **orally** (by mouth) or **parenterally** (by injection)
Injections may be intravenous, intramuscular, subcutaneous, intraperitoneal.
Other routes less commonly used include intracardiac and epidural.

Oral preparations
Tablets – Compressed, solid, rounded disks of oral medication composed of one or more drugs, a disintegrating agent such as starch and suitable binding agents.
Capsule – Gelatinous sheath containing a dose of a drug.
Granule – Any small sugar-coated or gelatin coated pill containing a minute dose of a drug.
Powder – A dry finely ground, homogeneous dispersion of one or more substances for external or internal use.
Mixture – A combining or blending of two or more substances without chemical reaction so that the properties of the components are retained.

Parenteral preparations
Injections – Drugs prepared for use either as a solution or, if the drug is insoluble, particles suspended in the liquid as a suspension.

Topical preparations
Cream – A semi-solid emulsion of oil or fat and water which usually incorporates drugs.
Ointment – A semi-solid preparation of one or more medicinal substances in a suitable base.
Lotion – A liquid preparation intended for application to the skin without friction.
Suppository – A solid body of various size, shape and constitution used for the delivery of an agent or drug into the rectal, vaginal or urethral orifices of the body.
Pessary – An alternative and more commonly used name for vaginal or uterine suppository.
Enema – Injection of a liquid per rectum.

Types of drugs in common use

Anabolics
Promote anabolism. ie. the conversion of food into body tissue.
Anabolic drugs with a steroid structure = anabolic steroids.
eg. nandrolone

Anaesthetics
Produce partial or complete loss of all forms of sensation such as cold,
heat, pain or touch.
**eg. Injectable: thiopentone sodium, ketamine hydrochloride, propofol
Inhalant: halothane
Local anaesthetics: lignocaine**

Analeptic
Stimulates the central nervous system, particularly with the property of
improving the strength and vigor of cerebral activity.
Used as a respiratory stimulant.
eg. doxapram

Analgesics
Relieve the sense of pain
eg. **paracetamol, flunixine meglumine, phenylbutazone**

Antibacterials
Impair the reproduction or survival of bacteria.
Bacteriocides kill bacteria: Bacteriostats inhibit bacterial growth.
**eg. Topical: chloromycetin ophthalmic
Injectable: amoxycillin, trimethoprim, tetracyclines, ampicillin
Oral: amoxycillin, ampicillin, cephalosporins, chloramphenicol,
metronidazole, neomycin, streptomycin, sulphonamides**

Anticoagulant
Interferes with or prevents normal clotting
eg. heparin

Anticonvulsant
Acts to prevent or control convulsions
eg. phenobarbitone, primidone

Antidiarrhoeal
Agents used to counteract diarrhoea
eg. kaolin, pectin

Antiemetic
Agents used to counteract vomiting
eg. metoclopramide, acepromazine

Antihistamines
Any agent that can prevent, reduce or oppose the pharmacologic effects
of histamine
eg. tripelennamine hydrochloride

Antiseptics
A substance capable of inhibiting or killing infectious agents
eg. chlorhexidine, iodine

Antisera
A serum that contains antibody

Antitussive   Prevents or relieves coughing
eg. butorphanol tartrate

Bronchodilators   Dilate the bronchus
eg. millophyline

Cardiac stimulants eg. digoxin

Corticosteroids   A steroid normally released from the adrenal cortex.
Any synthetic analogue of cortisol
eg. Injectable: dexamethasone, prednisolone
    Oral: dexamethasone, prednisolone
    Topical (skin): betamethasone, hydrocortisone
    Topical (eyes): hydrocortisone acetate

Diuretic   **Induces a state of increased urine flow**
eg. frusemide, hydrochlorothiazide, mannitol

Ear preparations   **eg. Antibiotics: neomycin sulphate**
    Corticosteroid: betamethasone
    Antifungal: nystatin
    Parasiticide: gamma benzene hexachloride

Ectoparasiticides Products used to treat skin disease caused by ectoparasites
eg. amitraz, permethrin, dichlorvos, phosmet

Emetics   Agents that induce vomiting.
eg. apomorphine, xylazine

Endoparasiticides Products used to control helminths of dogs and cats
eg. fenbendazole,oxfendazole,piperazine phosphate, praziquantel
nitroscanate, pyratel embonate

Eye preparations   **eg. Antibiotics (topical): chloramphenicol, neomycin**
    Antibiotics with steroids (topical): chloramphenicol
    hydrocortisone acetate

Fungicide/   Kills or stops the growth of fungi
fungistat   **eg. griseofulvin, nystatin**

Haemostats   An agent that arrests haemorrhage
eg. Injection: oxalic acid, malonic acid
    Swabs and dressings: calcium alginate

Hormones   Produced in the body by an endocrine gland (some can be produced
synthetically), and is transported by the ciculation before influencing the
metabolism of cells in other tissues.
eg. megoestrol acetate, insulin, oxytocin

Laxative and purgative	Promotes the onset of daefacation, stimulates a bowel movement. **eg. liquid paraffin**

Non-steroidal anti-inflammatory products
eg. paracetemol, phenylbutazone

Oestrus control	Products used to control oestrus in bitches and queens by suppression or postponement of heat. **eg. megoestrol acetate**
Sedatives	Produce mild depression of the central nervous system so that the subject is calm and possibly drowsy. **eg. xylazine, pentobarbitone**
Tranquillizer	Reduces anxiety without primary interference with consciousness and thinking. **eg. acepromazine**
Urinary acidifier	Makes the urine acidic **eg. ammonium chloride**
Vaccine	An antigenic preparation used to produce active immunity to a disease. **eg. infectious canine hepatitis vaccine, leptospirosis vaccine**

REFERENCES

BOOTH, N.H. and MCDONALD, L.E. (1988). *Veterinary Pharmacology and Therapeutics.* (6th Ed.). Iowa State University Press.

BOWER, J. (1990). Sale or supply of animal medicines by veterinary surgeons. *The Veterinary Record.* 127, 236

CHURCHILLS MEDICAL DICTIONARY. (1989). Churchill Livingstone Inc.

ETTINGER, S. J. (ed.). (1975). *Textbook of Veterinary Internal Medicine, Diseases of the Dog and Cat* (2nd Ed.). W.B. Saunders, Philadelphia.

EVANS, J. (1991/1992). *The Henston Small Animal Vade Mecum.* (10th Ed.). Emirates Printing Press, Dubai.

THE ROYAL COLLEGE OF VETERINARY SURGEONS, LONDON. (1991). *Legislation affecting the veterinary profession in the United Kingdom.* (6th Ed.).

HEALTH AND SAFETY

GENERAL SAFETY NOTES

1) **Good Housekeeping**   Efforts must be made to maintain a clean and tidy work area with stock properly stored and spillages or breakages dealt with at once.

2) **Safety and First Aid Equipment**   Always be familiar with type, position and operation of safety equipment, e.g. Fire Extinguishers and Protective Clothing.

3) **Warning Notices**   You must always make fellow workers aware of any dangers and special handling requirements by instruction and by drawing their attention to warning notices which are displayed in all work areas.

4) **Carrying Bottles**   Bottles should always be carried with both hands. Never carry a bottle by its neck.

5) **Toxic and Corrosive Materials**   Always treat all chemicals as potentially dangerous. Avoid direct contact with any breakages/spillages and never breathe in solvent vapours.
IN CASES OF SKIN CONTACT DRENCH WITH WATER, THEN WASH WITH SOAP AND WATER AND SEEK IMMEDIATE MEDICAL ADVICE.

6) **Waste Disposal**   A procedure operates in the surgery for the disposal of clinical waste. All such waste must be rendered safe and stored in a well-defined area prior to disposal. Clinical waste must not be disposed of with ordinary rubbish.

7) **Notification**   Every employee carries a responsibility to ensure that good housekeeping practices are maintained. Any accident, no matter how small, should be reported to a partner immediately, in order that everyone may all learn from the experience and possibly prevent further incidents of a similar nature.

HEALTH, ACCIDENTS AND FIRST AID

1) All accidents must be recorded in the Accident Book which is kept in a known place.
2) In the case of serious accidents, or those following which a member of staff will be absent from work for at least three days, the DHSS must be informed by completion of the RIDDOR forms available. All staff must know the location of the First Aid box.
3) The supply of First Aid contents is the responsibility of the First Aid Officer.
4) A list of individuals' next of kin and doctors' phone numbers should be kept.
5) Take care not to become a casualty yourself while administering First Aid. Be sure to use protective clothing and equipment where necessary. If you are not a trained first-aider, send immediately for the nearest first-aider where one is available.
6) If the assistance of medical or nursing personnel will be required, send for an ambulance immediately. When an ambulance is called, arrangements should be made for it to be directed to the scene without delay.
7) Notify the Safety Officer if:
   i) You have a history of eczema/allergies etc., which might influence the type of work within the practice that you can safely perform.
   ii) You suspect that you may be pregnant.

RADIATION PROTECTION

(Safety protocols as produced by the Radiation Protection Advisor) RPA.

Staff should be familiar with the following three publications:

1) *Radiation Safety in Veterinary Practice*
2) *The Ionising Radiation Regulations*, (1985)
3) *The Guidance Notes for the Protection of Persons against Ionising Radiation arising from Veterinary use*, (1988).

The "golden rules" are displayed in the X-ray room and form a summary of the above. However, they are not intended to replace the following:

LOCAL RADIATION SAFETY RULES

RADIATION PROTECTION SUPERVISOR (RPS) is..............................

A) Controlled area:
X-rays to be taken only in the operating room or wherever is the approved place.

B) Persons who can use X-ray machine:
Those staff over 16 years of age who wear radiation dosage monitoring badges.

C) Persons who cannot use, or be in the same room as the activated X-ray machine:
1) Part-time staff not having radiation badges.
2) General public and ex-members of staff.
N.B.
3) Persons under 16 years of age.
4) Pregnant women.

D) Protection:
1) Beam should only be pointed at the ground whenever possible and coned down.
2) Tranquiliser or, preferably, general anaesthesia should be used to immobilise.
3) No human should be X-rayed.
4) Any pregnancy of staff should be notified to RPS.
5) Use of X-rays in any direction other than vertically down should be authorised by RPS.
6) Staff should wear protective clothing provided.
7) Staff must not expose themselves to useful beam.
8) Any finger, etc., appearing on X-ray must be reported to RPS and notified in writing.
9) Staff should take care of X-ray protective clothing (which should not be bent or folded, etc.).
10) X-ray only if definite clinical indication.
11) No unnecessary repetition of radiography.
12) All animals should be positioned on special table provided in the X-ray room.
13) If animal restraint is necessary, the duty must be shared among designated persons.

Practical Veterinary Nursing

E) Badges: Should be –
   1) Worn near navel.
   2) Kept dry and away from heat and other X-ray sources when not worn.
   3) Not worn outside work.
   4) Changed for a new one every calendar month.
   5) Reported immediately to RPS if lost, damaged or laundered.

F) Management of controlled area:
   1) No entry or exit during X-raying.
   2) Minimum numbers only present.
   3) Protective clothing used at all times.
   4) Only specified persons present during X-raying.

G) Sequence to be undertaken during X-raying:
   1) Immobilise (in preparation area). Preferably anaesthetise.
   2) Take to X-ray area.
   3) Close door. Switch on warning light.
   4) Switch on machine.
   5) Select exposure.
   6) Position animal on table using troughs, sandbags or ties.
   N.B.
   7) Don protective clothing.
   8) Stand back and warn others.
   9) Expose (if switch jams on, turn off at mains and inform RPS).
   10) Switch off
   11) Remove protective clothing and store correctly.

X-RAY PROCESSING

1) The chemicals involved in X-ray development should be recorded. Chemicals for developing and fixing are harmful by inhalation, by contact with the skin and if swallowed. In case of contact with eyes, rinse immediately with plenty of water and seek medical advice.
2) When changing chemicals, wear disposable gloves, plastic aprons and wellington boots. Avoid contact with skin. Make up dilutions in well ventilated area.
3) Care should be taken in the disposal of spent chemicals.

LABORATORY PROCEDURES

1) Specimens should always be labelled with the patient's identity and the date of collection.
2) The request form should state the provisional diagnosis and type of specimen, e.g. throat swab, faecal swab. This facilitates a variety of techniques to be selected. Suspicion of T.B. or any other zoonosis should also be stated.
3) The correct container should be used. Most specimens should be received in a sterile container.

SAFETY PRECAUTIONS

1) Always wear a protective coat.
2) Never lay a culture tube on the bench; always place in a rack.
3) Always dispose of contaminated material in the clinical waste receptacle.
4) Keep working surfaces clear, and wipe up any spillages with correctly diluted disinfectant. (See Disinfectants and Floor Cleaning).
5) Clearly label all culture plates, tubes etc.
6) Do not smoke, eat or drink in the laboratory.
7) Do not lick gummed labels.
8) Always wash hands with antiseptic and dry using disposable paper towels after handling samples and before going off duty.
9) Note that a working fire extinguisher is available in the laboratory.

POSTAGE OF PATHOLOGICAL SPECIMENS

1) In general the despatch of deleterious substances by post is banned by the Royal Mail. However, there are special exemptions for pathological material sent to and from laboratories by veterinary surgeons and some others. Very highly infected material, such as that containing foot and mouth disease virus, or some especially dangerous human pathogens, are excluded from this exemption.

2) Members of the public may send specimens through the post only at the express request of a registered laboratory or a veterinary surgeon.

3) Only first class letter post or Datapost may be used. Parcel post must not be used.

4) The Royal Mail requires that all samples be packed in a particular way. These rules must be followed otherwise the Royal Mail may remove and destroy the specimen.

   a) Every specimen must be enclosed in a primary container which is securely sealed. This container must not exceed 50 ml. (although special multi-specimen packs may be approved).

   b) The primary container must be wrapped in sufficient absorbent material to absorb all possible leakage in the event of damage.

   c) The container and absorbent material must be sealed in a leak-proof plastic bag.

   d) This package must then be placed in either:
      i) a polypropylene clip-down container;
      ii) a cylindrical light metal container;
      iii) a strong cardboard box with full depth lid;
      iv) a specially grooved two-piece polystyrene box.

5) It is recommended that this completed package should then be placed in a padded bag.

6) Multi-specimen packs may be used provided that each primary container is separated from the next by absorbent packing.

7) Any other packaging systems must have the prior approval of the Royal Mail.

8) Labelling: The outer cover must be labelled "Pathological Specimen – Fragile. With Care". It must show the name and address of the sender, to be contacted in case of leakage.

9) Therapeutic and diagnostic substances, such as blood, serum, vaccines etc, are classified as pathological specimens.

Please be sure that anything you send by post complies with the regulations otherwise it may be removed from the mail and destroyed, and you will lose a valuable specimen. You may also be prosecuted by the Royal Mail. Even more importantly, you may cause injury or disease to someone handling the package either during its transit through the mail, or at the receiving laboratory.

Reprinted with the permission of the Royal College of Veterinary Surgeons

ANAESTHETIC GASES

LOCAL RULES FOR THE USE OF ANAESTHETIC GASES

Personal

No member of staff can be employed in a nursing capacity if she is pregnant, because of the potential danger to the unborn foetus from inhalation of certain anaesthetic vapours. It is the duty of all employees to inform the safety officer if such a situation exists.

Designated areas

Except in emergency, anaesthetic gases shall only be used in the following designated areas:

1) Preparation room.
2) Operating room.
3) X-ray room.

Agents

The following substances are extremely dangerous and some can give rise to explosions:

1) Ether.
2) Ether and oxygen.
3) Ether and nitrous oxide.
4) Ether, nitrous oxide and oxygen.
5) Compressed gases (air, oxygen and nitrous oxide), spirits (methylated) and spirit-based lotions e.g. Hibitane tincture.
6) Fluothane and oxygen.

Reduction of contamination: safety rules – designated areas

1) Avoid mask induction if a suitable, safe, injectable alternative is available.
2) Use closed circuit anaesthesia where possible.
3) Use inflated endotracheal tubes where possible.
4) Utilise scavenging ducts to outside where possible. In other cases use halothane absorbers (weigh regularly to check when full).
5) Anaesthetics must not be used for the disinfection or cleansing of skins, apparatus or surfaces.
6) Vapouriser - fill at the end of the day and ensure that it is off.
   Ventilate the room at the time of, and for half an hour after, filling.
7) Any spillage of anaesthetic liquids must be dealt with immediately.
8) Keep anaesthetic time as short as possible.
9) Connect patient before delivery of N_2O/Halothane and flush with O^2 before disconnection.

Reduction of explosive risks – designated areas

1) No naked flames or spark producing materials to be used in designated areas where explosive gases are used.
2) No electrically operated fires in designated areas where explosive gases are used.
3) No diathermy and thermocautery in designated areas where explosive gases are used.

Gas cylinders – safety rules

1) Any faulty cylinders must be reported to the safety officer and must be made safe until they can be exchanged.
2) All gas cylinders must be switched off at the end of each operating session.
3) All faulty gauges, regulators and equipment shall be reported to the officer as soon as possible.
4) Storage areas for gases should be adequately ventilated at all times.
5) Single cylinders kept for emergency use should be secured to prevent their being knocked over.

Maintenance of equipment: The anaesthetic machines and piped gas system are regularly maintained by technicians. Any problems noted during regular use shall be reported to maintenance personnel during routine visits.

DENTAL SCALER

1) Wear face mask to cover operator's eyes, nose and mouth. Dispose of mask after use.
2) Wear safety spectacles.
3) Use 0.2% solution of chlorhexidine as a bacteriostat in the coolant water bottle.
4) Ensure adequate anaesthetic gas scavenging.

STERILISERS

Operating
Care should be taken to operate sterilisers as per manufacturers' instructions.

Inspection/Service
1) Sterilisers must be inspected and/or serviced in accordance with manufacturers' instructions.
2) Service and inspection records should be kept on file.

Latent gas sterilisers
These should be used in well-ventilated areas.

SAFE PRESCRIBING AND HANDLING OF MEDICINES

The legal requirements with which veterinary surgeons must comply when handling and dispensing medicines are extremely detailed. You should refer to Chapter Eight, Pharmacy, for further details. The ability to supply and dispense medicines is a privilege granted to the profession under the Medicines Act 1968, and abuse of this privilege by failure to prescribe and dispense in accordance with the law jeopardises the case for veterinary surgeons to be permitted to continue this practice in the future.

House Rules

1) No smoking in the pharmacy.
2) No food or drink in the pharmacy.
3) Use the correct container with tamper-proof lid or seal.
4) Label the medicine correctly.
5) Use gloves when handling hazardous drugs (eg. cytotoxics, prostaglandins) or where there is a history of drug sensitivity.
6) Pregnant women should observe special precautions (eg. griseofulvin, prostaglandins).
7) If in doubt consult the data sheets.
8) Wear face masks if handling powders.
9) Use a product licensed for use in the appropriate species whenever possible.

INJECTIONS

1) Injections should only be drawn up into the syringe immediately prior to use.
2) Any spillage around the bottle should be wiped off with absorbent paper and disposed of as clinical waste.
3) At the time of injection every precaution should be taken to avoid accidental self-injection or injection of either a nurse or the owner.
4) Immediately after use the needle should be removed from the syringe and disposed of in the sharps container.
5) The empty syringe should be disposed of as clinical waste.
6) Disposable gloves should be used when handling drugs that can be dangerous if absorbed through the skin, e.g. prostaglandins, corticosteroids, cytotoxics.
7) Disposable gloves should be used if an individual has a history of sensitivity or allergy to specific drugs.

RESTRAINT OF ANIMALS

Animals must be suitably restrained at all times within the building.
1) **In the waiting room**
   The owner is responsible.
   All dogs must be kept on a suitably short lead. Muzzles should be worn if legally required.
   Cats should be held within escape-proof boxes.
   All other species should be kept in a suitable container or box to ensure their own safety as well as that of the other clients and their pets.

2) **In the kennels**
   Dogs to be restrained with choke chains while being moved. Use muzzles or tapes if there are any doubts about temperament. Use dog catcher to catch aggressive dogs within the kennel – do not take chances.
   Generally dogs should be given a "pre-med" on admission. Use other appropriate sedatives if necessary under the direction of a Veterinary Surgeon.
   Cats – to be given a "pre-med" on admission. Use wire baskets for transfer within the building.
   Aggressive cats should be restrained in a crush cage prior to sedation.

3) **Parrots and birds of prey**
   Use protective gloves.

UNDER NO CIRCUMSTANCES SHOULD RISKS BE TAKEN WHEN DEALING WITH POTENTIALLY AGGRESSIVE ANIMALS

KENNELS

1) Wear suitable protective clothing – gloves, aprons and footwear.
2) Always ensure adequate ventilation, fans should be set at the appropriate speed.
3) Disinfectants used in the kennels should be used at the recommended dilution rates (see Disinfectants and Floor Cleaning).
4) No refreshments should be taken within the kennel area.
5) Use non-slip stools to reach high cupboards.
6) Take care when handling animals, ensure adequate restraint.
7) Wash hands well after handling any animals.

MORTUARY

1) **Protective clothing**
   Use gloves, boots, coats or aprons as appropriate. Disposable items should be put in clinical waste.
2) **Face Masks**
   Wear a mask it there is a risk of respiratory disease, e.g. during parrot post-mortems.
3) **Disinfection**
   Thoroughly disinfect protective clothing, table and floor after use (see Disinfectants and Floor Cleaning). Ensure they are used at the recommended dilution.
4) **Refreshments**
   No refreshments to be taken in mortuary
5) **Lifting Aids**
   Use mechanical aids to move or lift heavy cadavers.
6) **Washing Up**
   Ensuring hands are washed throughly before leaving mortuary. Dry with dispoable paper towels.

WASTE DISPOSAL

1) **Sharps**
   Dispose of immediately after use in the yellow plastic containers. Full containers should be sealed and stored in the appropriate place, ready for collection.

2) **Clinical Waste**
   (i.e. syringes and materials contaminated with animal secretions or tissues)
   This should be placed in yellow sacks labelled "clinical waste". Where small bin liners are in use, these should be transferred at frequent intervals to the yellow clinical waste sacks. Full sacks should be stored in the appropriate place, ready for collection.

3) **Cadavers**
   Store individually in suitable bags sealed with a plastic tie. These should be transferred immediately to the mortuary for storage in the chest freezer.
   For individual cremation: store in bags and label with the name of the animal and the owner's name and address.

4) **Industrial Waste**
   All other waste to be stored in black sacks. Full sacks are sealed and transferred to metal bins prior to collection.

5) **Cardboard Boxes**
   Fold flat and store as appropriate.

DISINFECTANTS AND FLOOR CLEANING

A list of disinfectants used in the surgery should be kept. These should be used at the recommended dilution rates. For example:

Dettol	Chloroxylenol	3 tablespoons (90ml) per gal water
Savlon	Chlorhexidine gluconate, plus cetrimide	
		5ml in 1 litre (50ml in 2 gal)
Parvocide	Glutaraldehyde	10ml in 1 litre of water

Use disposable rubber gloves and suitable footwear. Plastic aprons should be worn if appropriate.

Avoid leaving pools of water on the floor, ensure that all fluids are adequately mopped up.

SPILLAGES

1) **Liquids/Caustics**

   Wear rubber gloves.

   In the case of small quantities, spillages should be mopped up with disposable paper towels which should then be disposed of in the clinical waste; the area should then be liberally washed with soap and water.

   For large quantities, sand should be used as an absorbent, and the contaminated sand put into sealed containers using a dust pan and brush. The dust pan and brush should then be thoroughly washed, as should the floor area.

2) **Inflammables**

   Generally treat as above.

   In addition open windows (do not use electric fan). Do not turn on any electrical equipment. Do not turn off electrical equipment already in use.

3) **Powder**

   Generally treat as in paragraph 1.

   In addition close windows and doors to avoid draught. Wear a face mask and gloves.

4) **Broken Glass**

   Sweep up with a dust pan and brush. Transfer this immediately to a sharps container, wash the area and the dust pan and brush after use.

5) **Infective Material**

   All blood, urine, and faecal material should be considered as potentially infectious. Disposable gloves should be worn and the material mopped up with disposable paper towels which can then be put in the clinical waste. The area should be cleaned thoroughly with antiseptic and water and sprayed with deodoriser/disinfectant.

6) **Hair/Dander**

   Sweep up at regular intervals to avoid accumulation of hair.

   Use vacuum cleaner if appropriate.

FIRE PRECAUTIONS

IN CASE OF FIRE

1) In the event of fire it is the first duty of all concerned to prevent injury or loss of life.

2) For this purpose, you should make certain that you are familiar with all the means of escape in case of fire. Since there may be an opportunity, in the event of fire, for you should also be familiar with how to use them.

3) IF YOU DISCOVER A FIRE, or one is reported to you, you should

SOUND THE ALARM

4) The Principal, or the authorised deputy, is repsonsible for ensuring that the fire brigade is called immediately on the sounding of the fire alarm.

5) Immediately after the fire alarm has been sounded you should:−

   a) See that any doors immediately surrounding the fire situation are closed.

   b) Escort the persons in your charge from the area, in accordance with the detailed fire drill procedure, ensuring that all doors through which you pass are closed after you.

   c) When the persons arrive at the assembly point, call the roll and notify the Principal, or the authorised deputy, at once of the result (e.g. all persons present or one missing, and the name and likely location, as the case may be).

INDEX

Practical Veterinary Nursing

Practical Veterinary Nursing